Korea in World Politics
1940–1950

Published under the auspices of
THE CENTER FOR JAPANESE AND KOREAN STUDIES
University of California, Berkeley

The Center for Japanese and Korean Studies of the University of California is a unit of the Institute of International Studies. It is the unifying organization for faculty members and students interested in Japan and Korea, bringing together scholars from many disciplines. The Center's major aims are the development and support of research and language study. As part of this program the Center sponsors a publication series of books concerned with Japan and Korea. Manuscripts are considered from all campuses of the University of California as well as from any other individuals and institutions doing research in these areas.

PUBLICATIONS OF THE CENTER FOR JAPANESE AND KOREAN STUDIES

Chong-Sik Lee
The Politics of Korean Nationalism. 1963

Sadako N. Ogata
Defiance in Manchuria: The Making of Japanese Foreign Policy, 1931–1932. 1964.

R. P. Dore
Education in Tokugawa Japan. 1964.

James T. Araki
The Ballad-Drama of Medieval Japan. 1964.

Masakazu Iwata
Ōkubo Toshimichi: The Bismarck of Japan. 1964.

Frank O. Miller
Minobe Tatsukichi: Interpreter of Constitutionalism in Japan. 1965.

Michael Cooper, S.J.
They Came to Japan: An Anthology of European Reports on Japan, 1543–1640. 1965.

George Devos and Hiroshi Wagatsuma
Japan's Invisible Race. 1966

Postwar Economic Growth in Japan. 1966
Edited by Ryutaro Komiya
Translated from the Japanese by Robert S. Ozaki

Robert A. Scalapino
The Japanese Communist Movement, 1920–1966. 1967

KOREA IN WORLD POLITICS 1940–1950

An Evaluation of American Responsibility

Soon Sung Cho

UNIVERSITY OF CALIFORNIA PRESS
Berkeley and Los Angeles 1967

University of California Press
Berkeley and Los Angeles, California

Cambridge University Press
London, England

Library of Congress Catalog Card Number: 67-14968
Printed in the United States of America

IN MEMORY OF MY PARENTS

Preface

I am indebted to many persons and institutions for help in the research and publication of this study. First, I want to express my great indebtedness to Professors Robert E. Ward and Russell H. Fifield of the University of Michigan. Without their suggestions and criticism as teachers, the preparation of the original manuscript would have not been possible. Special acknowledgment and gratitude are also due to Professor Robert K. Sakai of the University of Hawaii, Professor Frank Klingberg of Southern Illinois University, Professor Lee Chong-sik of the University of Pennsylvania, and Professor Glenn D. Paige of Princeton University for their kind and most helpful suggestions, as well as their pains in examining the manuscript for factual accuracy and textual correctness. I also extend my grateful thanks to my colleagues at Yun-sei University, Korea University, and International Christian University in Tokyo for their advice and helpful comments on the original manuscript. To Dr. Yu Chin-o, Dr. George Paik, and Dr. Ukai Sinsei, the presidents of the above three universities, and to Mr. William L. Eilers and Mr. James Stewart of the Asia Foundation, I express my special gratitude for financial assistance in various stages of the study. The University of Nebraska also generously provided me with a fund for typing the manuscript. I gratefully acknowledge the help of Professor Oval Alexander, Chairman of the Department of Government of Southern Illinois University, Professor Carl J. Schneider, Chairman of the Political Science Department of the University of Nebraska, and Professor George E. Taylor, Director of the Far Eastern and Russian Institute of the University of Washington, for their efforts in bringing me to their institutions as a visiting professor and continually encouraging me to complete this work. My sincere thanks go also to my editor, Miss S. Wander, for her patience and thoughtful guidance. To graduate assistants at the University of Nebraska, I extend my appreciation for their help.

I am deeply grateful for the constant advice and suggestions of the above persons. They are, in spirit, coauthors. But the contents and shortcomings of this book are, of course, solely mine.

In the romanization of Korean words this study follows the McCune-Reischauer system except for a few commonly accepted personal and proper names such as Syngman Rhee (Yi Sŭng-man), Lyuh Woon-hyung (Yŏ Un-hyŏng), Kimm Kiu-sic (Kim Kyu-sik), Kim Koo (Kim Ku) and Seoul (Sŏul). As a rule, with few exceptions, the family name is presented first, and the first and middle name are connected by a hyphen.

Contents

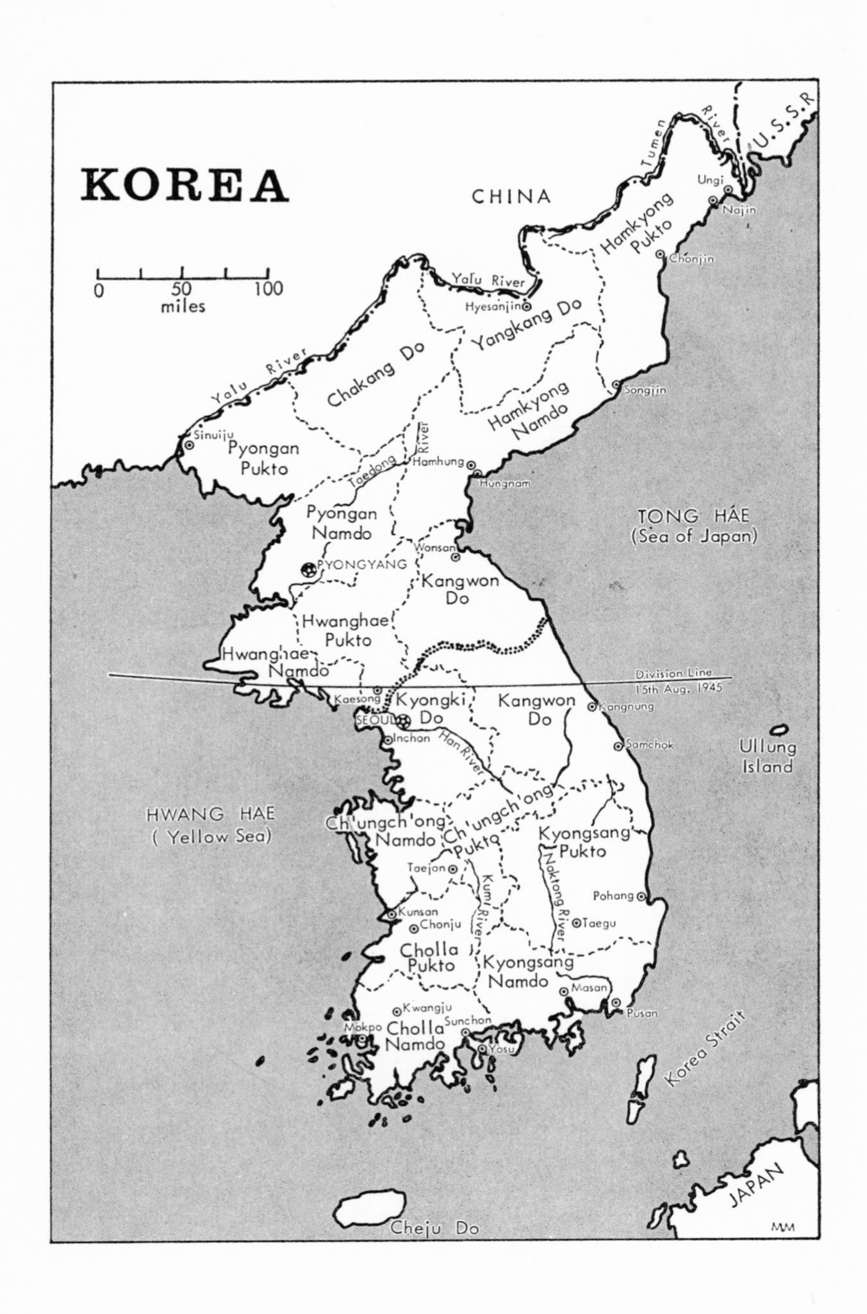
KOREA
0
50
100
miles
CHINA
U.S.S.R
Tumen River
Yalu River
Ungi
Najin
Hamkyong Pukto
Chonjin
Hyesanjin
Yangkang Do
Chakang Do
Songjin
Hamkyong Namdo
Sinuiju
Pyongan Pukto
Taedong River
Hamhung
Hungnam
TONG HAE
(Sea of Japan)
Pyongan Namdo
Wonsan
PYONGYANG
Kangwon Do
Hwanghae Pukto
Hwanghae Namdo
Division Line
15th Aug. 1945
Kaesong
Kyongki Do
Kangwon Do
Kangnung
SEOUL
Inchon
Han River
Samchok
Ullung Island
HWANG HAE
(Yellow Sea)
Ch'ungch'ong Namdo
Ch'ungch'ong Pukto
Kyongsang Pukto
Taejon
Kumi River
Naktong River
Pohang
Kunsan
Chonju
Taegu
Cholla Pukto
Kyongsang Namdo
Masan
Pusan
Kwangju
Sunchon
Mokpo
Cholla Namdo
Yosu
Korea Strait
JAPAN
Cheju Do
MM

Introduction

This study is concerned primarily with American policy toward Korea during a specific period—from the Cairo Conference in 1943 to the eve of the Korean War in 1950. Its particular focus is on those policy decisions which led, first, to the division of the country and then sought, unsuccessfully, to bring about its reunification. My aim has been to discover how and why the important policy decisions were reached; and to examine the reasons why those policies ended so dismally in failure. I have also attempted to find what the record may reveal of possible patterns in American responses to the international Communist challenge, and to internal political developments within Korea.

American policy toward Korean independence and unification evolved in distinct, though related, phases. In the interest of clarity, I have treated these phases separately and chronologically. The study is therefore organized into three parts, according to the shifts in United States policy which were called forth by Soviet challenges.

Part I deals with the wartime period from 1943 up to the end of hostilities. It examines the discussions and agreements concerning the future status of Korea and the trusteeship project which took place among the allied leaders at the various conferences of Cairo, Teheran, Yalta and Potsdam. An attempt is also made to clarify the origin of the 38th parallel as a dividing line between American and Soviet zones of military operations, showing how the decision was reached and why such a division was considered necessary.

Part II covers the period immediately following the end of the Second World War. This was the phase of "attempted cooperation" with the Soviet Union to establish "an effective, democratic, and unified Korean Government." Optimistic hopes could still exist for the settlement of Korean problems. If good faith on the part of the Soviet Union can be assumed, it was the last period during which some amicable arrangement might have been possible—had both the United States and the Soviet Union had effective, consistent, and constructive policies toward Korea. This portion of the study also deals with the initial period of American military government in Korea, and shows how that authority treated the *de facto* government in Korea. Finally, it analyzes the impasse reached in the Joint Commission, which had been brought into being ostensibly to carry out the agreement of the Moscow Foreign Ministers Conference regarding trusteeship for Korea.

Part III is devoted to the Korean policy of the United States during the period of containment, from 1947 to 1950. Although it was events in Europe that called forth the Truman Doctrine and the Marshall Plan, there were prompt repercussions in Asia. The containment policy ended any remaining prospects of a unified Korea: both the United States and the Soviet Union moved actively toward the establishment of two separate governments in Korea. The American containment policy in Korea was markedly different, however, from its counterpart in Europe. Analysis of these differences, both of scope and method, shows that, though containment may have been the intent, the reality was rather one of American resignation and withdrawal. This part also considers American motives in taking the question of Korean independence to the UN General Assembly, despite the knowledge that this would foster a permanent Korean division rather than unification. The last chapter analyzes the inadequate Korean aid program, which resulted in gross unpreparedness for the North Korean aggression of 1950.

It is difficult to determine causality for all the complex phenomena, large or small, in the field of international relations. This is particularly true in an analysis of a major political situation of such complexity and widespread ramifications as the problem of Korean unification and independence in the postwar period. The failure of these thirty-eight million people, with a rich tradition of cultural achievement and an independent political heritage, to take their rightful place in the world community as a free, united, and democratic country may be considered tragic. In attempting to trace the historical events that led up to this national calamity, it is impossible to single out any one factor as being solely responsible for the present division of Korea. Many factors have contributed to the impasse.

Principal contributing elements must certainly include: the deterioration of the relationship which had existed during the Second World War between the Soviet Union and the United States; the dramatic bipolarization of world power which took place as a result of that war; and the aggressive policy of the Soviet Union in the Far East.

The events following the war demonstrate the difficulty in trying to base foreign policy on laws, moral principles, or ideals, unless all parties approach the peaceful settlement of international disputes in the same spirit. Unquestionably, a major cause of the confusion that characterized Far Eastern politics in the postwar period was the refusal of the Soviet Union to honor its international agreements, notably those regarding the independence and unification of Korea which had been made at Cairo, Yalta and the Moscow Foreign Ministers Conference. Had the Soviet Union respected those agreements and shown a more compromising attitude at the negotiating table, there might well not be the problem of a divided Korea today. The unfortunate fact is that the national interests of the United States and the Soviet Union clashed and became dominant in the resolution of the Korean problem. The result was a permanent division, instead of the independence and unification that had been pledged.

It is also true that the events that lead to a divided Korea cannot be blamed wholly on international considerations. The Korean domestic situation after the defeat of Japan was itself a contributing factor. For thirty-five years the Korean people had been deprived of political training and the art of governmental administration. The sudden exodus of Japanese officials left a chaotic situation that was unparalleled elsewhere in the world. The lack of political experience, administrative acumen, and strong leadership made the Korean people easy prey for disorganized, irresponsible, and highly factious political parties which spawned overnight. Had there been strong leadership, and had the Koreans firmly agreed on the goal of unification of their motherland, the prospects would certainly have been improved.

Granting the complexity of the background and the presence of contributory factors, both domestic and international, it is nonetheless the major premise of this study that American policy toward Korea must be regarded, in the light of all available information, as a dominant factor in the situation which led to the division of Korea. This study, therefore, concentrates on American policy and its role in the creation of conditions under which Korean unification was frustrated.

In the course of the study, evidence will be offered in support of the following three hypotheses:

(1) The "personal diplomacy" of President Franklin D. Roosevelt, together with his own and President Truman's reliance upon the advice of military leaders in the period of wartime diplomacy, were major causes of the division of Korea.

(2) The almost complete lack of coordination between the local occupation authority in Seoul and the policy planners in Washington was a constant source of confusion and inconsistency and thus further hindered the unification of Korea.

(3) The failure of the United States to formulate an effective policy for Korean unification was due largely to Korea's remoteness from the presumed American national interest.

These hypotheses are interrelated and interacting. In analyzing the development of American policy toward Korean independence and unification with special attention to the above hypotheses, this study also attempts to shed light on such questions as: What American assumptions were made concerning Asian policy with reference to Korea? What were the Americans trying to achieve? What tactics and strategy were used to obtain this goal? To what extent did their policies reflect understanding of the aspirations of this newly emancipated people? And, finally, what were the alternative means of achieving unification besides those tried by the United States and the Soviet Union?

The reader who comes to a book such as this will already be generally familiar, I am sure, with at least the rough outlines of Korea's location and her unhappy history in modern times. A peninsula of only some 85,000 square miles, Korea commands the sea routes westward to Manchuria and the north Chinese mainland. To the east, it projects in such a way that it has been traditionally thought of by Japanese as "a dagger pointed at the heart of Japan." Looked at from the opposite direction, it becomes, with equal logic, "a hammer ready to strike at the head of China." To the north, the peninsula commands the port of Vladivostok, Russia's important naval base and vital outlet to the Pacific. Geography, then, has had a basic role in dictating Korea's dilemma.

Thus it was, by 1882, that impatient foreign pressures

forced this ancient, "Hermit Kingdom" reluctantly to open its doors to the world—and to be engulfed at once in the imperialistic ambitions of her far more powerful neighbors. Hampered by a weak economic foundation, confused leadership, political ineptitude, and a tardy start in facing the problems of modernization, Korea was the unwilling and largely helpless object of contention among the Powers. This phase was ended only when Japan succeeded in driving off her chief rivals—first China, and then Russia—and formally annexed Korea in 1910. It was not surprising, after the defeat of Japan in 1945, that Korea became once again the cause of friction between great powers.

One outstanding difference between the pre-1910 situation and that of 1945 was the changed, and now dominant, role of the United States. Great though America's part was in defeating the Axis in Europe, in the Far East its share in the crushing of Japan had been overwhelming.

Uniquely in Korea's experience of the modern world, her relationship with the United States had historically always been one of friendship. The United States had no territorial or political interests in the area and had attempted to protect it through policies such as the Open Door and the Most-Favored-Nation clause. Thus, from 1882 to 1902, the United States championed Korean independence and territorial integrity. But almost from the first American contact with Asia, United States policy toward Korea has been torn between allegiance to lofty moral principles and an acceptance of hard political and geographical realities. So, at a time in 1905 when American help to Korea was most needed, the United States, in a secret agreement between Prime Minister Katsura and Secretary of War Taft, officially approved Japan's suzerainty over Korea (in return for a Japanese disavowal of any aggressive designs on the Philippines).

After the Japanese annexation in 1910, Korea was all but forgotten by Americans until 1943. By then, the progress of the war against the Axis Powers forced consideration of postwar territorial arrangements and the Cairo Conference declared that the United States, the United Kingdom, and China, "mindful of the enslavement of the people of Korea, are determined that in due course Korea shall become free and independent." The Cairo statement marked a significant turning point in American policy toward Korea. It not only promised the formal return of the United States into Korean affairs, it was also an American commitment to the independence of Korea. It further took for granted, one might add, the unity of the Korean peninsula. The United States, by solemn undertaking, and by the logic of her new status as world power, assumed a position of vital importance for the destiny of Korea in the postwar era.

Unhappily, the United States was neither aware of the problems nor ready to carry out her commitment when the quick end of the war brought her directly into the Korean situation. Lacking an informed, effective or consistent policy, the result was frustration, fumbling, and finally only a half-hearted commitment to Korean defense. It is not too harsh, I believe, to say that the deficiencies of American policy in this period—basically a policy of resignation and withdrawal—contributed largely to the outbreak of the Korean War.

That event, and the related tensions between the free and Communist worlds, caused the American people and its leaders to obligate themselves firmly to defend the Republic of Korea. American policy toward Korea during the decade 1950 to 1960 was uncompromising in its determination. Korea was to be defended as an important part of blocking the advance of communism in East Asia. In addition, America seemed anxious to build the Republic of Korea as a "show-window of democracy" in Asia, perhaps in the hope that an economically prosperous South Korea could eventually play the role of another West Germany. One consequence was a decline of interest in discussing the possible reunification of Korea.

American policy toward Korea seems gradually to be moving toward a new turning point—as Korea itself is trying to find a role for itself in the free world. America's relationship toward Korea—like its relationships with Japan, the Philippines and Formosa—is slowly changing from that of protective guardianship to one of freer, but still undefined, association. But the fact is inescapable that American policy, however directed, will have great influence during the coming decade in determining Korea's future.

The Korean people, then, are entering a critical period. Will they remain a "free" nation? Will they be placed in the orbit of Communist China? Will they be neutralized by the power politics of their giant neighbors? These alternatives are not really new: they have their roots in the years before the Korean War. By examining the record—and inadequacies—of American policy during this period, we hope to obtain valuable historical lessons which may help in better understanding and more effective solution of the problems which lie ahead.

I have not intended to offer here a panacea for the current Korean impasse. At the present moment, there is probably no feasible means to bring about reunification. Nevertheless, the modern tragedy of Korea is one that neither Americans nor Koreans can neglect. Under the threatening conditions of the world today, American policy toward Korea cannot afford to be either stagnant or complacent. For success, that policy requires flexibility and imagination. And it must be based on comprehensive knowledge of the facts, and an awareness and consideration of—if not sympathy with—the Korean point of view.

I write, of course, as a Korean. Though I have tried, it is too much to hope that I have achieved complete objectivity. There are also limitations, I realize, in my knowledge of American foreign policy and other matters covered here. I can only say that I have written this book in the sincere hope that it may help to avoid a repetition of past mistakes, and contribute to the mutual understanding between the peoples of Korea and the United States which I believe so important.

Part I

Legacy of Wartime Diplomacy

1

Korea in Wartime Conferences: Cairo, Teheran, and Yalta

Following Japan's Twenty-one Demands on China in 1915, the United States rarely recognized arrangements in the area that violated its rights under the Open Door policy and the Most-Favored-Nation clause. Japan's actions in Manchuria, in violation of the Nine-power Treaty of 1922, and her subsequent withdrawal from the League of Nations in 1933, gradually turned American policy toward nonrecognition of Japanese claims to special interests in North China.

Nevertheless, the United States recognized Japan's predominant interests in Korea and treated Korea as an integral part of the Japanese Empire. Despite vigorous efforts by Korean leaders in exile and their friends to persuade the State Department that the Japanese annexation of Korea would eventually lead to armed conflict between the United States and Japan, the State Department remained apathetic regarding Korea. Korea had become virtually a forgotten nation. In truth, the United States could have done little even if it had wanted to, because the annexation of Korea was a *fait accompli* long before its formal proclamation.

The Atlantic Charter of August, 1941, incorporating the basic principles of future peace upon which President Roosevelt and Prime Minister Churchill agreed, asserted the right of national self-determination without defining the geographical areas affected.[1] For the United States, this meant accepting full responsibility for the defeat of the Axis powers and the establishment of a democratic peace.[2] The Eight Points of the Atlantic Charter encouraged people who had long hoped for a better world order, and especially gave hope to the conquered and exploited. The Korean leaders in exile were particularly encouraged by its promise: that people who had been denied the right to choose their own form of government would have that right in the future.

Subsequently, the Provisional Government of the Republic of Korea, then situated in Chungking, China, strenuously sought official recognition by the Chinese and American Governments. Its efforts won the sympathy of many Chinese leaders, and in April, 1942, the Chinese government proposed to "extend such recognition without delay." [3] However, the United States opposed the according of recognition to any one Korean group, in view of such factors as: (a) the lack of unity existing among Korean groups and (b) the possibility that the groups now existing outside of Korea have little association with the Korean population in Korea.

---

[1] For text, see U.S. Department of State, *Cooperative War Effort*, Department of State Publication 1732, Executive Agreement Series 236 (Washington, 1942), p. 4.

[2] William L. Langer and S. Everett Gleason, *The Undeclared War, 1940–1941* (New York, 1953), pp. 677–692.

[3] See the telegram by the Secretary of State to the Ambassador in China dated May 1, 1942. U.S. Department of State, *Foreign Relations of the United States: Diplomatic Papers, 1942* (Washington, 1960), Vol. 1, pp. 873–875. For the Chinese point of view, see Ko Chih-feng, *Ch'ao-hsien Ko-ming-shih* (History of the Korean Revolution) (Shanghai, 1945). For the Korean point of view, see Aeguk Tongji Wŏnho Hoe, *Han'guk Tongnip Undong Sa* (History of the Korean Independence Movement) (Seoul, 1956); Ch'oe Nam-sŏn, *Taehan Tongnip Undong Sa* (History of the Korean Independence Movement) (Seoul, 1946); Yi Sŏn-kŭn, *Han'guk Tongnip Undong Sa* (History of the Korean Independence Movement) (Seoul, 1956); and Pak Ŭn-sik, *Han'guk tongnip Ŭndongchi Hyŏlsa* (The Bloody History of the Korean Independence Movement) (Seoul, 1946).

Accordingly, the Chinese government withheld recognition.[4]

Despite their enlightened statement espousing the principle of self-determination, Roosevelt and Churchill apparently devoted little practical or detailed thought to an independent Korea. Diplomacy was influenced during this period more by military considerations than by possible future political developments. Statesmen and military men in both America and Britain were absorbed more in the immediate problem of winning the war than in long-range plans.

Following Japan's attack on Pearl Harbor, Churchill arrived in Washington on December 23, 1941, for strategic planning with Roosevelt and the British and American military leaders. It was decided at this conference to concentrate first upon the defeat of Germany and then upon that of Japan.[5] One consequence of this strategy was that the Pacific Theater suffered considerable delays in getting supplies; another was that China was virtually exhausted by the autumn of 1942.[6]

Japan's success in the Burma campaign effectively isolated China from her allies. The collapse of China would be a serious blow to the South Pacific Command, for it was imperative to have a large part of Japan's forces engaged in the China Theater so that American forces would be able to counterattack in the Pacific area. If China were to survive, it was essential to reopen a land route through Burma. To meet this goal, the Combined Chiefs of Staff, in a London meeting on May 8, 1943, proposed a program for an intensified China-Burma-India campaign, including a plan for an

---

[4] *Foreign Relations of the United States, 1942,* pp. 875–876.

[5] General Marshall was a strong advocate of this strategy; see Winston S. Churchill, *The Grand Alliance* (Boston, 1950), p. 705. See also General Marshall's report, "The Winning of the War in Europe and the Pacific, 1943–45," in *The War Reports of General of the Army George C. Marshall, General of the Army H. H. Arnold, Fleet Admiral Ernest J. King,* ed. Walter Millis (New York, 1947), p. 153.

[6] General Albert C. Wedemeyer, *Wedemeyer Reports* (New York, 1958), pp. 209–219, 275–301.

assault upon the Japanese forces in Burma by cooperating British, American, and Chinese forces.[7] The Chinese government, however, was reluctant to commit five divisions of her dwindling forces to Burma unless assured of British and American naval and air support, including an amphibious landing in southern Burma. In order to obtain more active Chinese cooperation, Roosevelt suggested to Chiang Kai-shek that they meet sometime during the autumn, at a place midway between their two capitals, to discuss mutual problems. This meeting took place in Cairo in November, 1943.[8]

Earlier, in March, 1943, Roosevelt had met with the British Foreign Secretary, Anthony Eden. In the course of their discussion, they touched upon their postwar policies regarding Manchuria, Korea, Formosa, and Indochina. They agreed that Manchuria and Formosa should be returned to China, and that Korea should be placed under an international trusteeship with China, the United States, and one or two other countries participating.[9] In October, 1943, just before Secretary of State Hull left for Moscow, Roosevelt conveyed these ideas to him. Roosevelt mentioned that Indochina and the Japanese-mandated islands might "be

---

[7] Charles F. Romanus and Riley Sunderland, *Stilwell's Mission to China* (Washington, 1953), p. 332. This volume is one of the series *United States Army in World War II* prepared by the Office of the Chief of Military History, Department of the Army. According to Sherwood, Churchill viewed the proposals with "scant enthusiasm." Robert E. Sherwood, *Roosevelt and Hopkins: An Intimate History* (New York, 1948), p. 772.

[8] For detailed information on the meeting, see Herbert Feis, *Churchill–Roosevelt–Stalin: The War They Waged and the Peace They Sought* (Princeton, 1957), pp. 237–256. For the Chinese side of the story, see Tang Tsou, *America's Failure in China: 1941–1950* (Chicago, 1963), pp. 63–73.

[9] Cordell Hull, *The Memoirs of Cordell Hull* (New York, 1948), Vol. II, p. 1596. See also the "Memorandum of Conversation by the Secretary of State, March 27, 1943" in U.S. Department of State, *Foreign Relations of the United States: Diplomatic Papers, 1943* (Washington, 1963), Vol. III, p. 37.

placed under international trustees, along with security points in other parts of the world." [10]

The President had long cherished the idea that the liberated Asian colonial peoples should come under the tutelage of the Great Powers and be educated in democratic institutions. He thought that the history of the Philippines in the last 44 years provided, in a very real sense, "a pattern for the future of other small nations and peoples of the world." As early as 1942, he expressed the ideas that "there [should] be a period of preparation through the dissemination of education" and that "there [should] be a period of training for ultimate independent sovereignty, through the practice of more and more self-government, beginning with local government and passing on through the various steps to complete statehood." [11]

THE CAIRO CONFERENCE

We can assume that these ideas were present in Roosevelt's mind when he met with Generalissimo Chiang Kai-shek at Cairo to discuss the future of Asia. At the time of this conference, Great Britain was not much interested in the discussion of future arrangements in the Far East. Churchill thought that Roosevelt's treatment of China as a Great Power was "a great illusion" and "a great farce," and he was disturbed when Roosevelt permitted Allied talks at Cairo to be distracted "by the Chinese story which was lengthy, complicated, and minor." [12] On the other hand, Roosevelt at this time believed that China should be considered one of the Great Powers in the world after the victory had been won.

---

[10] Hull, Vol. II, pp. 1595–1596.

[11] Speech of November 15, 1942. *The Public Papers and Addresses of Franklin D. Roosevelt,* ed. Samuel Rosenman (New York, 1950), 1942 volume, pp. 473–476.

[12] Winston S. Churchill, *Closing the Ring* (Boston, 1951), p. 328. See also Edward R. Stettinius, *Roosevelt and the Russians: The Yalta Conference* (New York, 1949), p. 71.

In fact, Roosevelt had decided to support China as one of the Great Powers long before the meeting at Cairo. Robert E. Sherwood writes that Roosevelt went to Cairo determined that "this conference should be a success from the Chinese point of view." [13] As for Korea, Britain had never supported Korean independence and had, in fact, positively favored Japanese hegemony over the peninsula since 1902. Sir Alexander Cadogan, British Undersecretary of State for Foreign Affairs, initially opposed the inclusion of any statement concerning Korean independence in the declaration that was issued at the conclusion of the conference.[14] His reasons are not stated in available sources, but we can speculate that he thought that if Japan were allowed to retain Korea, it would be possible to reach an agreement with her and thus shorten the war in the Pacific. Chiang Kai-shek bitterly resented what he considered the British attitude of appeasement. No Chinese leader could forget that the Japanese invasion of the Chinese mainland had its basis from the moment that Japan occupied the Korean peninsula. Thus, "deeply concerned as he was over the question of Korean independence, President Chiang made a special effort in enlisting President Roosevelt's support in our stand." [15] Having no immediate interest in Korea's future, Britain agreed to follow America's lead in settling the question of Korean independence.

The Conference communiqué was made public on December 1, 1943, and read as follows:

> The several military missions have agreed upon future military operations against Japan. The Three Great Allies expressed their resolve to bring unrelenting pressure against

---

[13] Sherwood, p. 773.

[14] Chang Chi-yün, *Record of the Cairo Conference* (Taipei, China, 1953), pp. 4–10. Since the United Kingdom has not released the documents on the Cairo Conference, there is no way to discover the given reasons of Sir Alexander Cadogan. No American sources recorded the British stand on Korea.

[15] *Ibid.*, p. 6.

their brutal enemies by sea, land and air. This pressure is already rising.

The Three Great Allies are fighting this war to restrain and punish the aggression of Japan. They covet no gain for themselves and have no thought of territorial expansion. It is their purpose that Japan shall be stripped of all the islands in the Pacific which she has seized or occupied since the beginning of the First World War in 1914, and that all the territories Japan has stolen from the Chinese, such as Manchuria, Formosa, and the Pescadores, shall be restored to the Republic of China. Japan will also be expelled from all other territories which she has taken by violence and greed. The aforesaid three great powers, mindful of the enslavement of the people of Korea, are determined that in due course Korea shall become free and independent.

With these objects in view the three Allies, in harmony with those of the United Nations at war with Japan, will continue to persevere in the serious and prolonged operations necessary to procure the unconditional surrender of Japan.[16]

By this statement, the three powers officially committed themselves to the independence of Korea after the war. However, the phrase "in due course" left some question as to the nature of this commitment. Dr. Syngman Rhee, the representative in the United States of the Provisional Government of Korea, was greatly alarmed by the phrase, for he believed that it could only mean the indefinite postponement of independence. He issued a series of statements condemning this restrictive phrase, and addressed letters to the State Department and to President Roosevelt asking for clarification of its intent, but he received no answers.[17]

Although the phrase "in due course" had a distinctively British flavor, it seems almost certain that the thinking behind it was Roosevelt's. The original draft of the Cairo Dec-

---

[16] U.S. Department of State, *In Quest of Peace and Security: Selected Documents on American Foreign Policy, 1941–1951* (Washington, 1951), p. 10.

[17] *Foreign Relations of the U.S., 1943,* Vol. III, p. 1096.

laration, dictated by Harry Hopkins, used the phrase "at the earliest possible moment." However, this phrase was revised to read "at the proper moment," apparently by Roosevelt. It seems probable that Churchill may have examined the revised draft and altered the phrase into its final form. The British draft of the communiqué, which is virtually identical with the final version of the declaration, used the unfortunate phrase "in due course." [18] According to the study of Herbert Feis, it is not recorded whether the draft was informally discussed with Chiang, but reliable Chinese sources reveal that Chiang had considerable influence at this conference.[19]

Secretary of State Hull later remarked in his memoirs that he considered the wording unwise for several reasons. One reason was that "the Koreans wanted their independence immediately [after] Korea was liberated and not in due course"; another reason was that this wording led the Koreans to fear that their country would be placed under the control of China. Hull also felt that the Soviet Union should have been consulted by the makers of the declaration, not only because she was their ally in Europe, but also because she had a traditional interest in Korea.[20]

Although Hull knew that the meetings at Cairo and

---

[18] U.S. Department of State, *Foreign Relations of the United States: Diplomatic Papers, Conferences at Cairo and Teheran, 1943* (Washington, 1961), pp. 399–404, hereafter cited as *Conferences at Cairo and Teheran*. The first draft was dated November 24, 1943, the day after the first formal meeting with Chiang.

[19] Chang Chi-yün, pp. 4–10. Hollington K. Tong, Chinese Ambassador to Japan, assured Mr. Oliver in August, 1953, that the Cairo pledge for Korean independence was inserted in the Joint Declaration only at the suggestion of Chiang Kai-shek. See Robert T. Oliver, *Syngman Rhee: The Man Behind the Myth* (New York, 1954), p. 365.

[20] Hull, Vol. II, p. 1584. The Korean representative in Chungking, China, expressed to the American Embassy his country's fear of Chinese intentions with regard to the postwar status of Korea and demanded clarification of the term "in due course." *Foreign Relations of the United States, 1943,* Vol. III, p. 1096.

Teheran were being planned, he did not actively share in the determination of American aims and decisions. The President did not consult with Hull before the meetings were arranged; nor did he consult with him before agreeing with Chiang Kai-shek and Churchill on a statement that independence would be restored to Korea "in due course." [21] President Roosevelt clearly dominated the wartime diplomacy of the United States. If he had better understood the problem of Korea; if he had consulted Hull and adopted his views on this phrase; and if he had been able to foresee the intense wave of nationalism that was to sweep over all of the colonial nations at the end of the war, this unfortunate wording might have been omitted from the declaration, and the ultimate division of Korea could well have been avoided.

STALIN AT TEHERAN

From Cairo, Roosevelt went to Teheran to meet with Marshal Stalin. Stalin had stayed away from Cairo, and had kept Molotov away, because he did not want the Soviet government to be associated at this stage in a conference with the Chinese government. He feared that Japan might close the port of Vladivostok in retaliation. Chiang Kai-shek was also hesitant about meeting the Russian leader face to face; he was not certain whether he could talk amicably with Stalin in such an encounter.[22] Therefore, Roosevelt arranged separate meetings with each of these two leaders.

At the meetings with the Anglo-American leaders in Teheran, Stalin officially reaffirmed what he had said to Cor-

---

[21] Hull wrote: "I learned from other sources than the President, what had occurred at the Casablanca, Cairo, and Teheran Conferences. I had no special occasion to interrogate Mr. Roosevelt on the developments at these conferences." Hull, Vol. II, p. 1110.

[22] Herbert Feis, *The China Tangle: The American Effort in China from Pearl Harbor to the Marshall Mission* (Princeton, 1953), p. 104. His accounts were based on the State Department documents and on a letter from Hurley to President Roosevelt from Cairo, November 20, 1943.

dell Hull at Moscow a few weeks earlier: that once Germany had been defeated, Russia would join in the war against Japan. Although Stalin's original promise to Hull had been "unsolicited" and, as far as Hull could judge, "had no strings attached to it," it became apparent at Teheran that Stalin expected substantial rewards.[23] He wanted all of Sakhalin and the Kurile Islands to be transferred to Russia to facilitate control of the straits leading to Siberia; he also expressed interest in Dairen and in the Soviet use of Manchurian railways. Recognizing that the Soviet Union had no ice-free port in the Far East, Roosevelt and Churchill agreed that Dairen should become "a free port under international guarantee."[24] The two western leaders also gave their consent to the other demands without hesitation.

Although Korea was discussed only briefly in the conference of Roosevelt, Churchill, and Stalin, the discussions had great significance for the future of Korea, inasmuch as Stalin tentatively agreed with Roosevelt's idea for Korean trusteeship.[25] Before the Teheran Conference went into formal session, Roosevelt reviewed with Stalin his conversations with Chiang Kai-shek and his plans for China and the Pacific areas. Stalin then remarked only that he thought China had fought very poorly because of incompetent leadership, and he expressed his opposition to granting China such a large part in the settlement of world affairs; he thought that the small powers would resent having China act against them.[26] At one of the first formal meetings at Teheran, on November 28, 1943, Roosevelt referred to one of his favorite topics, the

---

[23] Hull, Vol. II, pp. 1309–1310. See also U.S. Department of State, *United States Relations with China* (Washington, 1949), p. 113.

[24] Sherwood, pp. 791–792. A record shows that Roosevelt had discussed this matter with Chiang at Cairo. Chiang indicated that he would not object to this, provided Russia cooperated with China and that Chinese sovereignty was not impaired. See *U.S. Relations with China*, p. 558.

[25] *China Tangle*, p. 113; and *Churchill–Roosevelt–Stalin*, p. 254.

[26] *China Tangle*, pp. 111–114.

education of the people of the Far Eastern colonial areas in the art of self-government. He pointed with pride to the American record in helping the people of the Philippines to prepare themselves for independence. He continued, suggesting that Korea would "need some period of apprenticeship before full independence might be attained, perhaps forty years." [27] Subsequently, Stalin agreed with this proposal.[28]

One wonders why Roosevelt specified forty years for the tutelage of Korea. No available material reveals his reasons, but we can speculate that he intended to base the period of tutelage on the American experience in the Philippines. If this was the case, it indicates that Roosevelt's approach to the problem of Korean independence was lacking in insight, and that he failed to grasp the fact that no two nations are alike. Without studying the ability of the Korean people to govern themselves, and apparently without consulting the experts on Korean affairs, Roosevelt strongly influenced the fate of thirty million people by proposing to impose upon them a long and unnecessary period of tutelage. Even worse, he seemed unable to foresee the role of the Soviet Union in the future of Korea. In view of the century-long rivalry of great powers to control the Korean peninsula, and in view of the fact that Koreans had governed themselves effectively for more than a thousand years, Roosevelt's decision appears ill-considered.

Churchill reopened the discussion of the Far Eastern problems at a luncheon on November 30, 1943, by asking Stalin whether he had read the Cairo communiqué. Stalin answered that although he could make no commitments, he

---

[27] Sherwood, p. 777. Harry S Truman, *Years of Trial and Hope* (New York, 1956), p. 316.

[28] *Conferences at Cairo and Teheran,* p. 869. Upon his return from Teheran, Roosevelt summed up for the Pacific War Council the main points upon which agreement had been reached with Stalin and Chiang. Here he mentioned that they agreed "Korea was to be under forty year tutelage."

thoroughly approved of the communiqué and all its contents. He positively remarked that "it was right that Korea should be independent and that Manchuria, Formosa, and the Pescadores Island should be returned to China." [29] While the promise of Korea's independence was made in the spirit of historic justice and according to the humanitarian ideals manifested in the Atlantic Charter, the leaders of the Great Powers were hesitant to promise immediate independence to colonized peoples such as those in Korea, Burma, Indochina, and Indonesia. Restoration of the *status quo ante bellum* was more urgent for the Powers than the creation of a new order immediately after the victory.

NECESSITY FOR RUSSIAN HELP

The American leaders were delighted by Stalin's promise to enter the war against Japan; they believed that a joint attack by Chinese, Russian, and American troops would shorten the war by many months. The military and political leaders of the United States thought that the Japanese seemed determined to fight to the last man and that even trying to predict an approximate time for the total defeat of the Japanese was senseless. On December 29, 1943, less than two years before the Japanese surrender, one of the leading American experts on Japanese affairs implied in a speech that the war might last "ten or fifty [sic] years." [30]

American military planners wanted the Russians to engage Japanese forces on the mainland to facilitate an American invasion of the Japanese islands. As early as December 8, 1941, the day after the Japanese attack on Pearl Harbor, Russian participation was suggested to Soviet Ambassador Maxim M. Litvinov by both Roosevelt and Hull. On the same day, the Chinese government made a similar proposal to the Soviet government. On December 10, General Mac-

---

[29] *Ibid.*, p. 566.

[30] A speech by Mr. Joseph C. Grew, former American Ambassador to Japan, then Special Assistant to the Secretary of State. *Department of State Bulletin*, January 1, 1944, p. 17.

Arthur recommended Soviet participation to General Marshall. Within weeks after the American and Chinese proposals, the Americans, in the face of declared Soviet neutrality in the Far East, sought to reopen negotiations by asking the Russians to facilitate deliveries of lend-lease planes to Russia.[31] In March, 1942, the United States military leaders recommended to the President that he "initiate steps on the political level looking toward a more complete military collaboration" between the United States and the Soviet Union.[32] However, at that time the Soviet Union was facing Hitler's armies in the west and had little desire to stir up the famed Japanese Kwantung Army in Manchuria. At the Quebec Conference in August, 1943, military leaders reported that Russian participation in the war in the Far East would "save time, life, and resources," and also warned that should the war in the Pacific have to be carried on without Russian assistance, "the difficulties will be immeasurably increased and operations might become abortive." [33] Meanwhile, the Joint Chiefs of Staff estimated it would take eighteen months after the defeat of Germany and cost at least 500,000 American casualties to subdue the Japanese, even with Russian help.[34] Therefore, the cooperation of the Soviet armies was felt to be indispensable to meet American war aims.

NEGOTIATIONS AT YALTA

Thirteen months after the Cairo-Teheran Conferences, the United States, Great Britain, and the Soviet Union met at

---

[31] Maurice Matloff and Edwin M. Snell, *Strategic Planning for Coalition Warfare, 1941–1942* in the series *United States Army in World War II* (Washington, 1953), pp. 142–146.

[32] *Ibid.*

[33] U.S. Department of Defense, *The Entry of the Soviet Union into War Against Japan: Military Plan, 1941–1945*. Mimeographed report released on October 19, 1955. See also Sherwood, pp. 748–749.

[34] William D. Leahy, *I Was There* (New York, 1950), p. 260. Winston S. Churchill, *Triumph and Tragedy* (Boston, 1953), pp. 388–389.

Yalta. The Yalta Conference opened on Sunday, February 4, 1945, on a rising tide of Allied victories. The German counteroffensive in the west had been halted in the bloody battle of the Ardennes Forest, and the Allies were preparing to launch their main drive across the Rhine. First priority at Yalta was given, therefore, to European political and military problems, and to the creation of an international peace organization.

The Yalta Conference then focused on the question of the Soviet Union's participation in the Pacific war. The crucial question was whether Russia would join the war in time to assist the Allied invasion of the Japanese home islands. It was possible that the Soviet Union might wait until the Allies had defeated Japan at great cost, and then the Soviet Red Army would march into Manchuria and overrun a large area of North China. Therefore, the United States and Great Britain were primarily concerned with making certain that Russia's participation would be both reliable and effective.

The Pacific war and Far Eastern problems were discussed in a series of meetings. As America pressed for more Russian action in Asia, Stalin's price rose: "Mr. Stalin [was] not bashful about making demands."[35] Stalin stated that certain concessions desired in the Far East by the Russians were essential for Russian entry into the war against Japan. "Without these conditions," Stalin contended, "the Supreme Soviet and the Russian people would wonder why they had entered the war in the Far East." He elaborated that the Soviet people understood the German war because of the German attack on their country, but since the Japanese had made no overt move against Russia, concessions would be necessary to justify Soviet entry.[36] Using this argument, Stalin obtained many concessions which might otherwise have been impossible.

The final agreement reached by the three powers on the

---

[35] James F. Byrnes, *Speaking Frankly* (New York, 1947), p. 43.
[36] Stettinius, p. 92.

conditions of Russia's participation in the Pacific war was based primarily on military considerations, despite the ostensibly political nature of the meetings between Roosevelt, Churchill, and Stalin.[37] Although the Yalta Conference was one of the most carefully planned wartime summit conferences ever held, and although the United States had previously been made aware of the extent of Stalin's demands through Ambassador Harriman,[38] the final agreement illustrates that the United States went to Yalta inadequately and unrealistically prepared on Far Eastern problems. Nonetheless, pressured by American military leaders to secure Russian action "at the earliest possible date," [39] President Roosevelt signed the controversial document.

By this document, it was agreed that the Soviet Union would enter into the war against Japan on these conditions:

1. The status quo in Outer-Mongolia (The Mongolian People's Republic) shall be preserved;
2. The former rights of Russia violated by the attack of Japan in 1904 shall be restored, viz:
   (a) the southern part of Sakhalin, as well as the islands adjacent to it, shall be returned to the Soviet Union,
   (b) the commercial port of Dairen shall be internationalized, the preeminent interests of the Soviet Union in this port are being safeguarded and the lease of Port Arthur as a naval base of the U.S.S.R. restored,
   (c) the Chinese-Eastern Railroad and the South-Manchurian Railroad which provides an outlet to Dairen shall be operated by the establishment of a joint Soviet-Chinese Company, it being understood that the preeminent in-

---

[37] John L. Snell (ed.), *The Meaning of Yalta: Big Three Diplomacy and the New Balance of Power* (Baton Rouge, 1956), p. 136.

[38] Statement on the Yalta agreement by Harriman to the Committee on Armed Service and Foreign Relations, July 13, 1951, as cited in Richard H. Rovere and Arthur M. Schlesinger, Jr., *The General and the President* (New York, 1951), p. 347.

[39] U.S. Department of State, *Foreign Relations of the United States: Diplomatic Papers, Conferences at Malta and Yalta, 1945* (Washington, 1945), p. 396—hereafter cited as *Conferences at Malta and Yalta.*

> terests of the Soviet Union shall be safeguarded and that China shall retain full sovereignty in Manchuria;
>
> 3. The Kurile Islands shall be handed over to the Soviet Union. It is understood that the agreement concerning Outer-Mongolia and the ports and railroads referred to above will require concurrence of Generalissimo Chiang Kai-shek. The President will take measures in order to obtain this concurrence on advice from Marshal Stalin.
>
> The Heads of the three Great Powers have agreed that these claims of the Soviet Union shall be unquestionably fulfilled after Japan has been defeated.
>
> For its part the Soviet Union expresses its readiness to conclude with the National Government of China a pact of friendship and alliance between the U.S.S.R. and China in order to render assistance to China with its armed forces for the purpose of liberating China from the Japanese yoke.[40]

This secret document, signed also by Churchill and Stalin, did not contain a single reference to Korea, either directly or by implication. Although the Yalta Conference was not primarily concerned with the political problems of the Far East,[41] it is regrettable that the leaders of the three powers did not reach a formal agreement on the future status of Korea.

In preparing for the Yalta Conference, United States military planners had spent much care in outlining American strategy in the Far East, and the State Department had prepared a special briefing book for Roosevelt, setting forth United States political objectives in Asia, including one on Korea's postwar status.[42] In this briefing paper, the State Department recommended an agreement with Britain, China and, if possible, the Soviet Union, determining which countries should participate in the military occupation of

---

[40] *U.S. Relations with China,* pp. 113–114. Also, U.S. Congress, Senate, *A Decade of American Foreign Policy: Basic Documents, 1941–1949* (Washington, 1950), pp. 33–34.

[41] Only the meetings of February 8 and February 10 were devoted mainly to the problems of the Far East. *Meaning of Yalta,* pp. 148–150.

[42] *Conferences at Malta and Yalta,* p. 358.

Korea and in a possible temporary international administration or trusteeship for Korea.

With regard to the first problem, the State Department thought:

> The problems of Korea are of such an international character that with the completion of military occupation in Korea (1) there should be, so far as practicable, Allied representation in the army of occupation and military government in Korea; (2) such representation should be by those countries which have a real interest in the future status of Korea, such as the United States, Great Britain, and China and the Soviet Union if it has entered the war in the Pacific; and (3) the representation of other states should not be so large as to reduce the proportionate strength of the United States to a point where its effectiveness would be weakened.
>
> As regards the second part of the question, it is the Department's tentative opinion that (1) an interim international administration or trusteeship should be established for Korea either under the authority of the proposed international organization or independently of it; and that (2) the United States, Great Britain, China and the Soviet Union should be included in any such administration.[43]

In the briefing paper, the State Department emphasized that joint action of Allied powers for the establishment of Korean independence was "both important and necessary." It warned that the military occupation of Korea by any single power might have "far-reaching political consequences" because China and the Soviet Union are contiguous to Korea and have had a traditional interest in Korean affairs. Foreseeing the inherent danger of zonal divisions by military occupation, the State Department specifically recommended that such military government shall be an organized administration "with all of Korea administered as a single unit and not as separate zones."[44] The State Department had not yet decided which powers should partici-

---

[43] *Ibid.*, p. 359.
[44] *Ibid.*, p. 360.

pate in the military occupation. Yet it anticipated that the Soviet Union "will wish to participate in the military occupation of Korea even though [she] may not enter the war in the Pacific."

The State Department also felt that some form of international administration or trusteeship should be established "until such time as the Koreans are able to govern themselves." If such a trusteeship were established, this interim international administration should be under the authority of either the proposed United Nations or an interim administrative authority for Korea independent of the projected international organization. Either way, the State Department emphasized, "the position of the Soviet Union in the Far East is such that it would seem advisable to have Soviet representation on an interim international administration regardless of whether or not the Soviet Union enters the war in the Pacific." However, the Department stated that its studies had not progressed far enough to enable it to make a recommendation on either the precise structure for the proposed supervisory authority, or how long it should last.[45]

The State Department envisioned three steps to the establishment of Korean independence. The first stage was military occupation by Allied powers. The second was the establishment of military government under a single, unified administration. Finally, there should be a transfer of the military government's authority to a Korean government under the supervision of the trustee members, which would eventually lead to complete independence.

While the State Department predicted that occupation by any single power might have serious repercussions, it was shortsighted in not anticipating that an occupation by several powers would confuse the future political development of the Korean people. It rightly advocated that such military government should be organized on the principle of a cen-

---

[45] *Ibid.*, p. 361.

tralized administration for a single unit. The mistake was its failure to foresee that the occupation forces in their various zones would be reluctant to withdraw without leaving behind a government favorable to themselves. This problem was not unique to Korea after the war; it also existed with Nationalist Chinese forces in Indochina and with Russian troops in Manchuria. Further, the administrative ineffectiveness of a multipower military government and trusteeship system was not anticipated. Finally, the possibility that the Korean people might resist the plan for an interim administration imposed by the Allied powers, both because they had their own Provisional Government in exile and because they wished immediate independence, seems to have been overlooked.

Only two aspects of the Korean problem seem to have been touched upon at Yalta, and even those quite inconclusively. In a meeting with Stalin on February 8, 1945, President Roosevelt brought up the subject of Korea. He told Stalin that "he had in mind for Korea, a trusteeship composed of a Soviet, an American, and a Chinese representative." He stated that the only experience the United States had in such matters was in the Philippines. He added that it had taken about forty years for the Philippine people to be prepared for self-government, but "in the case of Korea, the period might be from twenty to thirty years." [46] Marshal Stalin replied: "the shorter the period, the better"; and inquired whether any foreign troops would be stationed in Korea. Roosevelt answered in the negative, to which Stalin expressed approval.[47] Presumably, this meant there would be no foreign troops during the trusteeship period following

---

[46] *Ibid.*, p. 770. Present at this meeting in Livadia Palace were Roosevelt, Harriman, Bohlen, Stalin, Molotov, and Pavlov.

[47] *Ibid.* See also Sherwood, p. 868. One source recorded that when Roosevelt proposed trusteeship for Korea, Stalin's response was "why was there any need of trusteeship if the Koreans could produce a satisfactory government." See *The Forrestal Diaries*, ed. Walter Millis (New York, 1951), p. 56.

the military occupation. The President said that "he personally did not feel that it was necessary to invite the British to participate in the trusteeship of Korea, but he felt that they might resist this." Stalin agreed that "they would most certainly be offended," adding that Churchill might "kill us." [48]

Since nowhere in the signed document was Korea mentioned, we can assume that Stalin and Roosevelt made no definite agreement at Yalta with regard to the future of the country. They did, however, reach a mutual, albeit informal, oral understanding on at least two points: that a multipower trusteeship should be established; and that no foreign troops would be permanently stationed in Korea.

In the light of subsequent events, the failure of Roosevelt to reach a formal agreement with Stalin at Yalta on the future political development of Korea must be considered a mistake of great significance. The effect of this mistake was heightened by the fact that, whereas the "Terms of Entry of the Soviet Union into the War against Japan" made no reference to Korea, it did contain a provision for the recognition of Russia's pre-1905 rights in Asia, especially in Manchuria. Thus, it should have been apparent that the Soviet Union, unless limited by formal agreement, would assert its historical interest in the political and economic affairs of Korea, even to the extent of occupying the whole or at least the northern part of the peninsula.

Although Roosevelt was certainly aware of Stalin's intent to fill the power vacuum in the Far East which would inevitably follow Japan's defeat, Roosevelt's decisions at Yalta were determined almost entirely by American military strategy, which seemed to dictate unreserved cooperation with the Soviet Union. We know now that Allied military experts continuously overestimated Japan's strength and that, even

[48] *Conferences at Malta and Yalta,* p. 770. Roosevelt said that he also had in mind a trusteeship for Indochina. However, he added that the British did not approve of this idea because they wished to return it to the French, fearing that trusteeship might affect Burma.

without the atomic bomb, Japanese industrial and military strength was nearly exhausted by the time of Yalta.[49] Many of Roosevelt's supporters defend the concessions to Russia on the ground that they were "generally matters which were within the military power of Russia to obtain regardless of United States military action short of war." [50] They believed that Russia was militarily capable of defeating the weakened Japanese defenders and seizing Karafuto, Manchuria, Korea, and North China before the United States forces could occupy these areas.[51] In spite of these justifications, subsequent events have shown that Roosevelt made too many concessions to the Soviet Union; he went too far indeed when he promised Stalin control over territories formerly under the domain of China, without having previously consulted the Chinese government.

Not only were the decisions made by the President at Yalta dictated by military considerations, he made them almost entirely alone, relying on his "personal diplomacy" as he had previously done at Cairo and Teheran. This was particularly the case regarding Korea, where Roosevelt decided almost everything on his own judgment. The talks at Yalta were essentially between Roosevelt, Churchill, and Stalin,[52] and the State Department delegation did not participate in the discussions. Although specific recommendations on Korea had been prepared by the State Department on the eve of the Yalta Conference (including a warning about zonal division for military occupation), Roosevelt did not discuss Korean problems on board the ship to Yalta, prob-

---

[49] Jerome Cohen, *Japan's Economy in War and Reconstruction* (Minneapolis, 1949), pp. 107–109.

[50] Statement of Secretary of War, Henry L. Stimson, as cited in *Meaning of Yalta,* p. 164.

[51] *Entry of the Soviet Union into War Against Japan,* p. 70.

[52] The only other persons present at the first of these meetings were Harriman and Charles E. Bohlen, who acted solely as an interpreter. Only once at Yalta did Secretary of State Stettinius have the floor concerning the Far East.

ably because of his illness. Moreover, it is also quite possible, as he mentioned none of its recommendations in his discussions with Stalin about Korea, that he had not read the briefing paper submitted by the State Department.[53]

Roosevelt's only concern seemed to be how to educate the Korean people for enlightened self-government after the model of the Philippines. Thus, he proposed forty years of tutelage at Cairo and then shortened this time limit to "twenty to thirty years" at Yalta. Without much study of Korea's cultural and political background, he accepted the phrase "in due course" at Cairo, and failed to understand the aspirations of the colonized peoples for immediate independence. Had he been better prepared, he might have effectively limited Russia's drive to dominate Korea. It certainly would have been wise to establish a time limit for the military occupation of Korea at Yalta; and a clearly defined agreement on the nature of both the occupation and the proposed interim government would have prevented the zonal division of Korea six months later. The developments in Eastern Europe as German armies were defeated and pushed back were already indicating that the Soviet Union would not abide by its agreements. Nonetheless, by failing to reach a formal agreement with Stalin on the future development of Korea, Roosevelt not only permitted the Soviet Union a free hand in Korea after the occupation, but he also prevented the Korean people from realizing the principle of self-determination that had been proclaimed in the Atlantic Charter.

---

[53] Byrnes, pp. 22–23. He wrote that "so far as I could see, the President had made little preparation for the Yalta Conference. . . . Later, when I saw some of these splendid studies [the briefing paper of the State Department] I greatly regretted that they had not been considered on board ship. I am sure the failure to study them while en route was due to the President's illness."

2

The Shadow of Roosevelt and the 38th Parallel

During the six months between the Yalta Conference and the Japanese surrender on August 14, 1945, the international pot was boiling. By the middle of March, Iwo Jima was occupied by the American marines. The American First Army had already crossed the Rhine at Remagen, and the German army was nearing collapse. Unexpectedly, President Roosevelt died on April 12, 1945, less than two weeks before the opening day of the San Francisco Conference. Germany surrendered on May 8; in July, the Allies met at Potsdam; in August, the atomic bombs were dropped on Hiroshima and Nagasaki; and on August 8, only six days before the Japanese surrender, the Soviet Union entered the Pacific war.

UNDER THE SHADOW OF ROOSEVELT'S POLICY

Roosevelt's death was a great blow to the Allied nations.[1] The war was ending, and the task of world organization and reconstruction had only just begun. It was Roosevelt who had arranged the peace settlement with Stalin and Churchill at Yalta. Almost single-handedly, he had drawn a new map of postwar Asia, with little or no reference to the State Department or to the government of China.

[1] Dwight L. Dumond, *America in Our Time: 1896–1946* (New York, 1947), p. 665.

After Roosevelt's death, great difficulties developed in Soviet-American relations. The Soviet armies were within thirty miles of Berlin and Germany's collapse was imminent. The Soviet Politburo no longer felt it essential to have America's help. In fact, Harriman had already warned that the Soviet government, once freed from the struggle against Germany, would become difficult to deal with and concerned only for Russian interests.[2] The situation was further aggravated by the fact that neither incoming President Truman nor the State Department knew much about the personal negotiations between Roosevelt and Stalin. Herbert Feis has written that Truman "knew nothing of" the contents of the Yalta Pact before entering the presidential office.[3]

What American foreign policy would have been, had Roosevelt lived, will never be known. With new men in charge, there could be no question that the ideas and methods would change. However, mainly because of his unpreparedness, Truman decided that he would stand behind what Roosevelt had done,[4] and it was only in the shadow of his predecessor that Truman was able to develop his own policy.

The State and War departments agreed that they would attempt to obtain the "unequivocal adherence of the Soviet Government to the Cairo Declaration" regarding the return of Manchuria to Chinese sovereignty and the future status of Korea as an independent nation, and to reach a definite

---

[2] Harriman's cable to the President and the Secretary of State, April 6, 1945, as cited in Herbert Feis, *The China Tangle: The American Effort in China from Pearl Harbor to the Marshall Mission* (Princeton, 1953), p. 282.

[3] Harry S. Truman, *Year of Decisions* (New York, 1955), p. 31; *The China Tangle*, p. 283.

[4] Herbert Feis, *Churchill–Roosevelt–Stalin: The War They Waged and the Peace They Sought* (Princeton, 1957), p. 599. Truman was acting in accord with the judgment of Admiral Leahy, Secretary Stimson, General Marshall, and other military advisers on whom Roosevelt had relied. Thus, the new President was able to continue his predecessor's policy without any drastic changes. *Ibid.*, pp. 596–600.

agreement with the Soviet Union that "when Korea is liberated, whether before final capitulation of Japan or after, it [can] be placed immediately under the trusteeship of the United States, Great Britain, China, and the Soviet Union." They further agreed that "this agreement should make clear that the four trustees are to be the sole authority for the selection of a temporary Korean government." [5]

If any new development of American policy on Korea under the new administration of President Truman can be pinpointed, it would seem to be that the State Department now specified four powers as members of the trusteeship for the Korean interim administration. At the time of the Yalta Conference, the State Department had indicated that its studies had not progressed far enough to enable it to make a recommendation on either the exact structure of any interim supervisory authority for Korea or the time when Korea should be granted independence.[6]

Since, as noted, the War Department had come to believe that Russia was militarily capable of defeating the Japanese and occupying Karafuto, Manchuria, Korea and Northern China before United States forces could occupy these areas, some agreement on Korean political problems was obviously crucial. Although Roosevelt had cleared the way for the trusteeship of Korea in the meetings at Cairo, Teheran, and Yalta, no agreement had yet been made on the nature of the interim international administration of Korea.

Therefore, in a meeting with President Truman on May 15, 1945, Acting Secretary of State Grew recommended that the questions of Chinese unity and of a trusteeship for Korea

---

[5] From the memorandum of the Secretary of War to Mr. Grew, Acting Secretary of State on May 12, 1945 and May 21, 1945, as quoted in Joseph C. Grew, *Turbulent Era: A Diplomatic Record of Forty Years, 1904–1945*, ed. Walter Johnson (Boston, 1952), Vol. II, pp. 1455–1458.

[6] U.S. Department of State, *Foreign Relations of the United States: Diplomatic Papers, The Conferences of Malta and Yalta* (Washington, 1955), pp. 359–361.

be immediately clarified with the Soviet Union. Truman agreed that Ambassador Harriman should not delay in returning to Moscow to clarify these matters [7]—although Harry Hopkins was eventually selected for the mission.

Following the Yalta Conference, the Soviet government had been inflexible in her relations with the Allied nations.[8] The Soviet approaches to such matters as the Polish question, the application of the Crimea agreement on Eastern European nations, and the voting procedure in the Security Council of the United Nations all served to illustrate that country's unyielding position.

While the State and War departments were discussing Far Eastern problems, Harry Hopkins set off for Moscow to talk with Stalin. It was agreed in Washington that if anyone could reassure Stalin that Roosevelt's policies would be continued under the new administration it was Hopkins, and that only he could induce Stalin to carry out the agreements reached with Roosevelt.[9]

Most of the talks between Stalin and Hopkins, which lasted from May 26 to June 6, 1945, were devoted to European affairs. However, at the third meeting, on May 28, 1945, Hopkins asked Stalin for the approximate date of the Soviet entry into the Pacific war and his views regarding trusteeship in Korea. Stalin answered that the Soviet Army would be prepared and in position by August 8th, and he definitely agreed that "there should be a trusteeship for Korea under the United States, China, Great Britain and the Soviet Union." At the same time, Hopkins suggested that the period of trusteeship might be twenty-five years or less, but "it would certainly be five or ten years." However, Stalin

---

[7] Participants in this meeting were Truman, Grew, Harriman and Bohlen. *Turbulent Era,* Vol. II, p. 1464.

[8] See a report of the State Department to Truman on April 13, 1945, as cited in *Year of Decisions,* pp. 14–17.

[9] Harriman recommended to Truman that Hopkins would be in a better position to impress upon Stalin the fact that Roosevelt's policy would be continued. *Ibid.,* p. 258.

made no comment on this specific suggestion.[10] Thus, in the early part of June, President Truman cabled Ambassador Hurley in China that "he [Stalin] agrees to a trusteeship for Korea under China, Great Britain, the Soviet Union and the United States." Hurley was instructed to obtain the concurrence of President Chiang Kai-shek in this matter, and in the other agreements affecting Chinese sovereignty that had been made secretly between the United States and the Soviet Union at Yalta.[11]

So far as Korea was concerned, Hopkins succeeded in obtaining from Stalin a reaffirmation of Roosevelt's idea of trusteeship. They did not discuss the nature of an interim administration under trusteeship or military occupation of Korea, nor did they discuss when Korea should be granted complete independence.

THE CONFERENCE AT POTSDAM

By the time of the Potsdam Conference, the Japanese position was hopeless. Her entire empire was now cut to pieces. Population and industrial centers, as well as transportation and communication networks, were being bombarded day and night. Her economic lifeline in the home front was completely disrupted, and at the same time her offshore islands were being captured one after another by American troops. While General Curtis LeMay boasted that his air power was turning Japan back to the stone age, American marines landed on Okinawa on Easter Sunday, 1945. Except for a small number of fanatic army officers, Japanese leaders had lost their will to fight. In fact, four days

---

[10] Robert E. Sherwood, *Roosevelt and Hopkins: An Intimate History* (New York, 1948), p. 903. U.S. Department of State, *Foreign Relations of the United States: Diplomatic Papers, The Conference of Berlin (Potsdam Conference) 1945*, two vols. (Washington, 1960), Vol. 1, pp. 47, 310–315. Hereafter cited as *Conference of Berlin.*

[11] For the text of Truman's instructions to Hurley see *Year of Decisions*, p. 269.

before the opening of the Potsdam Conference, the Japanese Ambassador in Moscow was instructed by his government to inform Foreign Minister Molotov that the Emperor wished peace and was sending a special envoy to Moscow to negotiate. This radio message to Ambassador Sato was intercepted by Allied intelligence.[12]

Truman, Churchill, and Stalin met at Potsdam on July 17 with their foreign and military staffs. With Attlee replacing Churchill on July 28 their deliberations lasted to August 2. The purpose of their meeting was primarily to deal with the European problems arising after the surrender of Germany, but also with the still unsolved problems in the Far East. News of the successful nuclear experiments in the New Mexico desert had reached Truman on July 16, and the report on the new weapon was brought to Potsdam by Secretary of War Henry Stimson.

But even after knowing that atomic warfare was a reality, United States military leaders insisted that the Soviet Union be brought into the Far Eastern war. They grossly overestimated the strength of the Japanese Kwantung Army in Manchuria, and thought that this self-contained force, with its autonomous command and industrial base, was capable of prolonging the war even after the Japanese islands had been subdued, unless Russia should enter the war and engage this army.[13] Stimson estimated that the fighting would not end until the latter part of 1946, at the earliest, and that such operations might cost over a million casualties to American

---

[12] Gaimusho (Japanese Ministry of Foreign Affairs), *Nihon Gaiko Hyakunen Shōshi* (A Short Hundred Years History of Japanese Diplomacy) (Tokyo, 1963), p. 235; and *The Forrestal Diaries*, ed. Walter Millis (New York, 1951), pp. 74–75.

[13] Edward R. Stettinius, *Roosevelt and the Russians: The Yalta Conference* (New York, 1949), p. 98. The fact was that with the impending American landing in the Philippines, the Japanese High Command drew heavily on the Kwantung Army to reinforce Formosa and the Japanese homeland.

forces alone.[14] Thus, on the 24th of July, 1945, the Combined Chiefs of Staff reported to President Truman and Prime Minister Churchill at Potsdam that the common policy should be "to encourage Russian entry into the war against Japan." There seemed to be no serious thought of opposing Russia's planned entry into the war, even though Churchill recorded that "the President and I no longer felt that we needed his [Stalin's] aid to conquer Japan."[15] Moreover, Truman stated emphatically in his memoirs that seven days after he had heard of the successful atomic test, it was still of great importance to the United States to secure Soviet participation in the war against Japan.[16]

The Joint Chiefs of Staff proceeded to hold military talks with Russian officials to coordinate strategy. The Russian Staff showed particular interest in plans to undertake operations in Korea or the Kuriles. General Marshall told them that American amphibious operations against Korea were not intended, "particularly not in near future." In fact, according to a secret briefing paper on Korea, American policy planners at this time considered that it would be "politically inadvisable for any one of the interested countries alone to invade Korea." They suggested that, if militarily possible, the invading forces be composed of units from the various

---

[14] *Ibid.*, p. 97. On June 29th the Joint Chiefs of Staff had already settled upon November 1st as the starting date of this operation. On the other hand, the American Joint Chiefs had come to recognize that the war might come to a quick end. In fact, the War Department warned MacArthur and Nimitz that it might "prove necessary to take action within the near future on the basis of Japanese capitulation, possibly before Russian entry." See messages, July 21st and 26th, Joint Chiefs of Staff to MacArthur and Nimitz. Ray S. Cline, *Washington Command Post: The Operations Division in United States Army in World War II* (Washington, 1951), pp. 348–349.

[15] Churchill, *Triumph and Tragedy* (Boston, 1953), p. 640.

[16] *Year of Decisions*, pp. 265, 381–382, and 416. U.S. Department of Defense, *The Entry of the Soviet Union into the War against Japan: Military Plan, 1941–1945*, mimeographed report released on October 19, 1955, pp. 90–91.

interested countries, such as the Soviet Union, China, and the United States, under an all-inclusive Allied command.[17] It was agreed that following Russia's entry into the Pacific war, there should be a line of demarcation in the general area of Korea between American and Russian air and sea operations. According to Truman, however, there was no discussion of zones for ground operations or military occupation, because it was not expected that either American or Russian troops would march into Korea in the immediate future. Nevertheless, as we shall see later, American military consideration of an army demarcation line in Korea began at around the time of the Potsdam Conference in July, 1945.[18]

During the last days (July 24–26) at Potsdam, in consultation with the Joint Chiefs of Staff, Truman and Byrnes decided upon the statement to be addressed to Japan. Its text was carefully examined by Churchill, who found no fault with it.[19] Chiang Kai-shek immediately approved the draft that was cabled to him, with the bitter comment that once again he had not been given a chance to share in the preparation of a document of vital importance to China. On July 26, the heads of the three governments announced the terms on which they would accept the Japanese surrender. They solemnly declared: "We call upon the government of Japan to proclaim now the unconditional surrender of all Japanese armed forces, and to provide proper and adequate assurance of their good faith in such action. The alternative for Japan is prompt and utter destruction." [20] The ultimatum then re-

[17] *Conference on Berlin,* Vol. II, p. 351 and Vol. I, pp. 925–926. See also William D. Leahy, *I Was There* (New York, 1950), p. 415.

[18] *Years of Trial and Hope,* p. 317. Roy E. Appleman, *United States Army in the Korean War: South to the Nakton, North to the Yalu* (Washington, 1961), p. 2.

[19] This action at Potsdam was one of Churchill's last as Prime Minister. Churchill departed to London and Attlee remained at the Conference.

[20] For the text see U.S. Congress, Senate Committee on Foreign Relations, *A Decade of American Policy: Basic Documents, 1941–1949* (Washington, 1950), p. 50.

affirmed the Cairo pledge to limit Japanese sovereignty to the "islands of Honshu, Hokkaido, Kyushu, Shikoku and such minor islands as we determine." Although the Soviet Union had already privately indicated agreement, it was not until August 8, when the Soviet Union officially declared war against Japan, that it publicly announced its adherence to the Potsdam and Cairo Declarations.

Truman wrote that Korean problems were not discussed at Potsdam with Stalin and Churchill even though these were briefly mentioned by Molotov.[21] During the sixth plenary meeting on July 22, Molotov had indeed raised the question of colonies and trusteeships, expressing the Soviet wish to share in the disposition of Italy's African colonies. He also requested an exchange of views on the trusteeship of the Korean peninsula, but this did not take place at this time because it was agreed that these matters should be referred to the foreign ministers.[22] However, by reaffirming the Cairo Declaration, the Potsdam Declaration made it clear that Japan would not be allowed to retain Korea.

The scant attention given to Korean problems at Potsdam may be easily understood; the Conference had to deal with such European problems as the Polish border question, German reparations, and the situation in Soviet-controlled Rumania and Bulgaria. In the Asian area, Chinese-Russian relations and the Soviet entry into the Pacific war were of more immediate concern, and thus more important than the mechanisms of the trusteeship or occupation of Korea, which were still remote from the focus of American strategy.

Yet, surprisingly, the Potsdam agreements were of great significance for the future of Korea. The promise of Soviet entry into the Pacific war on August 8, coupled with General Marshall's suggestion of American unpreparedness for Korean occupation, virtually conceded that the occupation of

---

[21] *Years of Trial and Hope,* p. 317. The content of Molotov's discussion is not known.

[22] *Conference of Berlin,* Vol. II, p. 253. See also Leahy, p. 408.

the peninsula would be left to the Soviet Union. And from the Russian actions in Eastern Europe after the German defeat, it was foreseeable that once the Soviet Union occupied the country, it would probably establish a *de facto* government that would be friendly only to Russia and a source of trouble to the free nations. It thus should have been extremely urgent to clarify the purpose and procedure of the occupation in order to limit future Soviet activity. But hope that wartime cooperation with Russia could carry over into the postwar period still survived among the Big Three leaders at the time of the Potsdam Conference.[23] They thought they could handle any issue that might arise during the military occupation of Korea, thus restraining the Communist advance. Potsdam was to prove the best and last chance to reach an amicable solution for the problem of the peninsula.

ON THE EVE OF THE JAPANESE SURRENDER

The Japanese surrender came so quickly that the American government was unprepared. Japanese Prime Minister Suzuki, the ex-Admiral who had initiated peace feelers in various countries, at first rejected the Potsdam ultimatum in a radio response. But new instructions were sent to Ambassador Sato in Moscow to try again to arrange with Molotov for the reception of Prince Konoye so that he might seek Soviet mediation to end the war with less than unconditional surrender.[24] Molotov refused to receive Konoye. Stalin had already told Truman at Potsdam that the answer would be

---

[23] Foster Rhea Dulles, *America's Rise to World Power: 1898–1954* (New York, 1955), p. 223.

[24] Toshikazu Kase, *Eclipse of the Rising Sun* (London, 1951), pp. 204–205 and 187–197. This book was published in America under the title *Journey to the Missouri* (New Haven: Yale University Press, 1950). For the American side of the story, see James Byrnes, *Speaking Frankly* (New York, 1947), pp. 211–213 and *The Forrestal Diaries,* pp. 74–75. For the Japanese side of the story see *Nihon Gaiko Hyakunen Shōshi,* pp. 235–244. See also Robert J. C. Butow, *Japan's Decision to Surrender* (Stanford, 1954), pp. 112–165.

no. At 8:15 a.m. on August 6, the first atomic bomb, with a destructive force equivalent to 20,000 tons of TNT, was dropped on Hiroshima; three days later the second one, an implosion bomb of plutonium, devastated Nagasaki.

On August 8, Molotov coldly read to Sato the prepared statement of the Soviet Union's entry into the war. Stalin did not wait as he had told western leaders, until China approved his Yalta claims. It was the date agreed upon at Potsdam, almost exactly three months to the hour after the end of the war in Germany. The Soviet Union, it may be assumed, feared that its interests in Asia would be neglected in the final settlement unless it entered before the impending Japanese surrender.

The Soviets ignored, of course, their neutrality pact with Japan, basing their entry on the Japanese refusal to capitulate completely to the Allies' Potsdam proposals. The war declaration was so phrased as to make it appear that "the Soviet Union had made this decision upon Allied request after the Japanese rejection of the Potsdam ultimatum." [25] The next day, Russian troops went into action in Manchuria and North Korea; within five days, by August 14, they had marched far inside the Soviet-Korean border.

Meanwhile, on August 10, the Japanese government had radioed through Switzerland its intention of accepting the conditions of the Potsdam Declaration, provided that the prerogatives of the Emperor as an independent sovereign were not to be diminished.[26] Immediately, the Allied

---

[25] For the text see U.S. Congress, Senate, *The United States and the Korean Problems, Documents, 1943–1953* (Washington, 1953), p. 2. For the Russian point of view see E. M. Zhukov, ed., *Kyokutō Kokusai Seiji Shi: 1840–1949* (History of Far Eastern International Relations: 1840–1949) (Tokyo, 1959), Vol. II, pp. 297–299. This is a Japanese translation.

[26] Kase, pp. 238–239; W. MacMahon Ball, *Japan: Enemy or Ally* (New York, 1949), p. 45. See also Hasegawa Saiji, "Hachigatsu Jugonichi eno Michi" (The Road to August 15), *Chūo Kōron* (August, 1964), pp. 239–244. This is a Japanese monthly journal published in Tokyo.

Powers refused this request and informed the Japanese that the surrender would be unconditional. On August 14, 1945, the Japanese Emperor finally issued an Imperial Rescript ending the war. General MacArthur, Supreme Commander for the Allied Powers, issued an order, with Truman's approval, that directed Japanese commanders within China, excluding Manchuria, Formosa, and French Indochina north of the 16th parallel, to surrender to Nationalist Chinese forces.[27] Enemy forces in Manchuria, in Korea north of the 38th parallel, and in Karafuto were to surrender to the Soviet army.

Now American strategy had to be switched abruptly from invasion to military occupation and disarmament of the enemy. During this time, Truman received a warning message from Ambassador Edwin W. Pauley, who was in Moscow to negotiate an agreement on reparation matters with the Russians: discussions on reparations and on other matters have "led me to the belief that our forces should quickly occupy as much of the industrial areas of Korea and Manchuria as we can, starting at the southern tip and progressing northward." [28] He added that all of this could be done at no risk to American lives after organized hostilities had ceased.

Ambassador Harriman similarly urged Truman to take drastic action. He recommended immediate landings of American forces to accept surrender of the Japanese troops, at least "on the Kwantung Peninsula and in Korea." "I cannot see," Harriman continued, "that we are under any obligation to the Soviets to respect any zone of Soviet military operation." [29]

---

[27] Molotov first proposed that there might be two Supreme Commanders, General MacArthur and Marshal Vasilevsky, but withdrew this demand because of Harriman's vehement opposition.

[28] *Year of Decisions,* p. 433.

[29] *Ibid.,* pp. 433–434; *Conference of Berlin,* Vol. I, p. 234.

DIVISION OF KOREA AT THE 38TH PARALLEL

Despite these timely warnings from the envoys in Moscow, sometime within the four days after August 10, 1945, the momentous decision was made to divide Korea at the 38th parallel in order to accept the surrender of the Japanese troops.

The idea of the division of the Korean peninsula by its neighbors can be traced all the way back to the latter part of the sixteenth century. In 1592 when an invading Japanese army swept through most of the peninsula, the helpless Korean government asked the Chinese Ming emperor to intervene. He did so, and the war became stalemated in the southern provinces with the help of a massive Chinese intervention. Toyotomi Hideyoshi, the strong man of Japan, then proposed as the condition for peace that the southern four provinces of Korea be ceded to Japan, leaving the remaining four northern provinces to the King of Korea.[30] Although Hideyoshi's proposal did not specify the exact boundary line for the division, it is believed that it lay at the Han River, roughly 45 miles south of today's 38th parallel.[31] The proposal was rejected by the Chinese; and the Japanese troops withdrew from Korea upon the death of Hideyoshi seven years later.

In 1894, three hundred years later, the division of the peninsula between Japan and China again became a major

---

[30] Kyōguchi Motokichi, *Hideyoshi no Chōsen Keiryaku* (Hideyoshi's Korean Policy) (Tokyo, 1939), pp. 244–250. See also Chindan Hakhoe, ed., *Han'guk Sa* (Korean History) (Seoul, 1960), seven volumes, Vol. III (Kŭnse Jŏnki P'yŏn), p. 643.

[31] For Korean sources on the negotiation, see *Sŏnjo Silrŏk* (Authentic Record of King Sŏnjo) and the memoirs of his Prime Minister Yu Sŏng-yong, *Chingbirok* (Pusan, 1960). King Sŏnjo (1552–1603) ruled Korea during the time of Hideyoshi's invasion. For a Japanese source see Kyōguchi, pp. 244–245 and pp. 427–428. For a more extensive study on this invasion, see Ikeuchi Hiroshi, *Bunroku Keicho no Eki* (The Japanese Invasion of 1592–1596) (Tokyo, 1914) and another volume under the same title (Tokyo, 1936).

issue. Since Korea had opened its doors to western nations in 1882, she had become the pawn of the big powers in Asian international relations. In 1894 under the leadership of a religious group called Tonghak (East Learning School), the long-suppressed and exploited South Korean peasants revolted against their weak government, as well as against foreign intervention in their domestic affairs.[32] When the revolt spread like a prairie fire through most of South Korea, the Korean King unwisely asked for Chinese intervention. As the Chinese soldiers landed, the Japanese dispatched an uninvited army to Seoul under the pretext of protecting their diplomatic mission in accordance with a previous treaty agreement between China and Japan.[33] When a clash between these two armies became imminent, the British government proposed that South Korea be occupied by Japan and North Korea by China. The exact line of demarcation for the division was not specified this time;[34] again division was rejected by both nations, mainly because neither was satisfied with only half the country. The Sino-Japanese war (1894–95) finally settled the problem and the Chinese lost their influence in Korea after their ignominious defeat.

---

[32] For one of the authoritative studies on the Tonghak rebellion see Kim Sang-gi, *Tonghak Kwa Tonghak Nan* (The East Learning School and Tonghak Rebellion) (Seoul, 1947). See also Chindan Hakhoe, ed., *Han'guk Sa,* Vol. VI, pp. 3–223 (this section written by Yi Sŏn-kŭn). In the English language, see Benjamin Weems, *Reform, Rebellion and the Heavenly Way* (Tucson, 1964).

[33] For an excellent study on Japan-Korean relations during this period, see Hilary Conroy, *The Japanese Seizure of Korea: 1868–1910* (Philadelphia, 1960), pp. 221–382. See also M. Frederick Nelson, *Korea and the Old Order in Eastern Asia* (Baton Rouge, 1946), pp. 203–212; and Fred H. Harrington, *God, Mammon and the Japanese: Dr. Horace N. Allen and Korean-American Relations, 1884–1905* (Madison, 1944), pp. 249–256.

[34] For the most comprehensive study on this issue, see Tabobashi Kiyoshi, *Kindai Nissen Kankei no Kenkyu* (Study of Modern Japanese-Korean Relations) (Seoul, 1940). See also Memorandum of the British Ministry of Foreign Affairs, No. 77, dated July 24, 1894, as cited in Loh Kei-hyun "Territorial Division of Korea—A Historical Survey," *Korean Affairs,* Vol. III, No. 1 (April, 1964), pp. 108–109.

Russia then replaced China as a major contender with Japan for power in the peninsula. Korea had been one of the prime targets of Russian policy in Asia since 1882. In 1896, and again in 1903, Russia and Japan had engaged in secret negotiations regarding the possible division of Korea between themselves along either the 38th or the 39th parallels. Aside from the usual considerations of trade, raw materials, territorial expansion and political domination, Russian interest centered around obtaining ice-free ports in Korea for convenient access to the sea and unhindered use of the Pacific. Czar Nicholas II once wrote to his foreign minister: "Russia absolutely needs a port free and open throughout the whole year. This port must be located on the mainland (southeast Korea) and must certainly be connected with our possessions by a strip of land." [35]

During the high tide of Russian influence, Japan proposed in 1896 that Korea be divided along the 38th parallel. Russia rejected this division because she still hoped to get control of the entire peninsula.[36] Later, when Japan regained ascendency, Russia made another proposal for division. In 1898 it was rumored that Spyer, then Russian minister to Korea, proposed to the Japanese minister that the two powers divide this strategic peninsula, with Russia taking the north with Pyongyang, and Japan the south with Seoul.[37] Again in

---

[35] Robert T. Oliver, *Why War Came in Korea* (New York: 1950), p. 5.

[36] William L. Langer and S. E. Gleason, *The Diplomacy of Imperialism* (New York, 1934), Vol. 1, p. 406. See also Gaimusho (Japanese Ministry of Foreign Affairs), *Nihon Gaiko Bunsho* (Japanese Diplomatic Documents) (Tokyo, 1954), Vol. 29, pp. 812–813. This proposal was made by General Yamagata to Alexis B. Lobanov, the Russian Foreign Minister. Zhukov, Vol. 1, pp. 164–221. For the Korean point of view, see Chindan Hakhoe, Vol. VI (Hyŏndae Pyŏn), pp. 756–777.

[37] William Franklin Sands, *Undiplomatic Memories* (New York, 1930), p. 158. Although Mr. Sands mentioned in this book that Mr. Pavloff made this proposal, the Russian Minister in Korea at this time was Mr. Spyer. This story was proved in the Japanese sources. See Gaimusho (Japanese Ministry of Foreign Affairs), *Komura Gaiko*

September, 1903, a few months before the outbreak of hostilities, Russian minister Rosen sought Japanese accord for an agreement making a neutral disarmed zone of Korea north of the 39th parallel while recognizing Japan's special interests in the south. The Japanese counterproposed a ten mile wide demilitarized zone along the boundary between Manchuria and Korea, that is, five miles to the north of the boundary and five miles to the south of it.[38] The proposal was turned down and the war between the two nations (1904–1905) finally settled the issue—Russian influence was ended by defeat.

Thus, the significance of the division of Korea and of the 38th and 39th parallels had been historically established, and even commented upon, in several instances well before the Second World War. Yet it appears that military planners in the Pentagon were unaware of these precedents when they proposed the 38th parallel to the Russian government as a basis for accepting the surrender of the Japanese forces in Korea.

At the time of the Potsdam Conference, the American and Soviet Chiefs of Staff had worked out an agreement to synchronize operations against Japan. As noted, when the Combined Chiefs of Staff met, they suggested invasion under a combined Allied command.[39] Forces would simultaneously be moved against Japan, Manchuria, and Korea from four different directions: from the north by the Soviets,

Shi (History of Komura's Diplomacy) (Tokyo, 1953), two volumes, Vol. I, p. 97. This book was published as a part of *Nihon Gaiko Bunsho.*

[38] Chindan Hakhoe, Vol. VI, pp. 896–904. *Nihon Gaiko Hyakunen Shōshi,* pp. 56–57. See also, *Nihon Gaiko Bunsho,* Vol. 33, pp. 699–705. See also *Komura Gaiko Shi,* pp. 334–335. For another useful study on this issue, see Kiyosawa Kiyoshi, *Gaiko Shi* (Diplomatic History) (Tokyo, 1941), pp. 319–322.

[39] The Russian staff comprised General Antonov, Red Army Chief of Staff, Admiral Kuznetsov, the People's Commissariat for the Navy and Marshall Fallalev, the Chief of the Soviet Air Staff. Antonov was accompanied by his deputy, General Salvin.

from the west by the Chinese, from the south and east by the United States and Great Britain. Though some division into zones of military operations was needed, these would not necessarily be zones of military occupation.[40] Agreement was reached two days later, on July 26, on an air and sea operational line that was to become effective when the Soviet Union entered the war. This was marked by a line running from Cape Boltina on the coast of Korea to a point 40°N, 135°E, then to a point 45°45′N, 140°E, and thence along the parallel 45°45′N to the line connecting Cape Crillon on the southern tip of Sakhalin with Cape Soya Misaki on the northern tip of Hokkaido.[41]

American forces were to operate south of, and Soviet forces to the north of this line. The division meant that part of southern Manchuria, and nearly all of Korea, as well as the Japanese island of Hokkaido were within the American zone of operation. But no line was set up for land operations since "it was not anticipated by our military leaders [the Americans] that we would carry out operations to Korea."[42] Yet, Marshall apparently did give some consideration to American military occupation. While at Potsdam, he and Admiral King told Harriman that American forces would land in Korea if the Japanese surrendered prior to Soviet occupation.[43] In fact, one day during the conference he asked Lieutenant General John E. Hull, then Chief of Operations Division, U.S. Army, to prepare for American troop

---

[40] *Year of Decisions,* p. 383. In this meeting General Antonov showed particular interest in any intention the United States might have of undertaking operations against the Kuriles and Korea. General Marshall, however, replied that America did not plan amphibious operations against Korea. Marshall felt that Korea could be brought under control without difficulty once the U.S. Air Force could operate from Kyushu.

[41] *Conference of Berlin,* Vol. II, pp. 410–411. *The China Tangle,* p. 326. Ernest J. King, *Fleet Admiral King: A Naval Record* (New York, 1952), pp. 616–617.

[42] *Year of Decisions,* p. 383.

[43] *Ibid.,* p. 434.

movement into Korea. After studying a map, Hull and some of his staff decided that somewhere near the 38th parallel would be a suitable dividing line for an army boundary between the U.S. and Soviet forces. Because the United States wanted to control at least two major ports in its occupation zone, Hull drew a line north of Seoul to include the ports of Inch'ŏn and Pusan. The line was "not on the 38th parallel but was near it and, generally, along it." The American and Russian delegates, however, did not discuss this dividing line in the military meetings of the Potsdam Conference.[44]

Although American military leaders were gravely mistaken in not clearly defining at Potsdam the zones of land operations, their tentative decision to divide Korea along the 38th parallel was an even more serious mistake. It implied that Soviet troops could occupy the area north of the 38th parallel without serious objection by the United States. It was by this time highly probable that the Soviet Union would launch a massive land operation in North Korea; protective measures would be necessary for their naval base in Vladivostok. And if they once occupied Korea, they would not withdraw without demanding concessions. Unfortunately, American military leaders overlooked the political implications of Soviet occupation.

As the war against Japan moved rapidly to its conclusion, War Department officials were working on instructions that MacArthur was to present to the Japanese on the procedure for the surrender of their armed forces. The Japanese offer of conditional surrender on August 10 brought the question of a demarcation line in Korea, hitherto merely a background question, abruptly to the fore. On August 11, a draft providing for the surrender of Japanese forces north of the 38th parallel to the Russians, and south of that line to American forces, was considered by the State-War-Navy Coordinating Committee. From August 12–14, the draft was in the hands

---

[44] Appleman, p. 3.

of the Joint Chiefs of Staff. Meanwhile, large-scale Russian attacks had begun on August 10 with amphibious landings at the extreme northeastern tip of Korea. These were followed by a landing at Ch'ŏngjin and Nanam on August 14 that proceeded to Wŏnsan farther to the south on August 16. During this time, the nearest United States forces were more than six hundred miles away from Korea. Though Byrnes had suggested that American forces receive the surrender of the Japanese "as far north as practicable," military leaders felt that the 38th parallel was too far away for troops to reach, should the Russians choose to disagree.

In this situation, those responsible for the drafting of the instructions apparently concluded that presence of Soviet forces on Korean soil precluded the possibility that the Japanese surrender in Korea could be accepted by American forces alone. A second-best choice was that the Americans occupy as much of Korea as was still feasible. Since the United States wanted to keep the capital city of Seoul in their zone along with the port of Inch'ŏn, the line of the 38th north parallel, which lay some 45 miles north of Seoul, was thus finally selected.[45] The dividing line was also practically identical with the line suggested to Marshall by Hull and his staff at the Potsdam Conference.

The draft instructions to MacArthur, including the provision specifying the 38th parallel, was reviewed and revised by the Joint Chiefs of Staff, approved by the State-War-

---

[45] The above information is based upon Arthur L. Grey, Jr., "The Thirty-Eighth Parallel," *Foreign Affairs* (April, 1951), pp. 482–487. Grey's suggestion that the line had been chosen because it was south of the Russian landings at Wŏnsan is difficult to accept because the document was drafted before the landing began. For the Russian landing operation, see Morita Kazuo, "Chōsen ni okeru Nihon Tōji no Shūen (End of the Japanese Rule in Korea)" in *Nikkan Kankei no Tenkai* (The Development of Japan-Korean Relations) (Tokyo, 1963), pp. 85–86. See also Kwahak Wŏn, Yŏksa Yŏn'gu So (North Korean Academy of Science, Division of History), *Chosŏn Kŭndae Hyŏngmyŏng Undong Sa* (History of Revolutionary Movement in Modern Korea) (Pyongyang, 1962), pp. 420–423.

Navy Coordinating Committee, and finally approved by President Truman on August 13. It was then communicated to the British and Soviet governments. Stalin requested minor changes but accepted the provision of the 38th parallel without objection.

Thus, contrary to a widely held view that the division of Korea was another secret agreement made either at Yalta or Potsdam, the truth would seem to be that the actual division had its origin in the War Department's recommendations in Washington.[46] The 38th parallel as a dividing line in Korea had never been the subject of international discussions among the wartime leaders. President Truman wrote that the line was "proposed by us as a practical solution when the sudden collapse of the Japanese war machine created a vacuum in Korea." [47] Knowing that Stalin had already concurred in the idea of a joint trusteeship, the United States expected that the division of the peninsula would be solely for the purpose of accepting the Japanese surrender and that joint control would then extend throughout Korea.[48] Thus, the line of demarcation was "intended to be temporary and only to fix responsibility" between the United States and So-

[46] Based on the statement of John M. Allison, Deputy Director of the Office of Far Eastern Affairs, Department of State, before the House Committee on Foreign Affairs. See U.S. Congress, House Committee on Foreign Affairs, 81st Cong. 1st Sess., Hearing on H. R. 5330, *Korean Aid* (Washington, June 8–23, 1949), pp. 118–119. In this hearing Under Secretary of State James Webb furnished the members of the Committee with a heretofore confidential explanation of the matter of the 38th parallel. This was the first time that a fairly complete official account of the decision had been made public. See also *The United States and the Korean Problems, Documents, 1943–1953,* pp. 2–3.

[47] *Years of Trial and Hope,* p. 317. Georg Schwarzenberger, however, speculated that "at Potsdam, or perhaps already at Yalta the military staffs contemplated a rough and ready demarcation line between Soviet and United States forces." See Georg Schwarzenberger, *Power Politics: A Study of International Society* (New York, 1951), p. 419.

[48] See the statement of Secretary Byrnes, *Department of State Bulletin,* December 30, 1945, p. 1035.

viet Russia for carrying out the Japanese surrender.[49] There was no thought, Truman recalled, of a permanent Korean division.

The instructions were dispatched on August 15 to General MacArthur in Manila as General Order No. 1 and at the same time communicated to the Russian and British governments. Not in Stalin's subsequent message to President Truman, nor in Antonov's to General MacArthur, nor in any other communication from Russia was there comment or question with regard to the line of demarcation for occupation of Korea.[50] The 38th parallel, which was destined to figure so importantly in Korea's tragedy in later years, was neither debated nor bargained for by either side.

Why was Stalin willing to accept the division of Korea, despite the fact that the Red Army was then in a position to occupy the entire territory? This is a moot question, as no materials are available at present to answer it. Probably he hoped thereby to improve his chances of sharing in the military occupation of Japan, inasmuch as he immediately requested that his troops accept the surrender on the island of Hokkaido.[51] He may also have hoped to gain more conces-

---

[49] See the address delivered before the Economic Club of Detroit, March 10, 1947 by General John H. Hildring, Assistant Secretary of State, *Department of State Bulletin,* March 23, 1947, p. 545.

[50] On August 16, 1945, Stalin sent a message to Truman stating that "I have received your message with the General Order No. 1. Principally I have no objections against the contents of the order." He asked that minor corrections be put into the order, but Korea was not included in this request. *Year of Decisions,* p. 440. According to Truman's memoirs this directive to MacArthur was approved by the President on August 13. See also *Stalin's Correspondence with Churchill, Attlee, Roosevelt and Truman: 1941–45* (London, 1958), pp. 266–268. This was originally published by Ministry of Foreign Affairs of the U.S.S.R. in 1957.

[51] See the cable of Stalin to Truman, dated August 18, *Year of Decisions,* pp. 440–441. In this cable Stalin stated that "I understand the contents of your message in the sense that you refuse to satisfy the request of the Soviet Union. . . . I have to say that I and my colleagues did not expect such an answer from you." See also John R. Dean, *Strange Alliance* (New York, 1947), pp. 278–284.

sions in Manchuria and Northern Japan. He was trying, in fact, to create in Japan the same kind of division zones as now existed in Korea and Germany. It is also possible that Stalin felt he did not have the military capacity to occupy the whole of Korea: the Red Army was still meeting stiff resistance from Japanese forces in Manchuria when he received the American proposal. Or he may have been relatively uninterested in the occupational phase of the Korean problem because of the previous agreement on Korean trusteeship. This seems, however, most unlikely.

In any case, it is apparent that the American proposal of the 38th parallel was motivated by certain specific political objectives. Although it was officially maintained that American troops entered Korea only to facilitate the surrender of the Japanese forces, the primary objective of the proposal was to prevent Soviet occupation of the entire peninsula, something considered inevitable in the absence of any agreement. Such an occupation would have been a great threat to Japanese security under the American military administration of Japan. In view of Soviet actions in Eastern Europe following Hitler's fall, it seemed very possible that Stalin might not abide by his agreement on Korean trusteeship. Furthermore, in order to be able to honor her Cairo pledge for Korea's ultimate independence, the United States had to maintain a foothold in Korea.

Unfortunately, the policy planners of the Truman administration accepted Roosevelt's idea of a trusteeship without criticism or scrutiny, and without foreseeing the difficulty of implementing the agreement without the close cooperation of the Soviet Union. The War Department, which decided at Potsdam on the dividing line and later drafted General Order No. 1, apparently had little knowledge of Korea. For example, as a better choice the 39th parallel could have been proposed, so that the American military forces could maintain the shortest possible boundary line. The 38th parallel, as would be expected of such a geodetic line, cut through individual farms and long-existing administrative units. More importantly, it severed Korea into two economically dependent zones. In this respect, too, the 39th parallel would have been advantageous to the South. Since Russia historically thought of the 39th parallel as the boundary of its sphere of influence, it might have accepted the line had it been proposed.

The Second World War made apparent the close connection between foreign and military policies. Foreign policy had been an adjunct of the military strategy of the United States; the War and Navy departments had had more voice in some foreign policy decisions than the State Department. The word of the Chiefs of Staff had been subject only to the consideration of the President. As John Foster Dulles put it:

> The military profession can produce great statesmen. General Eisenhower and General Marshall are two of our time. But when military people function in their military capacity, they are specialists. They do not purport to be judges of economics or of world opinion. They do not attempt to take account of possibilities that reside in moral forces. They do not claim to understand the working of organizations like the United Nations. . . . It is not their business to measure the resources of diplomacy and conciliation.[52]

The prestige of the State Department, which had severely declined under Roosevelt,[53] continued to decline during the initial period of the Truman administration; the President depended upon the military staff in the tradition of his predecessor. This dependence created immense problems that might have been avoided had a little more political judgment been exercised. Concerned only with the immediate defeat of the enemy, the military planners tended to be shortsighted. If Presidents Roosevelt and Truman had more

---

[52] John Foster Dulles, *War or Peace* (New York, 1957), p. 234.

[53] See Richard C. Snyder and Edgar S. Furniss, Jr., *American Foreign Policy: Formulation, Principles, and Programs* (New York, 1955), p. 287. See also John W. Spanier, *The Truman-MacArthur Controversy and the Korean War* (New York, 1965), p. 10.

seriously considered the recommendations of the State Department or their civilian ambassadors, such as Harriman and Pauley, many Korean problems could have been avoided.

At this time, there were within the Department of State and the Foreign Service many experienced officials who sent the White House repeated warnings against the "soft" course adopted toward the Soviet Union. But the Truman administration continued to pay little regard to the details of future Soviet-American relations in Korea. If the United States had landed its task forces by airlift or by warships in North Korea or in South Manchuria, as Harriman and Pauley had recommended, it might have been possible to accept the surrender of the Japanese as far north as Pyongyang or Dairen without sacrificing American soldiers. From General Wedemeyer's success in landing Chinese troops as far as Mukden by airlift, it seems possible that some contingents of American forces could likewise have been landed in Korea. Indeed, as will be seen later, Japanese troops in Korea preferred at this time to capitulate to American forces. The basic fault of American Korean policy during this period thus seems to lie in the political indifference, incomprehension, and unpreparedness of American military planners. To these military men, Korea seemed a never-never land in postwar international relations.

Part II

Period of Attempted Cooperation

3

Liberation and Military Occupation of Korea

The United States occupied a position of unprecedented power and prestige at the end of the Second World War. Its ability to influence the course of world events was immense; its willingness to help the underprivileged and its urge to liberate the colonial peoples had exalted its prestige among Asians who had just been liberated from the Japanese.

The United States has repeatedly advocated independence and self-government for all peoples qualified to govern themselves. The Cairo promise of independence for Korea was based upon this underlying philosophy. For Koreans, the victory of the Allied Powers meant not only liberation, but the rebirth of Korea as an independent state.

Nevertheless, upon the Japanese surrender, the United States found itself an occupying power along with the Soviet Union. The Koreans soon realized, to their great disappointment and dismay, that they had been freed from one master only to acquire two. It became apparent that the result would be more devastating than anything in Korean history.

The United States faced a situation in Korea for which it was completely unprepared and it has paid dearly for this error. The course of events dragged her into an increasingly complicated and seemingly unsolvable situation. Having no intentions of a lengthy military occupation, America had not expected such strong opposition from the Soviet Union against the establishment of a unified administration throughout the country. Lack of precedent, lack of information, and lack of experience and training in military government, caused critical problems. Despite American good intentions, the Korean people began to regard the American occupation with suspicion and discontent.

ON THE EVE OF LIBERATION

While it is true that the Japanese surrender came much sooner than had been expected, the Cairo Declaration had been in effect for twenty months; but during that period almost no American preparations had been made for the occupational phase in Korea.[1] With the sudden collapse of the Japanese Empire, the United States XXIV Corps, which had been getting ready at Okinawa to take part in the invasion of the Japanese mainland, received orders to land instead in Korea. Commanding General John R. Hodge was to accept the surrender of the Japanese forces in the zone south of the 38th parallel as prescribed in the General Order No. 1.[2]

Washington's instructions to MacArthur at this time only referred to the Cairo Declaration, and he quoted this in his own General Order to the people of Korea in asking their help and compliance. Part of his General Order reads:

> Having in mind the long enslavement of the people of Korea and the determination that in due course Korea shall become free and independent, the Korean people are assured that the purpose of the occupation is to enforce the instrument of surrender and to protect them in their personal and religious rights. In giving effect to these purposes, your active aid and compliance is required. . . .
>
> All power of government over the territory of Korea south

[1] Edward G. Meade, *American Military Government in Korea* (New York, 1951), p. 46.

[2] For the text of the General Order No. 1, see SCAP (Supreme Commander for the Allied Powers), *Official Gazette*.

of 38th north latitude and the people thereof, will be for the present exercised under my authority.[3]

The XXIV Corps had a long and excellent combat record in the Philippines and Okinawa, but it had no experience in the administration of civil affairs during the postcombat stage. It also had no personnel trained in government duties. Hodge himself received little or no concrete guidance on the problems of Korean independence, the methods of handling various political functions, or the removal of Japanese influence from Korea. There was almost no briefing on the Korean assignment and little information was available prior to his embarkation.[4]

On September 8, almost a month after the first Russian troops had entered Korea, 72,000 Americans, consisting of the Sixth, Seventh, and Fortieth Infantry Divisions under Hodge's command, landed in South Korea.[5] The next day the Japanese surrendered in Seoul, at the capitol building, to General Hodge and Vice Admiral Thomas C. Kinkaid, the Commander of the United States Seventh Fleet, amidst the wild enthusiasm of the Korean people.[6]

Hodge was assigned by the Joint Chiefs of Staff and the Supreme Commander of the Allied Powers to carry out the following missions:

(1) Take the Japanese surrender, disarm the Japanese armed forces, enforce the terms of the surrender, and remove Japanese imperialism from Korea; (2) maintain

[3] See *The Proclamation No. 1 to the People of Korea* in USAFIK (United States Armed Forces in Korea), *Official Gazette*.

[4] Carl J. Friedrich and Associates, *American Experience in Military Government in World War II* (New York, 1948), p. 355. See also Edgar S. Kennedy, *Mission to Korea* (London, 1952), pp. 10–11.

[5] According to the *New York Times*, May 20, 1949, the maximum number of United States troops in Korea was 77,643 in October, 1945. Before the Japanese surrender, 125,000 Russian troops under the command of Colonel General Ivan Chistiakov attacked North Korea and rapidly marched southward.

[6] U.S. Far East Command, TI and E Section, Hdqrs., XXIV Corps, *Korea* (Seoul, 1948), p. 46.

> order, establish an effective government along democratic lines and rebuild a sound economy as a basis for Korean independence; (3) train Koreans in handling their own affairs and prepare [them] to govern [themselves] as a free and independent nation.[7]

The first mission turned out to be comparatively easy, but the second and third were difficult and challenging tasks. They necessitated the substitution of a new regime for the Japanese machine. Also, they required many thousands of trained personnel for the effective management of the military government. Yet, the majority of the military government personnel assigned to the occupation were still in California awaiting embarkation. During the first few weeks the military government was under the control of untrained tactical forces.[8] Instructions from superiors were so sparse and ambiguous that Hodge, in hope of professional guidance, requested that a State Department representative be sent. A Class II foreign service officer was sent from Washington, but he could add "little to the sum total of knowledge on overall policy toward Korea." [9]

So, completely unequipped for their task, the American occupation forces made serious mistakes from the very beginning. For example, despite Korea's status as a friendly nation, one of MacArthur's first proclamations was to threaten with death anyone who violated USAFIK (United States Armed Forces in Korea) directions—a proclamation hardly conducive to good relations.[10] Also, immediately after the

---

[7] *Ibid.*, p. 11.

[8] Meade, p. 47. Even though it was assumed by the Joint Chiefs of Staff as early as 1943 that military government in Japan and Korea was to be the responsibility of the Army, little attention was paid to the preparation for Korean occupation. When the XXIV Corps landed in Korea, no trained personnel for the military government had been dispatched. See Hajo Holborn, *American Military Government: Its Organization and Policies* (Washington, 1947), pp. 87–104.

[9] Carl Berger, *The Korean Knot: A Military and Political History* (Philadelphia, 1957), p. 49. James A. Field, Jr., *History of United States Naval Operations: Korea* (Washington, 1962), p. 17.

[10] This order was mentioned in USAFP, OCG, Yokohama, Japan, September 7, 1945, *Proclamation No. 2 to the People of Korea.*

surrender ceremony, Hodge announced that the Japanese Governor General and other high-ranking Japanese officials would be retained in office temporarily in order to facilitate the administration of the military government and the orderly takeover of the civil government. He further declared that he would govern "through standing government bodies," that is, through the existing Japanese administrative machine. In fact, General Harris, who had arrived on September 6, confided in an interview with Mr. Endo, the Director General of Political Affairs in the Governor General's Office, that Korea would continue to be administered through the Japanese Governor General under the supervision of USAFIK commander.[11] The State Department quickly disclaimed responsibility for this statement, and two days later MacArthur ordered Hodge to replace Japanese officials as rapidly as possible consistent with the safety of operations.[12] But the mistake had been made; the dissatisfaction of the Koreans became so great that on September 12 Governor General Abe Nobuyuki was relieved of his duties and Major General A. V. Arnold was appointed Military Governor.

THE PEOPLE'S REPUBLIC

During the three-week interval between Japan's surrender and the arrival of the American troops, the situation in South Korea was extremely confusing. The Japanese, concerned about possible anti-Japanese riots in Korea, had hoped to create a pro-Japanese atmosphere before their evacuation by arranging for a group of prominent Korean leaders to form a transitional government.

---

[11] Bertram D. Sarafan, "Military Government: Korea," *Far Eastern Survey*, November, 1946, p. 350. Also see Morita Kazuo, "Chōsen ni okeru Nihon Toji no Shūen" (The End of the Japanese Rule in Korea) in Nihon Kokusai Seiji Gakkai (Japan International Political Science Association), *Nikhan Kankei no Tenkai* (Development of Japan-Korean Relations) (Tokyo, 1963), pp. 90–91. Mr. Morita is currently in charge of the Korean desk in the Japanese Ministry of Foreign Affairs.

[12] A. W. Green, *The Epic of Korea* (Washington, 1950), p. 52.

Three days before the public announcement of Japanese capitulation, the Japanese Governor General's office secretly approached Mr. Song Chin-u, a prominent right-wing nationalist leader, and asked his cooperation. They proposed to transfer the major functions of government to Song if he, in return, would guarantee the safety of the Japanese and their property. Song Chin-u, well known for his uncompromising struggle for Korean independence as a nationalist educator, and the publisher of the famed newspaper *Dong-A Ilbo,* rejected the offer. He made it clear that he would cooperate only with the Allied occupation forces.[13]

In desperation, the Japanese turned to Mr. Lyuh Woon-hyung (Yŏ Un-hyŏng), an equally well-known left-wing nationalist leader. Lyuh, educated in Nanking, China, was one of the original founders of the Korean Provisional Government in Shanghai. He had been closely associated with the left-wing movement of the Korean nationals in China since the early 1920's, and had traveled extensively for the cause of Korean independence until 1930, when he was sent back to prison by Japanese secret police. After his prison term, he became the publisher of another prestigious daily in Seoul, *Chung-Ang Ilbo,* and remained an important leader of the underground nationalist movement. A gifted orator, he strongly appealed to the Korean masses. In 1944, believing that the downfall of Japan was imminent, he had already organized a secret group to prepare for eventual Korean independence.[14]

---

[13] Hong Sŏng-myŏn *et al., Haebang Isip nyŏn* (Twenty Years of Emancipation) (Seoul, 1965), Vol. 1 (Kirok P'yŏn), pp. 297–298. See also Kim Sam-gyu, *Konnichi no Chōsen* (Today's Korea) (Tokyo, 1956), p. 20. Morita, p. 87.

[14] *Ibid.,* pp. 86–87. See also Lyuh's speech made on August 16, 1945 which reveals his negotiations with the Japanese. *Maeil Shinbo* (A daily paper in Seoul which subsequently on November 23, 1945, adopted the new name *Seoul Shinmun*), August 16–17, 1945. For a more comprehensive study on this period, Han Tae-su, *Han'guk Chŏngtang Sa* (History of Korean Parties) (Seoul, 1961), pp. 19–24.

On August 15, Lyuh laid down five conditions for his consideration of the Japanese offer. He demanded the transfer to himself of major governmental functions in order to preserve law and order, to prevent political chaos, and to establish a Korean government in harmony with the wishes of the people. Specifically, his five conditions were:

(1) immediate release of all political prisoners;
(2) noninterference in his activities for national reconstruction;
(3) freedom to organize the student and youth corps;
(4) free organization of labor unions by the working classes;
(5) and a guarantee of three months supply of food and grains.

His conditions were accepted with the understanding that the existing governmental structure would not be dissolved and that the Japanese and their property would be protected.[15]

We do not know why the Japanese asked the help of a left-wing leader at this critical moment. But we can speculate that it was not only because of Lyuh's reputation, but also because—lacking information on the Allied agreement concerning the 38th parallel—they thought that Russian troops would occupy the capital within two days. Apparently there was a complete breakdown of communication between the home government and the Governor General's office, as well as between the civilian government and the Japanese military commander in Korea. The latter belatedly, but without success, demanded that the civilian administrators annul the agreement.[16]

Lyuh then called the first open meeting of his secret 1944

---

[15] Morita, pp. 86–87. *Haebang Isip nyŏn,* Vol. 1 (Kirok Pyŏn), pp. 298–299. See also *Maeil Shinbo,* August 15–18. *Maeil Shinbo* is the major source of information on Korean political developments during this period until the time *Dong-A Ilbo* began its publication on December 1, 1945. Another important source of information is *Chosŏn Ilbo,* which recommenced publication on November 23, 1945.

[16] See Morita, pp. 86–87.

organization, Chosŏn Kŏn'guk Tongmaeng (the Alliance for Korean Independence), consulting many Korean leaders including Song Chin-u, Kim Chun-yŏn, Chang Dŏk-su, Ahn Chae-hong, all right-wing nationalists, and Yi Yŏ-sŏng, Yi Kang-guk, and other left wing leaders. Song, Kim and Chang refused their cooperation on the grounds that Lyuh should support the Korean Provisional Government in exile and that it would be unwise to help the Japanese at this moment. However, on August 16 Lyuh organized the Kŏn'guk Chunbi Wiwŏn Hoe (Committee for Preparation of Korean Independence, or CPKI) with himself as Chairman and Ahn as Vice-Chairman. Yi Yŏ-sŏng, Yi Kang-guk and many other leftists cooperated closely with the Committee.[17]

The CPKI became one of the strongest political forces in the early period of the occupation, partially controlling the existing administrative machinery, including the transportation and communication networks. It soon organized people's committees and security committees throughout the peninsula. In fact, the local committees effectively maintained order despite the lack of coordination with the central authority. Except for a few minor incidents involving notorious Japanese "thought control" police, the people behaved exceedingly well.[18] Indeed, there was a high spirit of cooperation as Koreans tried to prove their ability for self-government while the power vacuum lasted.

Lyuh and his followers wanted to organize a transitional government before the landing of American occupation forces. Only on September 2 did they finally learn that Korea would be divided at the 38th parallel. On September 6, the CPKI called a "National Assembly" meeting in Seoul, with approximately one thousand delegates who represented

---

[17] For the organization chart of the Committee and its initial activities, see Han Tae-su, pp. 33–39. See also Yi Ki-ha, *Han'guk Chŏngtang Baltal Sa* (History of the Development of Korean Political Parties) (Seoul, 1961), pp. 39–50.

[18] For the Japanese point of view see Morita, *op. cit.*

various groups and professions throughout the country. This Assembly, two days before the Americans arrived, declared themselves the People's Republic of Korea, and claimed jurisdiction over the whole nation.[19]

The People's Republic was composed of diverse political elements and contained men of all shades of political opinion. The assembly passed a resolution to appoint Syngman Rhee (Yi Sŭng-man) as Chairman of the Republic and Lyuh Woon-hyung as Vice-Chairman. It also selected Hŏ Hŏn as Prime Minister and appointed as its cabinet ministers, Kim Koo (Internal Affairs), Kimm Kiu-sic (Foreign Affairs), Cho Man-sik (Finance), Kim Sŏng-su (Education), Kim Pyŏng-no (Justice), Ha P'il-wŏn (Commerce), and Shin Ik-hi (Communication). As its main program, it advocated the establishment of a politically and economically independent state, the elimination of Japanese collaborators, the realization of a democracy based on fundamental human rights, social and economic reforms, and close cooperation with friendly nations to maintain international peace.[20]

When the United States occupation forces arrived in South Korea on September 8, they were surprised by a welcoming reception composed of delegates sent to Inchon by the People's Republic. General Hodge was completely unprepared for such a move: he had, of course, no knowledge even of the existence of such a body. His instructions clearly stipulated that he was to deal only with the Japanese Governor General in effecting the transfer of authority. Furthermore, MacArthur's General Order to the people of Korea had stipulated that the government of Korea south of the

---

[19] Han Tae-su, pp. 39–44. Yi Ki-ha, *loc. cit.* See also *Maeil Shinbo*, September 5–9, 1945.

[20] Han Tae-su, *loc. cit.* For the left-wing point of view on the establishment of the Republic see Kim Chong-myŏng, *Chōsen Shin Minshushugi Kakumei Shi* (History of Korea's New Democratic Revolution) (Tokyo, 1953), pp. 80–84. See also Minjujuŭi Minjok Chŏnsŏn, *Chosŏn Haebang Illnyŏn Sa* (One Year History of Korean Liberation) (Seoul, 1946).

38th parallel would be under his authority.[21] Hodge, therefore, declined to accept the offer of service by the People's Republic to the American occupation forces. Conflict became inevitable between the American commander and the national and local units of the Korean People's Republic.

Washington policy planners might have decided to ignore a *de facto* governing body in Korea, but the occupation forces could not dismiss it so easily. The Japanese Governor General had already gone so far as to allow the People's Republic to have access to press, radio and transportation facilities. As noted, order was relatively well maintained by the Republic's agencies, the people's committees, in each province. Its popularity and authority had already spread and no groups as strong had yet appeared.[22] It should have been immediately apparent that chaos would result if the *de facto* government was rejected. The Republic appeared to have a legitimate claim as the representative of the Korean people, and it refused to abandon its claim.

Hodge could not for some time obtain from Washington any clear-cut policy toward the Republic but the situation was clarified by a statement of President Truman on September 18. The President stated that "the assumption by the Koreans themselves of the responsibility and functions of a free and independent nation . . . will of necessity require time and patience. The goal is in view, but its speedy attainment will require the joint efforts of the Korean people and the Allies."[23] In his interpretation of this statement, General Hodge declared that "United States policy prohibits official recognition or utilization for political purposes of any

[21] U.S. Congress, Senate Committee on Foreign Relations, *The United States and the Korean Problems, Documents, 1943–1953* (Washington, 1953), p. 3.

[22] For detailed information see George M. McCune, *Korea's Postwar Political Problems* (New York, 1947). See also Ch'ŏn Kwan-u, "Haebang Simnyŏn Sa" (Ten Years' History of Korean Liberation), *Han'guk Ilbo* (a daily newspaper in Seoul), a series of articles which appeared from August 15, 1955 to December 1, 1955.

[23] *Department of State Bulletin,* September 23, 1945, p. 435.

so-called Korean provisional government or other political organization by United States forces."[24] On October 10, through his governor, Major General Arnold, Hodge reasserted that the military government was the "only government in Korea south of the 38th parallel."[25]

The Provincial People's Committees, however, continued to perform the main governmental functions in outlying areas until late October. By that time, American military government units had arrived and, replacing the tactical forces, assumed the government of the provinces. They also removed the representatives of the People's Republic from the local governments.

As it became clear that the United States had no intention of recognizing the *de facto* government of the People's Republic, conflict arose among Korean leaders. The split between the right and left wings accelerated the disintegration of the organization, while the conservatives began to form their own parties. As a result, Lyuh announced his resignation in order to form a new political group called Kŭnro Inmin Tang (the Korean People's Party). His departure with his followers left the Republic in the hands of the more radical leftist members.

The Republic was further weakened by the establishment of an eleven-member Advisory Council on October 5, appointed by Hodge to aid the military government. The Council, headed by Kim Sŏng-su, called the Republic an "irresponsible political group," an action which sharply antagonized the members of the Republic. They, in turn, began to label the military authority as "American imperialism" and publicly questioned the sincerity of American intentions for Korean independence. On November 20, a three-day "congress" of the People's Republic refused

---

[24] SCAP, *Summation of Nonmilitary Activities in Japan and Korea,* No. 1 (September, 1945), p. 177. Hereafter cited as *Summation.*

[25] American Military Government (AMGIK), *Chukan Digest,* No. 2 (October 25, 1945). See also *Maeil Shinbo,* October 10 and 11, 1945.

Hodge's request that it drop the title "Republic" and assume the conventional role of a political party by dissolving the Republic.[26]

To meet this refusal, the Commander of USAFIK took a more drastic measure. On December 12, he announced that the People's Republic was in no sense a "government," and denounced it by saying that the activities of any political organization in any attempted operations as a government are to be treated as unlawful activities.[27] This threat was effective, and the influence of the group subsequently declined as the conservative groups were strengthened by the influx of Korean leaders from America and China.

In retrospect, it appears that the independence and unification of Korea might have been achieved at an early stage (although at a considerable risk of eventual Communist domination) had the United States officially recognized the *de facto* government as it existed upon the arrival of the American forces. It was certainly true that the People's Republic was not dominated by American-style democratic thought and that it had a pinkish tinge. Nevertheless, it was the best opportunity to achieve the unification of Korea.

Was the establishment of an independent nation the only objective of United States Korean policy? The non-recognition policy reflected a fundamental attitude toward Korea after the war. America was not necessarily ready to grant Korean independence at the expense of its own national interests. It was true that she wanted the peninsula to be free, independent, and united, but not if it were to be governed along Communist lines. The American authorities viewed the People's Republic as a front organization for communist activity. This was, in fact, partially—but only partially—true. Among the group were also many prominent rightist leaders. Had the military government fostered the strength

---

[26] See *Chayu Shinmun,* November 20, 1945.

[27] *Summation,* No. 3 (December, 1945), p. 187 and AMGIK, *Chukan Digest,* No. 11 (December 29, 1945).

of these, while recognizing the People's Republic, Hodge's burdens might have been much lighter and Korean unification possibilities would have been substantially increased.

The non-recognition policy was a manifestation of power politics in international relations. Fundamentally, the objective seems to have been to keep South Korea out of the hands of any potential political enemy. Military occupation at the time was apparently aimed at keeping the Communists from gaining complete control of the entire peninsula.[28]

POLICY TOWARD KOREAN POLITICAL GROUPS

To create a counterforce to the People's Republic, General Hodge encouraged the formation of political parties, although there already existed the Han'guk Minju Tang (Korean Democratic Party) representing the conservatives. Partly through his encouragement, partly because of Korea's tendency toward political factionalism, dozens of new parties sprang up. As the General sealed the fate of the *de facto* government by treating the People's Republic as merely another party, he called for registration of all parties, their platforms, and their officers.[29] By October 24, 1945, there were 54 political parties registered with the headquarters of the military government, many with only a few hundred followers.[30]

The People's Republic was supported by several leftist

---

[28] In a policy briefing conference at Headquarters in Tokyo, General Christ gave the impression to the officials of USAMGIK that one of the principal missions of the military government in Korea was to "form a bulwark against Communists." Meade was one of the participants of the conference. Meade, p. 52.

[29] *Summation*, October, 1945, p. 178. See also Ordinance No. 55 in the *Official Gazette*. In this chapter, those who oppose the totalitarian concept of socialism are called the rightists. The leftists are those who favor the socialistic system of government.

[30] *Summation*, October, 1945, p. 178. See also, George M. McCune, "Occupation Politics in Korea," *Far Eastern Survey*, February 13, 1946, pp. 33–37.

parties. One of these was Lyuh's People's Party, whose members had once formed the core of support for the Republic. Originally fairly moderate and middle-of-the-road, this group was impelled by events to take an increasingly radical position. A second important leftist party was the Chosŏn Kongsan Tang (Korean Communist Party). This party had had some influence before 1945 among peasant and worker groups in the underground movement for Korean independence but had long been plagued by internal schisms. When Pak Hŏn-yŏng, a seasoned revolutionary, succeeded in unifying these groups in November, 1945, the Communist Party emerged as one of the strongest in Korea.[31] The *New York Times* reported on January 5, 1946, that the conservative groups had "fallen far behind liberal as well as radical factions" and that the People's Republic continued to gain strength in rural areas.[32]

Among the rightist elements also, two major parties emerged. The Han'guk Democratic Party, organized on September 8 under Song Chin-u and Kim Sŏng-su, was supported by landowners, manufacturers, bankers, businessmen, and some Christian organizations. After Song's assassination, Kim became its leader and advocated a moderate policy to achieve unification of Korea in close cooperation with the military government. The Kuk Min Tang (Nationalist

---

[31] For the origins of factionalism in the Communist Party, see Workers' Party of Korea, *Documents and Materials of the Third Congress of the Workers' Party of Korea* (Pyongyang, 1956), pp. 94–98. Mr. Pak became the Foreign Minister of the North Korean government in 1948, but was executed in 1955 on the charge of plotting "with American imperialists to destroy the Communist regime." *Ibid.*, pp. 99–104. For a detailed analysis of the origin of the Korean Communist Party, see Robert A. Scalapino and Chong-Sik Lee, "The Origins of the Korean Communist Movement," *The Journal of Asian Studies,* Vol. XX, No. 1 (Nov., 1960), pp. 9–31. For an official history of the party see *Chosŏn Rodongtang Yŏksa Kyojae* (Textbook for the History of the Korean Workers Party) (Pyongyang, 1964).

[32] *New York Times,* January 5, 1946. See also Yi Kiha, pp. 37–75.

Party), under the leadership of Ahn Chae-hong, merged with the Konghwa Tang (Republican Party) and three other small parties on September 24. This party grew rapidly in late 1946 with the semi-official support of the American occupational authority. The two rightist groups were in a powerful position because of their wealth, the political backing of the military government, and a conservative tendency within Korean society.[33] Nevertheless, the rightists were hopelessly divided and were therefore unable to serve as a unified force against the leftist groups.

The various political parties, which sprang up like mushrooms after rain, could be roughly divided into extreme rightists, centrists, and extreme leftists. By 1947, the number of political and social organizations in South Korea was to rise to 354.[34] The lack of strong leadership and political training, the lengthy suppression of political activities by the Japanese, the difficulties of conducting underground operations, the strong sense of provincialism, the division of the country into two diametrically opposed ideologies—all of these factors combined to cause factionalism. There were parties that emerged in the morning and were extinct by nightfall. About the only common aims were seizure of Japanese property, expulsion of the Japanese from Korea, punishment of collaborators, and immediate independence and

---

[33] George M. McCune and Arthur L. Grey, Jr., *Korea Today* (Cambridge, 1950), pp. 89–92. See also Pak Mun-ok, *Han'guk Chŏngbu Ron* (Korean Government) (Seoul, 1963), pp. 377–380. Han Taesu, pp. 296–297. Professor Han's book provides the best analysis of the development of Korean parties.

[34] USAMGIK, Department of Public Information, *Revised List of All Korean Political Parties and Social Organizations at the National Level under USAMGIK, Ordinance No. 55* (Seoul, January 22, 1948). This mimeographed pamphlet lists 354 political parties with the name of the group, registered number, English name, Korean name, address, date of organization, claimed membership and chairman. As prominent political parties in South Korea, it listed 18 as rightist, 6 as leftist, 14 as communist, and 10 as neutral.

self-government. It is thus almost impossible to make an authoritative analysis of Korean politics during the early period of the military occupation.[35]

There were several attempts to consolidate various parties into one group, and the return of Dr. Syngman Rhee on October 16, 1945, seemed to bring bright hope to this unification movement. Rhee, the first President of the Provisional Government of Korea in Shanghai, had long been a legend to the Korean people. He was not only the embodiment of the Korean independence movement but also a symbol of Korean pride. Due to his tireless fight for American recognition of the Provisional Government, he was not particularly liked by the State Department. Because of this, he promised the State Department, prior to his coming, that he would return to Korea in the role of a private citizen and not as a member of the Korean Provisional Government.[36] The prestige of Rhee was so great, however, that upon his arrival the leaders of nearly every political party in South Korea called on him and offered him the chairmanship of their parties. These included the leaders of the People's Republic and the Commu-

---

[35] For a more objective account of the political development of this period see Gaimusho (Japanese Ministry of Foreign Affairs), *Sengoni okeru Chōsen no Seiji Jōsei* (Korean Politics in the Post-war Era) (Research paper of the Research Bureau of the Ministry of Foreign Affairs, Tokyo, 1948), p. 46. For a brief survey of political development of this period, see also Tanaka Naokichi, *Nikkan Kankei* (Japan-Korean Relations) (Tokyo, 1963), pp. 46–48.

[36] For an account of Dr. Rhee's difficulty in obtaining permission to return to Korea, see Robert T. Oliver, *Syngman Rhee: The Man Behind the Myth* (New York, 1954), pp. 211–215. For a more critical analysis of Syngman Rhee, see Richard C. Allen, *Korea's Syngman Rhee: An Unauthorized Portrait* (Tokyo, 1960). On October 10, a preliminary meeting of representatives of 43 parties was held to discuss the unification of parties. As a result, a unification committee, composed of a communist, a nationalist, and a centrist, was formed to lay the groundwork for the movement. This committee failed, due chiefly to the lack of strong leadership as well as to the deep-rooted suspicion among the leaders. See *Summation,* No. 1 (September–October, 1945), p. 179. See also *Maeil Shinbo,* October 10–12, 1945.

nist parties.[37] Sensing the danger of becoming the puppet of these parties, he declined them all and made it clear that he would not affiliate himself with any one group. Instead, he undertook to organize the Tongnip Ch'oksŏng Chung'ang Hyŏbŭi Hoe (Committee for Rapid Realization of Korean Independence), asking all Koreans to join it.

On October 23, a meeting of 200 persons representing more than 50 political parties and social groups was held under the chairmanship of Dr. Rhee. Two days later the Central Committee for the Rapid Realization of Korean Independence was formed in the hope that it might unify all existing political parties. The Committee declared its complete support of the Provisional Government in Chungking and urged its immediate return to Korea. As a result, the Committee achieved a temporary consolidation of rightist political parties. However, the extreme leftists, including the Communists, refused to join this movement, while the People's Republic went ahead with its own program of expansion.[38] The cleavage between left and right became more and more serious after November 7, 1945, when Rhee flatly refused the official request of the People's Republic to be its chairman. The leftists began to realize that they could not compromise with Rhee, who now became the acknowledged leader of the rightists.

Mr. Kim Koo (Kim Ku), Chairman of the Provisional Government in Chungking, and his associates arrived on November 23, with the promise by Kim also that he would remain a private citizen. Kim's reputation was as remarkable in its own way as Rhee's. This self-educated leader was the one who had ordered countless acts of terror against the Japanese, including the assassination of General Shirakawa

---

[37] *Syngman Rhee,* p. 214. See also *Konnichi no Chōsen,* p. 21. See also Allen, pp. 76–79.

[38] *Summation,* No. 1, p. 180. See also Han Tae-su, pp. 64–90. The factual information on this period comes from *Maeil Shinbo* (Seoul Shinmun) if not otherwise specified.

and an unsuccessful attempt on the life of the Japanese Emperor. Upon his return, most of the rightist parties publicly announced their support of the Provisional Government.[39] Unlike the People's Republic, the Korean Provisional Government declared itself a political party in order to conform to the regulations of the military government.

During the initial period of American occupation, the military government nominally maintained a neutral attitude toward the various Korean parties, believing that democratic principles required that communists be treated like other political parties, provided no law was violated. The Communist Party occupied one of the best buildings in Seoul for its headquarters and their activities were not restrained by the military authorities. Nevertheless, "it was no secret that it [the military government] favored the right, and was anxious for the parties of the right to acquire strong popular support."[40] General Arnold instructed his subordinates that "political parties, organizations and societies will be placed under control. Those whose activities are consistent with the requirements and objectives of the military government will be encouraged. Those whose activities are inconsistent with military government will be abolished."[41] Actually, no parties were abolished, nor were they restricted

---

[39] *Summation,* No. 2 (November, 1945), p. 182. See also *Seoul Shinmun,* November 23, 1945. At first, the People's Republic was publicly bidding for the support of Kim Koo's Provisional Government. But Kim Koo and his group rejected an offer from the Republic for an equal division of offices in a proposed "cabinet" of the "Provisional Government." They offered, instead, to allow members of the Republic one or two places in the cabinet. *Summation,* No. 3 (December, 1945), p. 186. For detailed analysis of the Provisional Government, see Lee Chong-sik, *The Politics of Korean Nationalism* (Berkeley and Los Angeles, 1963). For the life of Kim Koo, see his autobiography, *Paekbŏm Ilchi* (Seoul, 1947).

[40] Bertran D. Sarafan, "Military Government in Korea," *Far Eastern Survey,* November, 1946, p. 349. For the left-wing point of view, see Kim Chong-myŏng, pp. 85–100.

[41] See the section "Public Relations and Politics in Chŏlla Namdo," Meade, pp. 103–104, and p. 71.

as long as they behaved as parties and not like a government.

DISCONTENT OF THE PEOPLE IN SOUTH KOREA

When the news was received on December 25 that the Moscow Conference had decided that a five-year trusteeship was to be imposed upon Korea, the growing discontentment of the people reached a climax. There was universal disapproval of trusteeship and of the military government, and the reaction was violent. All parties were hostile and even the conservative forces turned against Hodge's administration.

The conservative forces, strongly supported by the Provisional Government, immediately initiated a general work sabotage, and mass demonstrations broke out all over the country, with even the Korean employees of the military government participating. Hodge had almost no backing; he had already antagonized the People's Republic, and now the conservative forces withdrew their support. The popularity of the United States reached its lowest ebb.

Although, to placate the Koreans, the military government had expressed its intention of immediately removing all Japanese from public offices, the lack of trained civil servants caused it in reality to retain Japanese officials in important positions. This only aroused further resentment; Koreans preferred to suffer from their own administrative errors than to submit to government by their enemies, however efficient. Finally, to relieve this resentment, the change over from Japanese to Korean personnel was rapidly accelerated, and by the end of January, 1946, only 60 out of 70,000 Japanese officials remained in the military government. Later, Hodge requested his military governor to turn over various government departments to Koreans, with American personnel remaining only as advisors. This move was intended to encourage Koreans to operate their own government; but in fact, despite the change of status from director to advisor, Americans had to continue much of their direct control.[42]

To provide the Koreans a greater degree of self-government and thus recruit support for Hodge's administration, the military government moved to establish an advisory council of Koreans. The 25 members were appointed so as to give expression to various shades of political opinion, but not necessarily to represent the organizations to which they belonged. The Representative Democratic Council (Taehan Min'guk Taep'yo Minju Ŭiwŏn), with Rhee as its Chairman, was formed on February 14, 1946. The Council promptly met a cold response, particularly from left-wing groups.[43] For one thing, many of the appointees had backgrounds which (in leftist eyes at least) laid them open to charges of having been collaborators with the Japanese. Furthermore, the establishment of the Council was interpreted as giving substance to the fears that "in due course" meant not immediate independence but, rather, indefinite trusteeship. Leading liberals refused to participate, though some right-wing leaders did begin to align themselves with the American occupation authorities. In South Korea there seemed to be no way to pacify the people except by granting immediate independence, something which was beyond the power of the American military government.

[42] U.S. Department of the Army, "History of American Military Advisory Groups in Korea," MS, n. d., pt. 1, p. 32. See also *Nikkan Kankei no Tenkai,* pp. 91–92. At the time of occupation, there were 70,000 Japanese in the civil service of South Korea and more than 130,000 Japanese employees in minor positions. See *Summation,* No. 11 (August, 1946), p. 96. Also, *Department of State Bulletin,* January 27, 1946, pp. 104–110. For a more comprehensive study from the Japanese point of view, see Morita Kazuo, *Chōsen Shusen no Kiroku* (The Record of the End of the War in Korea) (Tokyo, 1964).

[43] The appointees were almost all right-wing conservatives. The Council finally lost its official status on December 18, 1946, with the establishment of the Interim Legislative Assembly. Critics likened the Council to the similar Central Advisory Council under the Japanese Governor-General. See *Korea's Post-war Political Problems,* p. 14. See also Pak Mun-ok, p. 333.

OCCUPATION IN NORTH KOREA

From the beginning Russia was much better informed about Korean internal affairs than the United States. There were far more Korean exiles in the maritime province of the Soviet Far East than in any other place except Manchuria. These exiles were well indoctrinated, had been trained as professional communists, and had maintained some liaison with the underground Communists inside Korea.[44]

When it marched in, Colonel General Ivan Chistiakov's XXV Army was accompanied by a Committee of Liberation and an embryonic Korean Army of hard-boiled Communists; the latter were placed in key positions of power.[45] With these trained forces, the Russians were able to set up a rigid communist control in the North.

In North Korea, as in the South, the People's Committee was established under the local leadership of both nationalists and communists. In the North, however, this Committee was formed with the sanction of the occupation forces. For example, as early as August 25, a meeting of the members of the Hamgyŏng Namdo Communist Council (Hamgyŏng Namdo Kongsanjuŭija Hyŏbi Hoe) and the nationalist members of the Committee for Preparation of Independence (Kŏn'guk Chunbi Wiwŏn Hoe) created the Hamgyŏng Namdo People's Executive Committee for the maintenance of law

---

[44] According to Professor Dallin, during the war many Communists in the Soviet Union were transferred to Yenan where they formed a Korean Emancipation League with a reputed membership of nearly 2,000. D. J. Dallin, *Soviet Russia and the Far East* (New Haven, 1948), pp. 255–258. According to Lee Chong-sik's study, the Soviet Union's relation with the underground Communist movement in Korea was not very close after 1941. See also Kim Ch'ang-sun, *Pukhan Sibo nyŏn Sa* (Fifteen Years of History in North Korea) (Seoul, 1961), pp. 51–61.

[45] Robert T. Oliver, *Why War Came in Korea* (New York, 1950), p. 5. The author indicated that the number could be 300,000, but this seems exaggerated. For more information, see Lee Chong-sik, "Korean Communists and Yenan," *The China Quarterly*, No. 9 (January–March, 1962), pp. 182–192.

and order. The Soviet occupation commander then formally confirmed the assumption by the Executive Committee of all administrative powers in the province, thus putting the People's Committee in nominal, if not actual, control of their own affairs.[46] This set a pattern for the role of the People's Committee throughout the North Korean provinces. In this way, the Soviet Union governed North Korea without establishing a military government.[47]

The People's Committee in North Korea had sent delegates to the congress at Seoul on September 6 which had established the People's Republic, under Lyuh, and the Central People's Committee. Since the Committee was created to represent the whole of Korea, the North Korean People's Committee did not establish a separate body. At the time, of course, it was hoped that the People's Republic would take over the administration of the entire country.[48] Therefore, the Northern group organized themselves as the Temporary Five Provinces People's Committee (Odo Inmin Wiwŏn Hoe), changing the name to the Five Provinces Administrative Bureau (Odo Haengjŏng Kuk) on October 19. Only much later, on February 9, 1946, was a Provisional People's Committee for North Korea (Puk Chosŏn Imsi Inmin Wiwŏn Hoe) established, replacing the Administrative Bureau as the central governing body. At that time, it adopted the political structure of the Soviet Union.

By the beginning of September, 1945, the Russians had es-

---

[46] "Unification Question in Historical Facts and Documents," *One Korea* (A monthly journal for Korean unification, published in Japan by Yi Yŏn Kŏn, an advocate of Korean neutralization), No. 31 (March, 1964), pp. 18–21.

[47] Yang Ho-min, "Chŏngch'i Ch'eje ŭi Pyŏnchŏn" (Transformation of Political System), *Sasangge* (a renowned monthly journal in South Korea), August, 1965, pp. 168–174. For a survey of the North Korean governmental structure, see also Kim Tae-ho, "The Ruling System of North Korean Regime," *Korean Affairs,* Vol. II, No. II, 1963, pp. 174–186.

[48] Kim Chong-myŏng, pp. 81–85. *Haebang Isip nyŏn,* pp. 299–300.

tablished their authority over the whole of North Korea and they were cautiously working toward the organization of a strong pro-Soviet Communist party as a reliable major political force. The task was difficult because, as in South Korea, numerous local communist as well as nationalist elements were competing with each other for power. The situation was further complicated by the heavy influx of Communists and nationalists from China, Manchuria, and the Soviet Union.

First, the Russians endeavored to eliminate the indigenous nationalist group led by Cho Man-sik, a famous Christian leader who was known as the "Gandhi of Korea" for his uncompromising nationalist fight against the Japanese. His popularity among the North Koreans was such that the Soviet authorities found it expedient to appoint him Chief of the Provincial People's Executive Committee rather than antagonize his followers by eliminating him immediately. In November, 1945, he was even allowed to form the Chosŏn Minju Tang (Korean Democratic Party, or KDP) which received substantial support from the middle class, Christians, and intellectuals. It was not until January, 1946, that the Soviet authority banished him from public office on the ground that he had opposed the Moscow Conference decision concerning trusteeship of Korea.[49] The arrest of Cho signalled the curtailment of the nationalist movement; the exodus of a large number of Christians to the South followed immediately. Although the headquarters of the party was moved to Seoul, the KDP itself was allowed to continue under the leadership of disguised communists so as to justify the communist line of the "New Democracy." [50]

The Korean communist movement had first begun in the

[49] For an excellent study on political developments in North Korea during this period, see Lee Chong-sik, "Politics in North Korea: Pre-Korean War Stage" in *North Korea Today*, ed. Robert A. Scalapino (New York, 1963), pp. 3–16.

[50] The party was reorganized in Seoul on April 26. For the slogan and policy of the party see Han Tae-su, pp. 214–218.

1920's among the Korean exiles in Siberia and China, but because of bitter nationalistic and ideological factionalism had not been able to create a single strong, unified party. Among the various surviving groups, that based on the Chinese Communist wartime center of Yenan, and led by Kim Tu-bong, was the strongest in terms of membership and prestige. They maintained a military organization with hundreds of veteran officers and a large number of well-trained troops for their resistance campaign against the Japanese.[51] After returning to North Korea, they preserved their political organization and steadily increased their strength, mainly by recruiting from the middle class and the white-collar intellectuals. In March, 1946, they changed their name from Chosŏn Tongnip Tongmaeng (the Korean Independence League) to Shinmin Tang (the New People's Party), and their activity became a major concern to the Soviet authorities until they were merged into the North Korean Workers Party at the end of July, 1946.

A third powerful political group facing the Soviet were the indigenous communists, who fought underground during the Japanese rule for their ideology as well as for Korean independence. They publicly emerged for the first time and quickly organized the northern branch of the Korean Communist Party. As mentioned earlier, they had new headquarters in Seoul under the leadership of Pak Hŏn-yŏng. Their followers and strength came largely from the small proletarian labor class. Because of their training in underground activities within Korea, they were able to reorganize their cells quickly, and easily infiltrated the local People's Committees.[52]

Although the leaders of the Korean Independence League and the indigenous communists were well-known and popu-

---

[51] *North Korea Today*, p. 9.

[52] *North Korea Today*, pp. 3–16. The principal leaders of the group in the north were Hyŏn Chun-hyŏk, O Ki-sŏp, Yi Chu-ha and Chŏng Tal-hyŏn. See Kim Ch'ang-sun, pp. 65–66.

lar, the Soviet authorities preferred to depend upon Soviet-trained communists. Some of these were ex-partisans who had fled to Siberia in the 1940's from Manchuria; others were party cadres who were drawn from Soviet citizens of Korean origin in Uzbekistan and Kazakhstan.[53] In the hectic postwar confusion and emotionalism, the Russians installed their own henchman as the leader of the communist groups in North Korea. The man whose name, South Korean sources claim, was Kim Sŏng-ju, had led a guerrilla group in Southern Manchuria and then had suddenly disappeared into the Soviet Union around 1941. He returned to Korea at the age of thirty-three in the uniform of a Red Army major using the alias of Kim Il-sŏng, the name of a legendary hero of the Korean resistance movement in Manchuria. Although he may well have been in North Korea from the beginning of the Soviet occupation, he did not publicly appear until October 3, 1945, when he was dramatically introduced to the North Koreans by Cho Man-sik as the true national hero, Kim Il-sŏng.[54]

According to an official North Korean source, Kim was elected on October 10, 1945, seven days after his public appearance, as the First Secretary of "the North Korean Central Bureau of the Korean Communist Party" at a meet-

---

[53] For an objective study see U.S. Department of State, *North Korea: A Case Study in the Techniques of Takeover* (Washington, 1961), pp. 12–16.

[54] For a general study of the political developments in North Korea see Kim Ch'ang-sun, pp. 54–61. For an official biography of Kim Il-sŏng, see Han Sul-ya, *Hero General Kim Il Sŏng* (Tokyo, 1962). For Kim's activities, see also Kwahak Wŏn, Yŏksa Yŏn'gu So (The North Korean Academy of Science: Division of History), *Chosŏn Kŭndae Hyŏngmyŏn Undong Sa* (History of Revolutionary Movement in Modern Korea) (Pyongyang, 1959). See also Kwahak Won, Yŏksa Yŏn'gu So, *Chosŏn T'ongsa* (Outline History of Korea) (Tokyo, 1959), Vol. III, pp. 15–20. See also Han Im-hyŏk, *Kim Il-sŏng Tonji e ŭihan Chosŏn Kongsantang Ch'anggŏn* (The Foundation of the Korean Communist Party by Comrade Kim Il-sŏng) (Pyongyang, 1961); and Pak Sang-hyŏk, *Chosŏn Minjok ŭi Witaehan Yŏngdoja* (The Great Leader of the Korean Nation) (Tokyo, 1965).

ing of the North Korean Five Provinces Party Conference. It is now claimed that this was the first Korean Communist Party organized by "the true communists." Kim, with the strong backing of the Soviet occupation authority, began to place his ex-partisan followers and the Soviet Koreans in key positions within the party and governmental administrative machinery. After the elimination of Cho Man-sik, no one was able to compete effectively with Kim. Kim's success owed more, however, to organizational strength and Russian backing than it did to genuine popularity.

In the process of establishing a regime wholeheartedly loyal to the Soviet Union, the Soviet authorities acted "with purposiveness and a considerable degree of finesse."[55] In the initial occupation period, nominally important positions were given to men with strong national appeal—but the positions of real power were filled by followers of Kim Il-sŏng, or trusted Soviet Koreans who retained their membership in the Russian Communist party. Even while holding vitally important posts, these Soviet-trained party members generally remained in the background of the political stage. The nationalist leaders and indigenous communists were used as figureheads to be discarded later as the pro-Soviet communists gradually consolidated their power in North Korea.[56]

Furthermore, the Soviet command—from the very beginning of the occupation—pursued a policy of complete elimination of all vestiges of the Japanese regime. Most of the high-ranking Japanese officials had already fled to South Korea; but the organizational forms, as well as all remaining Japanese personnel, were speedily removed. At the same time, the Soviet command did not "waste its energies in the morass of military government." Instead, it wisely sought to avoid any appearance of direct control of the Korean people. This was done by hiding behind the existing People's Com-

[55] Kim Ch'ang-sun, p. 61. *North Korea: A Case Study in the Techniques of Takeover*, pp. 12–16.

[56] *Ibid.*, pp. 2–9, 15–16, and 100–105; Yang Ho-min, *loc. cit.*

mittee—though there were few illusions as to where the real power lay. It is quite clear, nonetheless, that the Russians permitted the Koreans to exercise much wider authority than did the Americans.[57]

Although Soviet policies and propaganda were successful during the initial period of occupation in promoting the image of the Russians as the true liberators, their economic policies were not so readily accepted. The Soviet Army demanded a regular supply of food, at the expense of the country. New money, printed and put into circulation in large amounts, added to inflation. The removal of some industrial equipment caused concern.[58] The tight Russian control of the Korean economy alienated many of the farmers—who wanted a free market for their produce. The undisciplined conduct of Russian soldiers also gradually antagonized Koreans. By November, there were several revolts of youth and student groups, indicating dissatisfaction with the Soviet occupation.[59] Freedom of political activity was then restricted and various political parties were forced out of

---

[57] For a broad study of the transformations of governmental structure in North Korea, see Pak Tong-un, *Pukhan T'onch'i Kigu Ron* (Theory of North Korean Government) (Seoul, 1964), pp. 7–16. See also F. I. Shabshina, "Korea after the Second World War" in *Krisis Kolonialism Sistema,* translated by the Chosen Historical Society, Pyongyang, Korea, as it appeared in *Chōsen Minzoku Kaiho Tōsō Shi* (History of the Korean People's Struggle for Liberation) (Tokyo, 1952), pp. 363–368.

[58] *North Korea: A Case Study in the Techniques of Takeover,* pp. 67–84. Chung Kyung-cho, *Korea Tomorrow: Land of the Morning Calm* (New York, 1956), pp. 194–197. It is interesting in this connection to note that Ambassador Edwin W. Pauley, U. S. Reparation Commissioner, toured North Korea and reported on June 4, 1946, that the Russian commander stated that there were no removals of industrial equipment of any kind to the Soviet Union. Pauley himself added that "only on two or three occasions did we view anything that would indicate that such removals had taken place, and those only to minor extent. . . ." *Summation,* June, 1946, pp. 17–18. See also Edwin W. Pauley, *Report on Japanese Assets in Soviet-Occupied Korea to the President of the United States* (Washington, 1946).

[59] Kim Sam-gyu, *Chōsen Gendai Shi* (Modern History of Korea) (Tokyo, 1963), pp. 51–53.

existence. Political activity came to be limited to members of only the Communist, Chosŏn Democratic, and Ch'ŏndokyo parties.[60]

At the risk of repetition, it may be useful to summarize some of the basic differences between Soviet and American policy during the first postwar phase. In the first place, the Russians established no military government as such. Soviet control operated through the recognition and utilization of the People's Republic and People's Committees at all levels. The Americans not only established a military government, they insisted that it be the only governing body in Korea. The effect of this was to refuse the Koreans any share in administrative responsibility and to emphasize the strictly military character of American control.

In the second place, the Russians came with a background of knowledge and with well-prepared plans. They aimed at close political, social and economic integration of North Korea into the Soviet sphere of influence, and they were prepared to indoctrinate the Korean people to this end as thoroughly and speedily as possible. The Americans, on the other hand, were entrusted primarily with merely receiving the surrender and carrying out the repatriation of Japanese forces and nationals. Beyond this limited goal, they were not equipped with detailed or long-range administrative plans and political policies to cope with the problems of Korea.

One of the local factors assisting the Russians was that the People's Republic and its local committees were dominated by leftist and revolutionary elements. These bodies were thus amenable to Russian direction through Communist

---

[60] The Ch'ŏndokyo Ch'ŏng-u Tang is the party organized by a nationalistic religious group called Ch'ŏndokyo, the changed name of Tonghak—which spearheaded the Tonghak rebellion of 1894 and later played the important role in the independence movement of March 1, 1919. The party was formally organized in February, 1946, drawing its strength mainly from the farming population, but soon became a satellite organization of the Communist party. See Kim Ch'ang-sun, pp. 164–166.

members, who quickly succeeded in effectively taking control. This revolutionary character of the People's Committees, obviously unlike the democratic American system, only convinced the Americans all the more, however, that military government was needed until anti-Communist (or non-Communist) groups could have a chance to develop and mature. From the beginning, therefore, both sides were actively engaged in fostering forces that would strengthen their own positions. The result was that North and South Korea were being made, by the two occupying powers, into two distinct political and economic entities.

To the Americans, it seemed that the Korean people devoted most of their efforts to criticizing American occupational policy and were unappreciative of the liberation which American war sacrifices had brought them. As I have already mentioned (in the Introduction), the Korean people themselves cannot escape all the blame for political chaos and ineffectiveness. Although the division of the country was beyond their control, the conflicts among the Korean leaders were disastrous and self-defeating. The lack of wise and mature leadership—like that of Gandhi in India, for example—made it difficult for the Korean people to unite and present their case strongly to the occupying powers and the world. One can say that this was part of the legacy of nearly four decades of Japanese denial of all rights of self-government and of brutal secret police suppression of all indigenous national leadership. The return from exile of those old leaders who had been able to escape the country did not satisfactorily fill this gap: though they shared an ardent nationalism, they lacked fresh roots in the country, were without practical experience of political leadership and responsibility, and grievously split along ideological lines. It is true, too, that the people were not educated or trained for sophisticated management of a democratic system of government. Yet, had they joined firmly in an unselfish desire for national unification and united behind either the Provisional Government or the People's Republic, they might at the least have retained a strong bargaining position vis-à-vis the American and Russian occupation authorities. Unfortunately for Korea, the leaders of both right and left, from the day of the Japanese surrender, had different visions of a future government and were never willing to reconcile those views.

One can have some sympathy, then, with American discouragement and resentment of Korean attitudes. Yet it was the American lack of imagination and initiative, and American failure to understand the basic feelings of the people and the political realities within the country that contributed to those attitudes and increased the fractiousness of the Korean problem. If the representatives of the United States had only been willing to utilize the Provisional Government, avoiding direct involvement in the civil administration of the country, their prestige as liberators would have been immeasurably increased. On this basis, it might have been possible with patience and skill to mediate the conflicts between the People's Republic and the Provisional Government and thus to bring about a coalition government acceptable to both powers. The Soviet command had already accepted the People's Committee as the official governing body of North Korea. The establishment of a unified Korean government might in this way have become a reality.

Is this suggestion overly optimistic? I submit that it is not. The forces of both right and left had not yet hardened and were still more or less in the embryonic stage. Although there was an influx of Communists from the Soviet Union, their power in North Korea during this early period was still far from secure. The Chinese Communists were not yet a factor. A coalition of forces centered around the Provisional Government was quite within the bounds of realistic possibility: all parties, including the People's Republic, had pledged their support to Rhee and Kim Koo upon their arrival in the country. With effective economic aid, understanding political support, and the gradual reform of this coalition government, the United States might well have been successful in establishing a strong and stable democratic Korean government. The opportunity, however, was lost.

Lamentable though it was, the failure to see and grasp this opportunity is not the basic count against American policy. Contemporary developments in Eastern Europe and China were not encouraging for the concept of a coalition government. The important charge against American policy is that of grossly and inexcusably inadequate preparation. Because no agreements on Korean policy had been reached with Russia at Yalta or Potsdam, it was all the more dangerous that American policy was unformed and uninformed, vague and ambiguous, arbitrary and yet uncertain. Because of this lack of preparation, there were frequent policy changes, deviations, mistakes and lack of coordination. They could have been avoided if American policy toward Korea had been thoughtfully planned, and if competent, trained administrative personnel had been ready. Use could have been made, for instance, of the many Korean exiles in the United States and China by training them for the post-occupation transfer of administrative functions. An American expert on Korean matters summarized the military administration as follows:

> In the government administration of southern Korea, the American command was handicapped, particularly in the early stage when precedents were being established, by a lack of adequate planning and guidance from Washington and by a lack of advisors possessing either political "know-how" or a broad understanding of Korean psychology and political background. As a result, certain early actions of the American authorities had a cooling effect upon the predominantly pro-American feeling of the Koreans.[61]

---

[61] Benjamin Weems, "Behind the Korean Election," *Far Eastern Survey*, June 23, 1948, p. 144.

4

Hodge's Dilemma: The Moscow Agreement on Korean Trusteeship

The Korean people are of one race, with one language and one homogenous culture. It was clear that division, though temporary, would violate this fundamental unity.[1]

When the American occupation forces landed in Korea, they found an economic situation most difficult to handle. The Americans controlled the best of the country's farmlands, but they were also responsible for feeding more than two-thirds of the nation's population. Over a million Koreans in Japan returned to their homes in South Korea and nearly one hundred thousand came back to South Korea from China and other overseas areas. In addition, about a million North Koreans migrated to the south for better living conditions and more freedom.[2] By the end of 1945 more than 10

---

[1] See Matsumoto Hirokazu, *Gekido suru Kankoku* (Korea in Turmoil) (Tokyo, 1963), pp. 16–31.

[2] Official figures indicate that approximately 800,000 left North Korea during the first two years of occupation. USAFIK (United States Armed Forces in Korea), *Summation of U.S. Army Military Government Activities in Korea,* No. 24 (September, 1947), p. 3. Hereafter cited as Summation. See also Edward W. Wagner, *The Korean Minority in Japan: 1904–1950* (New York, 1951), pp. 43–49; and Shinozaki Heiji, *Zainichi Chōsenjin Undo* (Movement of Korean Minority in Japan) (Tokyo, 1956), pp. 38–46.

percent of the people in the South were refugees.[3] Consequently, South Korea suffered an acute food shortage.

The 38th parallel not only cut indiscriminately across mountains and plains, hamlets and towns, communication and transportation networks; [4] it separated the predominantly agricultural South from the more industrial North. For a healthy Korean economy, it was necessary for the two zones to complement one another.[5] The South heavily depended on the North for electric power and semifinished raw materials, whereas the North depended on the South for its consumer goods and food supply. With no fertilizer from the North, South Korean food production could not even meet the local demand. Without chemicals, coal, and raw materials, the Southern economy was faced with complete paralysis.[6] In November, 1945, the price index in the American zone began to rise in an uncontrollable inflationary spiral.

---

[3] James Shoemaker, *Notes on Korea's Post-war Economic Position,* mimeographed, Secretariat Paper No. 4, Institute of Pacific Relations, New York, 1947.

[4] Shannon McCune, "Physical Basis for Korean Boundaries," *Far Eastern Quarterly,* May, 1946, pp. 272–288. For an authoritative work on the regional and social geography of Korea, see Shannon McCune, *Korea's Heritage: A Regional and Social Geography* (Tokyo, 1956), pp. 82–189. A most authoritative analysis of the effect of the zonal division in the areas of economic and social development, is George M. McCune and A. L. Grey, Jr., *Korea Today* (Cambridge, 1950), pp. 52–60 and pp. 93–220. An excellent work on the Korean economic structure for this period is Ko Sŭng-je, *Han'guk Kyŏngje Ron* (Theory on Korean Economy) (Seoul, 1958), pp. 10–33.

[5] For the complementary nature of the Korean economy, see *Korea's Heritage,* pp. 100–189. See also Lawrence K. Rosinger and Associates, *The State of Asia: A Contemporary Survey* (New York, 1953), p. 133.

[6] The following commodities reported to be available in the Russian zone were needed in the American zone: coal, soybeans, wheat, salt, pig iron, aluminum, ferro-molybdenum, ferro-tungsten, fertilizer, sulphur phosphate, and ammonium sulphate. *Summation,* No. 1 (October, 1945), p. 181.

HODGE'S ATTEMPT TO NEGOTIATE WITH CHISTIAKOV

As the economic situation in South Korea became critical, the American commander tried to effect a relaxation of travel restrictions, and to secure unification of the economy and civil administration of the country. But aside from agreeing to establish a tactical liaison at the 38th parallel, the Soviet authorities remained almost entirely unresponsive to General Hodge's overtures. Actually, it had become evident within a very few days after the American entry on September 8 that the Russians were not going to cooperate. When Hodge sent a trainload of supplies to the North to be exchanged for a load of coal, the Soviet command sent no coal and even kept the train. Next, the Russians cut off electric power service for the area north of Seoul.[7] This strict interpretation by the Soviets of their responsibilities changed the 38th parallel from a dividing line into a barrier.

In an effort to solve these difficulties, Hodge twice invited Chistiakov, the Soviet commander in the North, to fly to Seoul to discuss the various economic and political problems resulting from the zonal division. The Russian commander, however, replied in a letter of October 9, 1945, that he could not take such an action without instructions from his government because the matter of unification could be solved only by the governments of the two occupying powers.[8]

It seems that Chistiakov was given no authority to initiate any policy toward the unification of Korea and was restricted to matters of occupational conduct.[9] On the other hand, Hodge was fully empowered to negotiate for a unified

---

[7] For detailed information on the problems of electricity, see *Korea Today*, pp. 146–152. Despite many difficulties, the transmission of electricity across the 38th parallel continued until May 14, 1948.

[8] Carl Berger, *The Korean Knot: A Military and Political History* (Philadelphia, 1957), p. 56.

[9] Max Beloff, *Soviet Policy in the Far East: 1944–1951* (London, 1953), p. 159.

administration and to settle with the Soviet commander any local problems caused by the unnatural division of the peninsula.[10] Understandably, Hodge reported to MacArthur that the liaison with the Russians in Korea was anything but satisfactory.

As the difficulties increased, the United States government approached the Russian government in Moscow and suggested that practical problems be solved either through local negotiations between the two commanders or on a governmental level.[11] Practical problems included the reintegration of communications, the economic unification of the two zones, and the problem of currency. These were later to be discussed directly between Secretary of State Byrnes and Foreign Minister Molotov at Moscow.

SEARCH FOR A KOREAN POLICY: TRUSTEESHIP

In Washington, authorities faced the necessity of forming a definite Korean policy that the local commander could implement effectively. As a result, the State-War-Navy Coordinating Committee on October 20, 1945, laid down a general policy on Korea which clearly stated that "the present zonal military occupation of Korea by the United States and Soviet forces should be superseded at the earliest possible date by a trusteeship for Korea." [12]

The next day, John Carter Vincent, the State Department's Chief of Far Eastern Affairs, publicly announced that: "Korea, after years of subjection to Japan, is not immediately prepared to exercise self-government. We, therefore, advocate a period of trusteeship during which Koreans

---

[10] For an official statement see *Department of State Bulletin,* November 18, 1945, p. 813.

[11] *Department of State Bulletin, loc. cit.* The letter was delivered by Ambassador Harriman on November 8. Harry S. Truman, *Years of Trial and Hope* (New York, 1956), p. 319.

[12] U.S. Department of the Army, "History of United States Military Advisory Groups to the Republic of Korea," unpublished MS., Pt. II, Chapter II, pp. 57–58.

will be prepared to take over the independent administration of their country. How long that will require neither you nor I can say; we will agree, however, that the briefer the period, the better." [13]

On November 10, 1945, President Truman met in Washington with Prime Minister Attlee and Prime Minister Mackenzie King of Canada to discuss various world problems, including the Far Eastern situation. With regard to Korea, it was agreed that immediate steps would be taken by the United States to set up a trusteeship under the direction of Great Britain, Russia, China, and the United States.[14]

As we have seen in previous chapters, trusteeship had been discussed since 1943. However, it was not until May, 1945, that a gentlemen's agreement [15] was reached between Stalin and Hopkins, who was then in Moscow to clarify Truman's policy after Roosevelt's death. The agreement was not written. When T. V. Soong, the Chinese Foreign Minister, went to Moscow in July, 1945, to discuss the pending Russo-Chinese treaty, Marshal Stalin confirmed his agreement to establish a four-power trusteeship. At this time, Stalin said that "there should be no foreign troops or foreign policy in Korea." Molotov interjected that this was an unusual arrangement with no precedent and that, therefore, it would be necessary to come to a detailed understanding.[16]

Despite this timely warning, American policy planners still felt the necessity of a trusteeship.[17] Prophetic vision

---

[13] Statement by John Carter Vincent at the Foreign Policy Association Forum. *Department of State Bulletin,* October 21, 1945, p. 646.

[14] Harry S. Truman, *Year of Decisions* (New York, 1955), p. 540.

[15] Robert E. Sherwood, *Roosevelt and Hopkins: An Intimate History* (New York, 1948), p. 903; see also Chapter 2 of this book.

[16] *Year of Decisions,* p. 317.

[17] *Ibid.* Truman recorded Soong's warning in his memoirs: ". . . the Russians have 2 Korean divisions trained in Siberia. He [Soong] believes that these troops will be left in Korea and that there will be Soviet-trained political personnel who will also be brought into the country. Under those conditions, he is fearful that even with a four-power trusteeship the Soviets will obtain domination of Korean affairs."

was certainly not needed to predict that this would fail without the close cooperation of the Soviet Union. Even if there were four-power guarantees, it was highly probable that Russia would dominate Korea through well-trained Korean Communists unless the United States actively fostered a strong counterforce; this would be most difficult if the Soviet Union were to have a strong voice in the trusteeship.

The United States had ample time to contrive a more secure plan for Korea, such as the establishment of an interim government by a general election under the supervision of the United Nations or the Allied powers. As noted earlier, the prestige of the already existing Provisional Government in Chungking could have been utilized, and a compromise mediated between it and the People's Republic so that the conservative Provisional Government could control the country with a minimum of concessions to the left. Additionally, since there was no written agreement on the Korean trusteeship, nor any concrete plans, there would have been no impediment to the introduction of a better unification program had the consent of the powers concerned been obtained. There was no reason to believe that the Soviet Union favored the idea of trusteeship, if indeed it did not actually dislike it. Nevertheless, the United States now made public her policy for the establishment of a trusteeship.

By the statement of Mr. Vincent, the abstract term "in due course" was clarified for the first time for the Korean people. Previously, the exiled Provisional Government had taken the phrase in the Cairo Declaration to mean "immediately" or "within a few days" and this interpretation had been widely circulated.[18] Even the official translation by the Chinese government contained some assurance for "immediate independence."[19] Moreover, the phrase "in due course" in a

---

[18] *Survey of International Affairs: The Far East, 1942–1946,* ed. F. C. Jones *et al.* (London, 1955), p. 431.

[19] See the Chinese official text, Chang Chi-yün, *Record of the Cairo Conference* (Taipei, 1953), pp. 4–5.

Chinese or Korean translation has such a vague and ambiguous meaning that many Koreans interpreted it as they wished. At any rate, no one had dreamed that Korea would be placed in a trusteeship system for an undefined length of time, and once this became apparent, "trusteeship" met with universal disapproval. The Communist Party, the Nationalist Party, the People's Republic, the Han'guk Democratic Party, and all others were united in denouncing the decision.[20] The press carried on a loud and continuous clamor —every issue of every paper contained adverse comments. Korean leaders organized a Committee for Anti-Trusteeship, which included almost all parties and challenged the unilateral decision of the American government. The prestige of the United States and its military government fell even further.

Observing the vehement Korean opposition, the American commander in Korea and his newly assigned diplomatic advisors themselves gradually became strongly opposed to the idea of trusteeship. After three months of occupation, Hodge told the Joint Chiefs of Staff that the Allied interim solution was so strongly disliked that "if it is imposed now or at any future time, it is believed possible that the Korean people will actually and physically revolt."[21] Hodge further reported that although by occidental standards the Koreans were not ready for independence, it was growing more apparent daily that Korea's capacity for self-government would not greatly improve as long as the dual occupation continued. He pointed out that "the U.S. occupation of Korea under present conditions and policies is surely drifting to the edge of a political-economic abyss from which it can never

---

[20] *Summation*, No. 1 (October, 1945), p. 181. On October 25, the Communist Party spokesman called the trusteeship "a great insult to Korea." Two months later the Communist Party reversed its position and began to support the trusteeship. See *Seoul Shinmun* (October 26, 1945).

[21] The text of Hodge's report as cited in *Years of Trial and Hope*, p. 318.

be retrieved with any credit to the United States' prestige in the Far East." The urgency for either positive action on the international level, or the seizure of complete initiative in South Korea by the United States in the very near future was stressed.

The General's specific recommendations were: (1) clarification and removal of the 38th parallel so as to unify Korea; (2) a clear statement of policy regarding the status of, and reparations as applied to, former Japanese property; (3) reiteration of the Allied promise of Korean independence; (4) establishment of the complete separation of Korea from Japan in the minds of the press, the public, the State and War departments, and Allied nations. He further recommended that under present conditions, with no corrective action forthcoming, the United States should seriously consider agreeing with Russia that both powers withdraw their occupation forces simultaneously and "leave Korea to its own devices and an inevitable internal upheaval for its self-purification." [22]

These recommendations were both timely and practical. Since no party had yet consolidated its powers, it might have been possible for the United States to create a genuinely democratic government. Though there was a good chance of civil war or communist domination if a coalition were set up, it was most unlikely that Korea would become another satellite state in Asia if its sovereignty and neutrality could be specifically guaranteed by the powers concerned. The American military government might have taken steps to strengthen the position of the Provisional Government, led by Rhee and Kim Koo, before withdrawing. At this time, the prestige

[22] *Ibid.* According to *The Forrestal Diaries,* a State Department dispatch from Korea, dated December 11, 1945, also suggested abandoning international trusteeship if adequate specific guarantees for unification and independence could be obtained from the Soviet Union. It stated: "It might be more realistic to bypass trusteeship and seek guarantees directly." *The Forrestal Diaries,* ed. Walter Millis (New York, 1951), p. 125.

of the Provisional Government was so high that Communist domination might not have been possible unless there was some split between the two leaders. In addition, the Communists were still far from their victory in China and the country was substantially under the Nationalist government. Without direct intervention from outside Korea, there seemed to be a fair chance of establishing an independent nation friendly to the West.

On November 29, 1945, Secretary Byrnes replied to General Hodge. He said that if, during the approaching Moscow Conference, adequate guarantees could be obtained from the Russians for unification and independence, it might be possible for the United States to discontinue its support of trusteeship.[23] However, other policy planners in Washington apparently did not pay much attention to Hodge's recommendations. Judging from events at the Moscow Conference, the United States appeared to believe that only a trusteeship of the Four Powers could prevent ultimate Soviet domination of Korea.

KOREAN TRUSTEESHIP DECIDED AT THE MOSCOW CONFERENCE

To deal with the many postwar problems among the Allies, the Foreign Ministers of Great Britain, the Soviet Union, and the United States met together at Moscow from December 16 to 26, 1945. At these meetings, informal and exploratory discussions eventually led to agreements on many world problems, including Korea. For this nation, the Conference was most important; it was here that a concrete plan for future Korean unification through a trusteeship system was decided.

In the meeting that opened at 5 p.m. on December 16, with Mr. Molotov as chairman, it was agreed that "the creation of a unified administration for Korea as a prelude to the

---

[23] U.S. Department of the Army, "History of the USAFIK" MS. pt. II, Chapter 4, p. 62, as cited in Berger, p. 58.

establishment of an independent Korean government" should be included in the agenda. This item was introduced by Secretary Byrnes,[24] who then introduced the letter that Ambassador Harriman had addressed to Molotov on November 8, asking that the Soviet commander be given authority to consult the American commander, with a view to working out practical problems. Molotov, however, stated that "this letter dealt with matters other than government administration and therefore had no connection with the topics on the agenda." He wanted the discussion to be confined only to matters of administration and trusteeship.[25]

The following day, Byrnes made a statement of United States policy toward Korea, emphasizing the Cairo pledge which committed the Allied Powers to the establishment of an independent and unified Korea. He proposed immediate action to abolish the separate zones of military administration as a preliminary to a trusteeship under the United Nations. He also recommended that independence might then be granted within five years: [26] it was made clear that this four-power trusteeship would "endure for no longer a period than necessary to allow the Koreans to form an independent, representative, and effective government." After studying Byrnes' paper, Molotov submitted on December 20 a Soviet proposal for the establishment of a joint commission on urgent problems of economic unification, of a provisional government, and of a four-power trusteeship to last for five years. Byrnes accepted this draft with two minor changes, and it was included in the Moscow protocol [27] which Great Britain subsequently accepted. Thus, the Soviet proposal became the basis for the Korean decision adopted by the

---

[24] James F. Byrnes, *Speaking Frankly* (New York, 1947), p. 111. *Soviet Policy in the Far East,* p. 159. The Korean problem was discussed on American initiative at the conference.

[25] Byrnes, p. 222. *Years of Trial and Hope,* p. 319.

[26] *Ibid.*

[27] Byrnes, p. 222. Truman's memoirs mention that there were two minor changes, but does not explain them.

Moscow Conference. The full text of the Moscow agreement on Korea, published on December 28, 1945, was as follows:

1. With a view to the re-establishment of Korea as an independent state, the creation of conditions for developing the country on democratic principles and the earliest possible liquidation of the disastrous results of the protracted Japanese domination in Korea, there shall be set up a provisional Korean democratic government which shall take all the necessary steps for developing the industry, transportation, and agriculture of Korea and the national culture of the Korean people.

2. In order to assist the formation of a provisional Korean government and with a view to the preliminary elaboration of the appropriate measures, there shall be established a Joint Commission consisting of representatives of the United States command in Southern Korea and the Soviet command in Northern Korea. In preparing their proposals the Commission shall consult with the Korean democratic parties and social organizations. The recommendations worked out by the Commission shall be presented for the consideration of the governments of the Union of Soviet Socialist Republics, China, the United Kingdom and the United States prior to final decision by the two governments represented on the Joint Commission.

3. It shall be the task of the Joint Commission, with the participation of the Provisional Korean Democratic Government and of the Korean democratic organizations to work out measures also for helping and assisting the political, economic, and social progress of the Korean people, the development of democratic self-government and the establishment of the national independence of Korea.

The proposals of the Joint Commission shall be submitted, following consultation with the Provisional Korean Government for the joint consideration of the Government of the United States, the Union of Soviet Socialist Republics, United Kingdom, and China for the working out of an agreement concerning a four-power trusteeship of Korea for a period of up to five years.

4. For the consideration of urgent problems affecting both Southern and Northern Korea, and for the elaboration of measures establishing permanent coordination in administrative-economic matters between the United States com-

mand in Southern Korea and the Soviet command in Northern Korea, a conference of the representatives of the United States and Soviet commands in Korea shall be convened within a period of two weeks.[28]

According to the Soviet sources, the decision on Korea adopted by the Moscow Conference differed from the initial American draft on a number of essential points.[29] First, the Americans proposed to begin by setting up a single administration, headed by the two military commanders, to govern Korea until the establishment of a trusteeship. Koreans were to participate only in the capacity of administrators, consultants, and advisors; and there was no provision for the creation of a National Korean Government during that period. It was Soviet pressure that forced the inclusion in the final text of the phrases setting forth the urgency of forming "a provisional Korean Democratic government" to meet the common aspirations of the Korean people, and calling for "the earliest possible liquidation of the disastrous results of the protracted Japanese domination in Korea."

Secondly, the American draft, according to these sources, proposed that an administrative body with representatives of the United States, the U.S.S.R., Great Britain, and China should be set up to exercise executive, legislative, and judicial power during the period of trusteeship. But by Soviet

---

[28] U.S. Department of State, *Moscow Meeting of Foreign Ministers: December 16–26, 1945* (Washington, 1946), pp. 14–16. See also *Department of State Bulletin,* December 30, 1945, p. 1030.

[29] The following information is based upon *The Soviet Union and the Korean Question: Documents* (London, 1950), pp. 9–11; and F. I. Shabshina, "Korea after the Second World War," in *Chōsen Minzoku Kaiho Tōsō Shi* (History of the Korean People's Struggle for Liberation), translated into Japanese by the Chōsen Rekishi Kenkyu Kai (Tokyo, 1952), pp. 368–370. This book contains a detailed account of the Moscow Conference. See also Yu Ho-il, *Gendai Chōsen no Rekishi* (History of Modern Korea) (Tokyo, 1953), pp. 17–21; and Kim Chong-myŏng, *Chōsen Shin Minshushugi Kakumei Shi* (History of Korea's New Democratic Revolution) (Tokyo, 1953), pp. 100–101.

proposal, it was decided that the trusteeship was to be exercised through a Provisional Korean Government, rather than through such a four-power body. Finally, the Soviet sources assert, the Americans proposed a provision that would permit the extension of the five-year trusteeship into ten years; the Soviets were responsible for limiting the period to only five years.[30]

To these assertions of the Soviet press, Acting Secretary Dean Acheson later remarked that the so-called original American plan was not a plan in the sense that it offered a specific series of proposals.[31] He defended it as a statement of the general problems and possible lines of solution, asserting that the paper stressed the necessity of a unified Korean administration, something which was to be brought about by the two commanders. But he did concede that the United States proposed a possible five-year extension.

The idea of a five-year trusteeship with the possibility of an additional period reflected the ideas of President Roosevelt and the State Department. It also reflected the American belief that only trusteeship would be able to check possible Soviet domination in Korea. Though Byrnes claimed to consider the peninsula as "an economic and administrative whole," he apparently made no attempt to change the basic zonal division. He still seemed naively to believe—at this late stage—that the Russians would cooperate with the United States in administering a united Korea and that, once the proposed Joint Commission was established, the 38th parallel as an impenetrable barrier would disappear. In fact, there was ample reason to anticipate that the trusteeship, as prescribed in the Moscow agreement, would not work out. Frequent conflicts between the two powers on administra-

---

[30] *Tass* was authorized to publish detailed proceedings of the Moscow Conference with regard to Korea on January 25, 1946, to defend the Soviet position there. *The Soviet Union and the Korean Question,* p. 9.

[31] See his statement at the press and radio conference on January 25, 1946. *Department of State Bulletin,* February 3, 1946, p. 155.

tive procedure could be expected to diminish the effectiveness of the system. They would also inevitably produce political forces friendly to each of the trustee nations. The power struggle among Korean leaders would thus be intensified, hindering the establishment of a stable government. Furthermore, the ever-increasing conflicts between the Soviet and the West in regard to Eastern Europe had already made it clear that the spirit of cooperation that had prevailed during the war was rapidly fading.

Fatal to the plan for a trusteeship, however, was the fact that no one considered the Korean reaction. Even if the Four Powers agreed on the trusteeship, what would happen if the Korean people would not accept it? In the South, it already was apparent that there would be resentment and possibly a revolt, as Hodge had reported. A careful analysis of the practical problems would have made it easy to foresee what might happen.

KOREAN REACTION AGAINST THE MOSCOW AGREEMENT

The news of the Moscow Agreement reached Korea on the morning of December 29, 1945. The reaction was immediately hostile.[32] Premature and inaccurate press releases contributed to the great confusion. The South Korean press described the Agreement as "a second Munich," "another Mandatory Rule," "an insult to Korea," "another agreement for international slavery," and "a violation of international treaties."[33]

The main objections were to the trusteeship provisions. It was argued that any trusteeship, no matter how temporary, would mean a postponement of independence. The rightist

---

[32] *Seoul Shinmun,* December 30, 1945.

[33] A. W. Green, *The Epic of Korea* (Washington, 1950), pp. 78–80; and *Summation,* No. 3 (December 30, 1945), p. 189. See also *Seoul Shinmun,* December 30, 1945; and *Dong-A Ilbo,* December 30–31, 1945.

groups, especially, opposed any interim international control in which the Soviet Union was to participate. Rhee and Kim issued a denunciation, calling for a protest strike by all government workers and the organizing of mass demonstrations in the streets of Seoul and provincial capitals.[34] These demonstrations continued throughout January, 1946, and for a while completely paralyzed the military government.[35]

Hodge did his best to clear up the inaccuracies in the press statements and to interpret the decisions of the Conference. He called in representatives from each political faction and from the newspapers and declared that "the Moscow declaration was designed to give full aid and protection to Korea in establishing itself as an independent nation." [36] Subsequently, he sought to interpret the meaning of trusteeship as "cooperation and help" and stressed the differences between it and a mandate. But only a few Koreans accepted these interpretations; most remained adamant or became even more hostile.

Upon receiving General Hodge's report of the Korean reaction to the Agreement, Byrnes in a December 30 broadcast to the American people on the results of the Moscow

---

[34] For another interpretation of this situation, see Ralph Izard, "Close-up of Korea," *New Masses,* Vol. 63, No. 9, pp. 8–11; and Kim Sam-gyu, *Chōsen Gendai Shi* (Modern History of Korea) (Tokyo, 1963), p. 40.

[35] For the first few days after the announcement of the Moscow agreement, the left-wing parties, led by the Communist party, also vehemently protested, but on January 3, 1946, they suddenly announced their acceptance of the decision. The XXIV Corps later obtained a document with this date, containing North Korean Communist Party "instructions to all levels and branches concerning the decisions on Korea made at Moscow." This sudden change stimulated a marked polarization of the political elements; hereafter, the rift between left and right became more and more obvious and irreconcilable. Terrorism by youth groups of both sides became widespread and virtually uncontrollable (it was at this time that Song Chin-u, the Chairman of the Han'guk Democratic Party, was assassinated by a fanatic youth.)

[36] *Summation,* No. 3 (December, 1945), p. 189. See also *Seoul Shinmun* (December 29, 1945).

Conference, stated that "the Joint Soviet American Commission working with the Korean provisional democratic government may find it possible to dispense with a trusteeship." [37] He also asserted that it was the goal of the United States to hasten the independence of Korea. Finally, President Truman, in his State of the Union message of January 14, 1946, announced it was "the purpose of the government of the United States to proceed as rapidly as is practicable toward the restoration of Korea and the establishment of a democratic government by the free choice of the people of Korea." [38]

HODGE'S DILEMMA

Without knowing what had happened at Moscow, General Hodge and his associates (who had recommended immediate Korean independence) concluded that the trusteeship was the result of Soviet machinations. The American commander emphatically assured Korean leaders that it was not a certainty, and might be dispensed with if better cooperation could be obtained from the Koreans.[39] He and Military Governor Lerch issued warnings that continued demonstrations could only create an unfavorable impression in the United Nations of Korean political capabilities, and that a repetition of disturbances might well postpone the ultimate attainment of independence.[40] Reluctantly, the right-wing leaders ordered the strike ended. They continued, however, to demonstrate against the Soviet Union and the Communist party, accusing the Russians of delaying the independence. Indeed, the acceptance of the

---

[37] *Department of State Bulletin,* December 30, 1945, p. 1036.

[38] "The State of the Union" message to Congress, *Department of State Bulletin,* February 3, 1946, pp. 135–145.

[39] *Summation,* No. 4, pp. 282–283.

[40] Korean Affairs Institute, *Voice of Korea,* May 22, 1946 and February 15, 1947, Washington, D.C. This was issued semi-monthly. See also *Dong-A Ilbo,* January 22, 1946.

trusteeship seemed to have weakened the South Korean leftist parties.

The Soviet command in North Korea, of course, did not remain unresponsive to Hodge's interpretation. The Americans, *Tass* charged, "had assumed a position of inspiring reactionary demonstrations against the decisions of the Moscow Conference, in which, as is known, the Government of the United States participated." [41] In response, on January 26, Hodge asserted that the *Tass* statement was "without basis in fact." The same day, Colonel General Terenti Shtykov, the head of the Soviet military mission in Seoul, called a press conference and unilaterally released account of the proceedings of the Moscow Conference. Charging that the newspapers in South Korea were victims of false and unscrupulous information, and denying the alleged report that the Soviet Union insisted on the establishment of trusteeship, General Shtykov stated that the purpose of the release was to inform Koreans of "the true standing of Russia in regard to Korean problems." [42]

The Soviet press release was a mortal blow to the prestige of the United States and its military government. The Korean people were shocked and dumbfounded. The news indicated: first, that it had been the United States (and not the Soviet Union) which had originally proposed trusteeship; second, that the trusteeship might last—again, by American suggestion—as long as ten years; and third, that the United States had had no interest in the establishment, prior to the setting-up of trusteeship, of a unified national government for all of Korea. Russia now appeared to be the true protector of Korean interests.[43]

As can be imagined, the American command in Seoul was greatly embarrassed by the Shtykov press release. Hodge's

[41] *New York Times,* January 23, 1946.

[42] *The Soviet Union and the Korean Question,* pp. 9–11. See also *Seoul Shinmun* and *Dong-A Ilbo,* January 27, 1946.

[43] *New York Times,* January 25 and January 26, 1946.

confusion was immediately compounded when Acheson, in a Washington press conference on the same day, gave implicit confirmation to the Soviet version.[44] Greatly disturbed, Hodge cabled Tokyo and Washington pleading for information and guidance so that he could align policies and, if possible, try to allay the damaging effects of the Soviet statements. The State Department's reply, received on January 30, gave him neither aid nor solace. The Department not only verified the Russian version, it went on to explain that trusteeship was considered essential in order to "prevent the Russian domination of Korea." The rationale for this was that, in the absence of trusteeship guarantees, it might be impossible to prevent a Russian take-over of a democratic "Provisional Government."[45]

The United States had taken a stand that General Hodge and his staff had assured the Korean people it would never take. The Koreans believed they had been betrayed and the whole nation, it now seemed, had no hesitation in giving vent to its feeling of outrage. To this Korean uproar, and to the obvious desirability of trying to save some face for Hodge and the United States, the State Department suddenly reacted: it drastically changed its attitude toward Korean trusteeship. On January 27, 1946, just a month after the announcement of the Moscow Agreement, John Carter Vincent reiterated Secretary Byrnes' statement of December 30 that "trusteeship is only a procedure, which may or may not be necessary since independence of Korea is the goal."[46]

---

[44] See the statement by Acheson, *Department of State Bulletin*, February 3, 1946, p. 155. Mr. Acheson practically acknowledged all the Soviet charges as correct. However, as noted previously, he stressed that the American idea had not been put forward as a concrete plan but only as a basis of discussion.

[45] U.S. Department of the Army, "History of USAFIK," MS, pt. II, Chapter 4, p. 88, as cited in Berger, p. 64.

[46] Statement by John Carter Vincent, *Department of State Bulletin*, January 27, 1946, p. 108. According to his view, if the Koreans co-operated satisfactorily with the U.S.–Soviet Commission, there would

Vincent went on to state that whether there was to be a trusteeship depended upon the ability of the Koreans to work with the Soviet-American Joint Commission in forming a democratic provisional government capable of unifying and governing Korea.

Beset with confusion, General Hodge sent another message to General MacArthur, his superior in Tokyo, complaining of the lack of guidance from higher authorities. He protested that the Shtykov statement would cause the Koreans to believe it was the Americans who had sold them out although, in his opinion, the Russians themselves had no intention of permitting the unification of Korea so long as any American occupation forces remained in the country. Having "the distinct feeling of being let down by the authorities in Washington," he insisted that he be kept informed of American policy. Finally, in the hope of restoring American prestige in Korea, Hodge offered to be relieved from his command and to play the role of a "sacrificial goat" if it was thought that such action might be useful.[47]

If there had been closer coordination between Washington and the military government in Korea in the formulation of policy, vast confusion and fatal mistakes might have been avoided. The United States appears to have been as ill-prepared for the formulative as for the administrative processes of its foreign policy for the occupied area. Responsibilities for Korea were divided between various departments, without close coordination. The military government operations were carried out by the Civil Affairs Division of the Army. In theory, the War Department was responsible only for the execution of overall policy formulated by the

---

be no trusteeship. However, the Commission would probably continue in existence for some time, that is, until the provisional government was well established and free elections held to provide a democratic government. *Ibid.*, p. 100.

[47] U.S. Department of the Army, "History of USAFIK," pt. II, Chapter 4, p. 88, as cited in Berger, p. 65.

Department of State,[48] and on August 30, 1945, the President had issued an executive order to that effect. Though consideration was given to the transfer of responsibility for administration to the Department of State, the Secretary of State resisted—feeling his Department was ill-equipped for this.

A situation continued for several years, therefore, in which: (1) the Department of State was responsible for the formulation of general policy, (2) the War Department (and its successor, the Department of the Army) was responsible both for carrying out policy and for all phases of administration, and (3) the officials having authority in the field were expected to exercise it with discretion when unable to obtain workable instructions from above. A major difficulty was that, because the State Department had no concrete Korean policy except for a vague idea of trusteeship, workable instructions were hard to come by. The frequent near-vacuums that resulted had necessarily to be filled by the commander of the occupation forces. From the beginning, Hodge repeatedly complained of his lack of directions.[49] Moreover, additional confusion was caused by the activities of departments and agencies other than the State Department. These seriously affected the conduct of foreign affairs, yet they were not coordinated with policies of the State Department.[50] Of course, the State-War-Navy Coordinating Committee existed, but it was not responsible for the making of policy on Korean occupation matters.[51] In this

[48] U.S. Department of State, *American Policy in Occupied Areas*, Publication 2794 (Washington, 1947), p. 1. See also Brookings Institution, *The Administration of Foreign Affairs and Overseas Operations* (Washington, 1951), p. 27.

[49] *The Forrestal Diaries*, p. 135.

[50] The Commission on Organization of the Executive Branch of the Government, *Task Force Report on Foreign Affairs* (Washington, 1949), Appendix H, p. 2. See also the same Commission's *Administration of Overseas Affairs* (Washington, 1949), pp. 4–17.

[51] For the text on organization and procedure for the development and promulgation of U.S. policy with respect to occupied areas, effec-

situation, it is clear that the official Washington decisions should have been shaped or modified in close cooperation with the military commander.

Since there was no direct connection between the American command and the State Department, the conflict in formulation and interpretation of policy between the two was inevitable. The Hoover Commission found the situation unsatisfactory when it reported in 1949. It stated that "the conduct of foreign affairs within the executive branch, more than ever, requires action, supervision, and coordination from the office of the President and cannot be solely the special province of the State Department."[52] To meet these problems, the Commission recommended that the President establish a Cabinet-level committee to advise him on both domestic and foreign matters affecting foreign affairs and involving more than one department or agency of the executive branch.[53]

The State Department at this time was apparently torn between the conviction that only trusteeship could protect Korea from the impending danger of Communist domination, and the fear that any form of trusteeship would arouse such violent opposition in Korea as to render doubtful its successful realization. The policy planners in Washington must expect to have to deal with some situations where knowledge is incomplete and the potential effects of policy factors are obscure. This was not the case in this instance. Hodge's experience was immediate and his information ac-

---

tive as of April 8, 1946, see *Department of State Bulletin,* April 28, 1946, p. 734.

[52] The office of Assistant Secretary of State for Occupied Areas was created on April 8, 1946. Before then, the military government of Korea had almost no connection with the State Department. The Japan-Korean Secretariat, under the chairmanship of Hugh Borton, Chief of the Division of Northeast Affairs, was responsible for coordinating and expediting the State Department's political policy in Korea. Department of State, *American Policy in Occupied Areas,* p. 8.

[53] The situation was somewhat improved by the establishment of the National Security Council in 1947.

curate. The judgment of the local commander should have been given much greater weight and consideration. If the State Department had acted on the basis of his recommendation that immediate independence be given to all of Korea without trusteeship, the future would have been much more promising than it turned out to be.

5

Impasse in the Joint U.S.-Soviet Commission

The Moscow Agreement had specifically provided that a conference of the United States and Soviet commands in Korea would convene within two weeks to find a means of solving the urgent problems affecting both the South and North.[1] In accordance with this provision, General Hodge addressed two communications (January 2 and 4) to the Soviet command in North Korea, expressing American willingness to meet as soon as convenient. The Soviet Union had said it fully supported the Moscow Agreement "as the first practical solution for the unification of Korea,"[2] and the Soviet command immediately announced its willingness to convene the conference.

PRELIMINARY CONFERENCE

The Soviet delegation of 73 persons arrived in Seoul on January 15, 1946. Their chief, Colonel General Terenti Shtykov, was accompanied by a political advisor, Semyon K.

---

[1] Paragraph 4 of this agreement, U.S. Department of State, *Moscow Meeting of Foreign Ministers: December 16–26, 1945* (Washington, 1946), pp. 14–16.

[2] See the editorial of the *Moscow News* as quoted in *Manchester Guardian,* December 31, 1945.

Tsarapkin, and by Major General Parin, Major General Romanyenko, and other advisors and technical personnel.[3] On the American side, Major General A. V. Arnold, former Military Governor of South Korea, was appointed by Hodge to head the American delegation, with Mr. H. M. Benninghoff as diplomatic advisor. Thus, Hodge and Chistiakov took no formal part themselves in the discussion.

The first meeting opened January 16 with Hodge's welcoming speech in which he expressed his desire for an agreement to eliminate the 38th parallel boundary, and so bring to an end many of the difficulties of the Korean people.[4] It became immediately apparent that the two sides had different approaches to the problem.

The American representatives wished to discuss the 38th parallel and prompt administrative integration of the two zones, following which there should be a speedy restoration of the economy of the whole country. To implement their plan, they sought a broad agreement for unified operation of the railroads, electric power, and communications, a single currency throughout the country, the free flow of goods, and the free passage of certain categories of persons. They also proposed the establishment of joint control points along the 38th parallel, which would remain unfortified. The Soviet representative, however, wanted the discussion limited to a few specific subjects, such as the delivery of northern electric power in exchange for rice, the exchange of certain commodities and equipment, and the reestablishment of rail and automobile traffic between the two zones.[5] They were par-

---

[3] From the letter of Chistiakov to Hodge, dated January 8, 1946, *Department of State Bulletin,* January 27, 1946, p. 111.

[4] *Seoul Shinmun,* January 16–17, 1946. For a North Korean source on this meeting see Kim Hi-il, *Mije ŭi Chosŏn Ch'imyak Sa* (History of the Invasion of American Imperialism in Korea) (Pyongyang, 1962), pp. 49–60.

[5] The following information, if not specified otherwise, is based on U.S. Department of State Document, *Korea's Independence,* publica-

ticularly interested in getting rice from the American zone; but, because of the shortage in the South, the American delegation disclosed that no rice would be available. At this point the Russians ruled out the exchange of needed electric power, raw materials, fuel, industrial equipment, and chemical products.

Finally, after three weeks of tedious discussion, limited accord was reached on: (1) railroad, motor, and coastal water-borne transportation; (2) movements of certain groups of Korean citizens between the two zones; (3) exchange of mail; (4) radio broadcasting frequencies; and (5) the establishment of liaison between the two commands to coordinate economic and administrative matters. Also, weekly American convoys were to be permitted to travel 25 miles across Soviet-occupied territory in order to reach the isolated Ongjin peninsula in the American zone. But the general movement of Koreans across the parallel was denied.[6] Nor was there any progress toward a uniform currency, a unified telecommunication system, or the free circulation of newspapers,[7] though proposals for these matters were presented by the Americans. Furthermore, subsequent efforts to implement even the few limited agreements were unsuccessful, owing to the Soviet refusal to honor them.[8] The actual

---

tion 2933, Far Eastern Series 18, released in October, 1947 (Washington, 1947), pp. 3–4. See also U.S. Department of State, *The Record on Korean Unification, 1943–60* (Washington, 1960), pp. 5–6.

6 The American delegation sought a boundary adjustment in Kyŏnggi and Hwang-Hae Do in order to create more effective local government, but without success. Edward G. Meade, *American Military Government in Korea* (New York, 1951), p. 92.

7 American journalists were not allowed to enter the Soviet Zone, and in retaliation Soviet correspondents were excluded from the South. Mark J. Gayn, *Japan Diary* (New York, 1948), pp. 378–384.

8 One source said that Shtykov consented to allow Koreans to cross the 38th parallel, but his superior Chistiakov cancelled this arrangement without explanation. Henry Chung, *The Russians Came to Korea* (Seoul, 1947), p. 88.

results of the conference, except for intermittent exchanges of mail and military liaison teams, were thus virtually nil.

It was, however, during this preliminary conference that the two Commands arranged the establishment of the U.S.-Soviet Joint Commission to implement Paragraph 2 of the Moscow Agreement. Both delegations announced that "the Joint Commission is to help in the establishment of a provisional Korean government." It was also decided that the proposed Joint Commission would start its work not later than one month after the end of the preliminary conference; and that the permanent seat for the Commission would be Seoul, but that it would visit Pyongyang and travel to other points in the country.

The Commission was to consist of ten men, five from the Soviet and five from the American commands, with necessary advisors and assistants. They were to consult with the democratic, political, and social organizations of both North and South Korea as a prelude to the establishment of the provisional Korean government as agreed at Moscow.[9] Thus, the military command conference led, in effect, to setting up a body to negotiate concerning Korean unification, although this was not its original aim.

THE FIRST TRIAL OF THE JOINT U.S.–SOVIET COMMISSION

On March 11, 1946, the American commander explained to the Korean people the purpose of the Joint Commission soon to convene in Seoul. Hodge announced that its main objective was to assist in the formation of a provisional Korean government. He carefully stated that his country did not

---

[9] USAFIK (United States Armed Forces in Korea), *Summation of U.S. Army Military Government Activities in Korea*, February, 1946, p. 285. This *Summation* is the continuation of the SCAP *Summation*. These two are the most exhaustive sources of information on the United States military government in Korea. Hereafter cited as *Summation.*

want to bring about a form of government representing only a particular group, but wanted one that would correspond to the wishes of the majority of the people.[10]

In its own preparatory meetings, the American delegation agreed that the Soviet Union's long-term strategic aim would be the establishment of a communistic state in Korea by manipulating a subversive movement through loyal party members. To expedite this aim, the Russians would probably try for the early establishment of a provisional Korean government so that the American occupation forces could be quickly eliminated. The Americans felt it was essential to obtain some form of guarantee for Korea's territorial integrity, so that the government of the peninsula would be protected from direct or indirect Communist attacks.[11]

The Joint Commission convened on March 20, 1946. In the American delegation were: Major General Arnold, Chairman; William R. Langdon, a career Foreign Service Officer with experience in China and Japan; Charles W. Thayer, also a Foreign Service Officer and a former Embassy Secretary in Moscow; Colonel Robert N. Booth, formerly executive assistant to the military governor in Korea; and Colonel Frank M. Britton, formerly with General Headquarters of the Southwest Pacific area.

Formal ceremony and high expectations marked the opening at the Dŏk Su Palace. Here, General Shtykov emphatically claimed that "the Soviet Union has a keen interest in Korea being a true democratic and independent country, friendly to the Soviet Union, so that in the future it will not become a base for an attack on the Soviet Union." He stated that "certain reactionary anti-democratic groups" had undermined the work of creating and firmly establishing a democratic system and that "the future provisional Korean

---

10 Korean Affairs Institute, *Voice of Korea*, April 6, 1946.

11 U.S. Department of the Army, "History of USAFIK," MS., pp. 154–155 as cited in Carl Berger, *The Korean Knot: A Military and Political History* (Philadelphia, 1957), p. 67.

democratic government must be created on a basis of wide unification of all the democratic parties and organizations, supporting the decisions of the Moscow Conference of the Ministers of Foreign Affairs." [12]

Following the opening ceremony, the Commission held closed sessions. Immediately there arose the situation that the American delegation had anticipated in its preparatory meetings. The Soviets demanded that those organizations and individuals that had carried on anti-trusteeship activities be excluded from consultation.[13] Since these groups comprised almost all the right-wing parties, such a policy would have barred a large segment of the anti-communist parties in South Korea, and a majority of rightist leaders would have been excluded from participation in the provisional government. Acceptance of the Russian proposal would have allowed only Communists and their sympathizers to be consulted in the formation of a unified government.

The American delegation argued that the Koreans ought to be permitted to express their views on any issue, including that of trusteeship. Under the terms of the Moscow Agreement, the nature of the trusteeship was a future issue dependent upon the decisions reached by the Four Powers after consultation with a Korean provisional government. Therefore, according to their interpretation, vocal Korean objection to it was "fully within the right of freedom of expression." [14] Finally, the American delegation suggested two criteria for determining eligibility for consultation with the Commission: an individual or a group, first, should be

---

[12] *Source Materials on Korean Politics and Ideology,* comp. Donald G. Tewksbury (New York, 1950), mimeographed, p. 78. Also, *Voice of Korea,* April 6, 1946.

[13] *Korea's Independence,* pp. 3–5. This booklet contains many of the very important documents on the negotiations for Korean independence during 1946–1947.

[14] *Summation,* August, 1946, p. 101. The following information was based on the *Summations, Seoul Shinmun, Dong-A Ilbo,* and *Korea's Independence,* if not otherwise specified.

truly democratic in aim and, second, should be prepared to cooperate in forming a provisional government and working out proposals concerning the trusteeship.[15] The Americans also insisted that the Commission give the "reactionaries" an opportunity to "reform" themselves along "democratic" lines.

After seemingly endless discussions of proposals and counterproposals, a formula was agreed upon that provided for the future cooperation of individuals and groups in implementing the Moscow decisions. This formula was incorporated in what came to be known as Communiqué No. 5 which was publicly issued on April 18, 1946. It reads:

> The Joint Commission will consult with Korean democratic parties and social organizations which are truly democratic in their aims and methods and which will subscribe to the following declarations: "We . . . declare that we will uphold the aims of the Moscow Decision on Korea as stated in paragraph 1 of this decision, namely: The re-establishment of Korea as an independent state, the creation of conditions for developing the country on democratic principles, and the earliest possible liquidation of the disastrous results of the protracted Japanese domination of Korea. Further, we will abide by the decisions of the Joint Commission in its fulfilment of paragraph 2 of the Moscow decision in the formation of a Provisional Korean Democratic Government: further, we will cooperate with the Joint Commission in the working out by it with the participation of the Provisional Korean Democratic Government of proposals concerning measures foreseen by paragraph 3 of the Moscow decision.
>
> Signed ____________
> Representing the ________
> Party or Organization"
>
> The procedure for inviting representatives of Korean democratic parties and social organizations to consult with the Joint Commission is being worked out by Joint Sub-

---

[15] *Survey of International Affairs: 1942–46,* ed. F. C. Jones *et al.* (London, 1955), p. 439. See also Communiqués No. 2 and 3, in *Seoul Shinmun,* March 31, 1946.

Commission No. 1. When details of the procedure are completed it will be announced publicly.[16]

This seemed to be a reasonable compromise. The actual mechanics governing the consultation were to be worked out as follows: the Joint Sub-Commission No. 1 and Joint Sub-Commission No. 2 would prepare a charter in which would be incorporated the structure and operation of the provisional government at all levels, and Joint Sub-Commission No. 3 would work out the political, economic, and cultural plans.[17] With the publication of Joint Communiqué No. 5, everything seemed to be going in the right direction.

Then, suddenly, the Russians hardened their policy. In a complete reversal, they insisted that regardless of adherence to the formula contained in Communiqué No. 5, no party could be represented by an individual who had opposed the trusteeship provision of the Moscow Agreement.[18] They demanded that members of the Representative Democratic Council not be consulted unless they renounced their opposition to trusteeship.[19] The U.S. delegation, on its part, maintained that such action was not only contrary to the Moscow Agreement, but also violated freedom of speech. General Arnold again emphasized that from the American viewpoint it was of prime importance to maintain this principle.

Unfortunately, neither side was able to agree on the

---

[16] *Korea's Independence,* pp. 19–20. For a good summary of the work of the Joint Commission, *Haebang Isip nyŏn* (Twenty Years of Emancipation), ed. Hong Sŭng-myŏn *et al.* (Seoul, 1965), Vol. 1 (Kirok Pyŏn), pp. 305–308.

[17] *Summation,* No. 7 (April, 1946), p. 15.

[18] See the letter of Secretary of State Marshall of April 8, 1947, to Molotov. *Korea's Independence,* pp. 32–34.

[19] Hodge initiated the formation of this Council on February 14, 1946, to enlist Korean support for the military government. It was an advisory organ. All appointees were right-wing conservatives because liberals refused to join. The Council finally lost its official status on December 18, 1946, with the establishment of the Interim Legislative Assembly.

nature of "democratic" parties and social groups. The Americans argued that the use of the word "democratic" throughout the world was not restricted to organizations or parties belonging to a school of social thought favoring certain classes over others.[20] The Russians countercharged that it was necessary to consider "not the declarative announcements of the party," but the actual policies it pursued.[21] In response, the Americans labeled many leftist bodies (such as the Korean Revolutionary Party, the All Korean Confederation of Labor, the All Korean Peasant Union, and the All Korean Youth Union) as "undemocratic" organizations, demanding that they be excluded from consultation with the Joint Commission. On this basis, the Russians later attributed the failure of this Conference to the fact that the Americans "excluded participation by a whole series of large democratic organizations in South Korea." [22]

The United States delegation finally sought to discuss (under Paragraph 2 of the Moscow Agreement) the integration of the country's economy and administration. The Russians, however, refused to consider this question before the settlement of the problems on the consultation of the "democratic" parties. For six weeks the Commission debated without finding a single compromise.

At 2 p.m. on May 8, 1946, General Shtykov called upon General Hodge and informed him that after having communicated with a higher authority, he had received orders to stop work and return to North Korea with his entire delegation. In a final statement on the Soviet position, Shtykov told Hodge:

> The main reason why the Soviet Delegation insisted on barring certain persons from consultation is that Russia is a

---

[20] Letter from Hodge to Chistiakov, August 12, 1946. *Korea's Independence*, pp. 22–23.

[21] Letter from Chistiakov to Hodge, October 26, 1946. *Ibid.*, pp. 23–26.

[22] Letter from Molotov to Marshall, April 19, 1947. *Department of State Bulletin*, May 4, 1947, p. 812.

> close neighbour to Korea and, because of this, is interested in establishing in Korea a provisional democratic government which would be loyal to the Soviet Union. [The Koreans who objected to the Moscow decision and] raised their voice against the Soviet Union slandered the Soviet Union and smeared it with mud. If they seized power in the government, the government would not be loyal to Russia, and its officials would be instrumental in organizing hostile action on the part of the Korean people against the Soviet Union.[23]

Thus, after 24 fruitless sessions, lasting from March 20 to May 6, 1946, the Joint Commission was adjourned *sine die* on May 8. Not a single problem concerning the 38th parallel boundary had been solved.[24]

THE SEARCH FOR MODERATE PARTIES

To Koreans, the realization of a united independent country now seemed much further away than before the Moscow Agreement. At that time, there were still high hopes for unification through direct negotiations between the two occupation commands. Most of the parties were then still in their embryonic stages, both in terms of their organizational strength and their ideology. Animosity among party leaders was not yet deep enough to cause the sacrifice of national interests to personal party advancement. Furthermore, the people were still rejoicing over their recent liberation from Japanese domination. It might have been possible to bring about a peaceful unification at that pre-Moscow Agreement stage if these parties had not been stimulated.

The Moscow Agreement, however, aggravated the situation. Parties of the left and right consolidated their powers and hardened their ideologies. The line between them was

[23] "History of USAFIK," MS., pp. 212–213, as quoted in Berger, p. 69.

[24] Hodge informed Shtykov that, in the American view, it would be possible to resume work at once if the Joint Commission agreed to recognize the right of all democratic groups and individuals in Korea to freedom of speech. But no date was set for the next meeting. *Summation,* No. 8, May 1946, p. 17.

clearly drawn, not only by ideological differences, but also by attitudes toward the Agreement. Whoever supported the trusteeship was automatically considered a leftist, while anyone opposing it was a rightist.[25] The middle-of-the-roaders were decried as opportunists by both extremes. Korean parties and social groups seemed to be equally divided into two large camps: the rightists in the Representative Democratic Council, and the left-wing parties in the Chosŏn Minjujuŭi Minjok Chŏnsŏn (the Korean National Democratic Front).[26]

This bipolarization was most unfortunate for General Hodge. Prior to the Joint Commission meeting, the American Commander had found that his most active supporters were rightists who had been antagonistic to any kind of trusteeship. If the American delegation supported a trusteeship program in the forthcoming meeting, Hodge would automatically forfeit the support of these groups, who were led by Syngman Rhee and Kim Koo. Yet if he tried to win Korean support by violating the international agreement, the Russians and leftists would certainly accuse the United States of bad faith. It was nearly impossible to satisfy both sides, as neither was willing to make any concessions. Were Hodge able to go his own way, and had there been no American commitment to trusteeship, he might have chosen to support the Korean cause. But he had been instructed differently. Shortly before the convening of the Joint Commission, the State Department had belatedly informed him that

[25] In this chapter the criterion of right, left, and moderate is derived more from attitudes toward the trusteeship proposal than from ideological principles.

[26] To counteract the rightist movement, the leftist parties assembled together under the flag of this Council. Chairmen were Kim Wŏnbong, Hŏ Hŏn, and Lyuh Woon-hyung. Gaimusho (Japanese Ministry of Foreign Affairs), *Sengo ni okeru Chōsen no Seiji Josei* (Korean Politics in the Post-war Era) (Tokyo, 1948), p. 14. See also Han Taesu, *Han'guk Chŏntang Sa* (History of Korean Political Parties) (Seoul, 1961), pp. 39–155. In this chapter, the factual information is based on *Seoul Shinmun* and *Dong-A Ilbo* if not otherwise specified.

American support was to be shifted away from the Rhee-Kim forces to progressive leaders.[27] Directives from the Joint Chiefs of Staff further stated that only those groups who truly represented the "views and aspirations of the Korean people as a whole" and who were acceptable to both America and Russia should be permitted to consult with the Joint Commission. It was made clear that Communists or extreme rightists could not be "considered as representative of the Korean people." [28]

Hodge was at first unable to follow these instructions at the Joint Commission meeting because he could not find strong "progressive leaders" upon whom he could rely. Just at the time, therefore, that the Joint Commission meeting was opening, Hodge was having to look for new political elements that could bolster the American position in the Joint Commission and at the same time check the spreading pro-Communist trend in Korea. In this desperate situation, he tried to lure some influential leftists, such as Lyuh Woon-hyung, into the Representative Democratic Council in hopes of recruiting Korean support for the military government.[29] The American command eagerly hoped that the Council might thus supply the "unity" which it had long sought. However, the followers of Rhee and Kim Koo—who were the central forces of the Council—refused to accept unity at the cost of coalition with leftists who supported the trusteeship, and instead denounced them bitterly. Here began the fundamental conflict between Hodge and Rhee. Their relationship became even more strained when Hodge appointed "a censor to read all of Rhee's speeches prepared for delivery over the Korean radio net work and had him de-

---

[27] Berger, pp. 66–67.

[28] *Ibid.* This information is based upon U.S. Department of Army, "History of USAFIK," MS., p. 145.

[29] *Summation,* No. 5 (February, 1946), pp. 283–284. See also George M. McCune, *Korea's Post-war Political Problems* (New York, 1947), p. 14.

lete all criticisms of Russia and of communism."[30] As the bitterness between the two men increased, the Council became useless and the whole scheme collapsed.

Talks between Kimm Kiu-sic (Kim Kyu-sik), a moderate leader of the rightists and a founder of the Provisional Government in Shanghai, and Lyuh Woon-hyung resulted in the formation of a Coalition Committee (Chwau Hapchak Wiwŏn Hoe) on October 7, 1946, working under the joint chairmanship of the two leaders. They declared that they would establish "a democratic transitional government" in accordance with the decision of the Moscow Conference, securing the independence of Korea by unifying the right and left wings throughout the nation.[31] This movement was strongly supported by Hodge.

Meanwhile, American-Soviet relations were further deteriorating with the expulsion of the Soviet Consul from Seoul in retaliation for the Russian refusal to permit establishment of an American consulate in Pyongyang. With the failure of the Joint Commission and subsequent hostile developments, the 38th parallel became virtually an impassable barrier, and the American command realized the inevitability of a prolongation of the military government. Consequently, both commands began actively to foster the stabilization of their political, economic, and social situations as separate entities. This could be done only through the elimination of hostile groups from their respective zones.

At about this time Ambassador Edwin W. Pauley made an extensive tour in North Korea as the personal representative

---

[30] Robert T. Oliver, *Syngman Rhee: The Man Behind the Myth* (New York, 1954), p. 219.

[31] *Dong-A Ilbo*, October 7 and 8, 1946. *Summation*, October, 1946, pp. 16–18. Kimm was the one-time Vice-President of the Korean Provisional Government in Chungking. Later, in December, Lyuh withdrew from the Committee, probably under pressure from his own party, with a statement that "his withdrawal did not mean that he had withdrawn his support." *Summation*, No. 15 (December, 1946), p. 17.

of the President, and it seems that his report made a definite change in American policy. He said that judging from their action the Soviet Union has "no immediate intention of withdrawing from Korea," that actually it was planning for a long stay, and he warned that "if it is an ideological battleground upon which our entire success in Asia may depend," Korea was not "receiving the attention and consideration it should." [32]

THE SITUATION IN THE NORTH

With the rise of Kim Il-sŏng as the head of the Communist party, the Russian authorities hastened their moves toward the creation of a strong indigenous North Korean regime fashioned after the Soviet political system. This was welcomed by the Korean Communists who had already resolved, in their Central Committee meeting of December, 1945, to make North Korea "a democratic base for the Korean unification." [33] In communist jargon "a democratic base" meant, first, establishing a strong socialistic or communist regime in the North; and then using the regime as a base to take over the South by various revolutionary means, such as subversive movements.

As noted earlier, a central government had been established in February, 1946, under the name of the Provisional People's Committee for North Korea, with Kim Il-sŏng as its chairman and Kim Tu-bong as its vice-chairman. The Committee immediately took over the existing central administrative bureaus and then gradually developed its own network of local administrative structures, including court, po-

---

[32] Harry S Truman, *Years of Trial and Hope* (New York, 1956), pp. 320–322. See also another report in *Department of State Bulletin*, August 4, 1946, p. 233.

[33] Pak Tong-un, *Pukhan T'ongch'i Kigu Ron* (Theory on North Korean Government) (Seoul, 1964), p. 3. See also Kim Hi-il, *Choguk ŭi P'yŏnghwajŏk T'ongil e Taehan Uri Tang ŭi Pangch'im* (The Policy of Our Party toward the Peaceful Unification of the Fatherland) (Pyongyang, 1962), pp. 262–264.

lice, and procurator systems similar to those in the Soviet government. The North Korean Army, with border constabulary units, was also established by August, 1946.[34]

On October 3, the first local elections were held to choose the members of province, city, county, and district People's Committees. In February, 1947, the "Supreme People's Assembly" (Puk Chosŏn Inmin Hoeŭi) was inaugurated as the highest legislative body in North Korea. It created an executive branch called the "Central People's Committee" (Puk Chosŏn Inmin Wiwŏn Hoe), consisting of various ministries and bureaus. The form of this North Korean governmental structure remained unchanged until 1948.

In the beginning, many of the ministries were nominally headed by locally prominent Communist or nationalist leaders, but the actual power was located in the strategic position of the vice-minister of each ministry who was, in most cases, a trusted lieutenant of either Kim Il-sŏng or the Soviet Koreans. Furthermore, Soviet advisors were assigned to each ministry and to the important government agencies (such as the army and major industrial plants) and they appear to have had more power than an ordinary advisor would enjoy. Thus, the Soviet control mechanism in North Korea was cleverly hidden under the surface of the nominally Korean administrative structures.[35]

Meanwhile, Kim's ex-partisan followers and the Soviet Koreans steadily penetrated into most of the key positions within the Communist Party. As a result, the influence of the indigenous communists was definitely on the wane. The New People's Party merged, on August 28, 1946, with the Communist Party, taking the name of the North Korean

---

[34] Park Tong-un, pp. 8–9. Kim Sam-gyu, *Chōsen Gendai Shi* (Modern History of Korea) (Tokyo, 1963), p. 52. See also Kim Tal-su, *Chōsen* (Korea) (Tokyo, 1962), p. 200. For an excellent analysis of politics in North Korea see Glenn D. Paige, *The Korean People's Democratic Republic* (Stanford, 1966).

[35] U.S. Department of State, *North Korea: A Case Study in the Techniques of Takeover* (Washington, 1961), p. 15.

Workers Party (Puk Chosŏn Rodong Tang), with Kim Tu-bong, the leader of Yenan faction, as its chairman and Kim Il-sŏng and Chu Yŏng-ha, leaders of the domestic factions, as its vice-chairmen.[36] Hŏ Ka-i, a Korean party organizer in the Soviet Union, was named First Secretary of the new party, the position that controls all the organizational and administrative functions. The other positions of vital importance were also occupied by Kim's immediate followers or by Soviet Koreans.

With the emergence of the North Korean Workers Party, the other existing groups—the Korean Democratic Party and the Ch'ŏndokyo Party—barely maintained their skeleton organizations and henceforth played a clearly secondary role in the politics of North Korea. The Workers Party, on the other hand, concentrated on expanding its membership by recruiting grass roots support from the labor and peasant classes. It was reported that membership reached about 600,000 by December of 1946.[37] As the ruling party, it directed, coordinated, and supervised all activities in North Korea, both governmental and nongovernmental. It also expanded its front organizations, such as the Democratic Youth League, Women's League, Workers' League and Farmer's Federation. In short, Kim and the Russian authori-

---

[36] The reason why Kim Il-sŏng was chosen as a vice-chairman is not known but it seems to indicate his political agility. It was desirable to avoid antagonizing the Yenan and domestic factions, and to disguise the fact that the union was an absorption, rather than a merger, of the New People's Party into the Communist Party. For a different interpretation, see Kim Ch'ang-sun, *Pukhan Sibo Nyŏn Sa* (Fifteen Years of History in North Korea) (Seoul, 1961), pp. 99–101. Kim interprets the election of Kim Tu-bong as chairman of the Communist party as the result of tactical mistakes of Kim Il-sŏng at the party assembly. For an official interpretation of the party, see *Chosŏn Rodongtang Yŏksa Kyojae* (Textbook for the History of the Korean Workers Party) (Pyongyang, 1964), pp. 185–192.

[37] *North Korea: A Case Study in the Techniques of Takeover*, p. 14. *Chosŏn Rodongtang Yŏksa Kyojae*, p. 192.

ties created a machine that could effectively regiment the North Korean people.

With this monolithic organizational strength, the North Korean regime initiated a series of drastic social and economic reform programs in early 1946. Land reform distributed the land that had been owned by the Japanese, and by Korean landlords, churches, and monasteries, to the "tilling farmers" who received up to a maximum of 2.45 acres without compensation.[38] It also cancelled all debts owed by the peasants to the landlords, and distributed all farm equipment and animals. By the law of August 10, more than 90 percent of the industrial plants were nationalized, as well as banks, transportation and communication facilities, public utilities, and large-scale private enterprises. A series of laws were enacted to improve working conditions for the laboring class, to set up welfare programs, to guarantee the equality of women, and to reform the taxation system. Finally, the regime launched, in 1947, a One Year Economic Plan to improve the unsatisfactory economic conditions resulting from Japanese colonialism and the division of the country.[39] Although these reform programs were not always successful, they did create conditions for stable government. Since more than 50 percent of the population of the North consisted of landless tenant farmers, they must have had considerable influence on the thought and feelings of the majority of the North Korean people. Moreover, despite the increasing in-

---

[38] For an excellent analysis, see Lee Chong-sik, "Land Reform, Collectivisation and the Peasants in North Korea" in *North Korea Today*, ed. Robert A. Scalapino (New York, 1963), pp. 65–81. For an official analysis of the North Korean regime, see *Chōsenni okeru Shakaishugi no Kiso Kensessu* (Construction of the Foundation of Socialism in Korea), ed. Chōsen Minshushugi Jinmin Kyowakoku Kagakuin Hōgaku Kenkyu Sho (Tokyo, 1962), pp. 25–45.

[39] Yoon T. Kuark, "North Korea's Industrial Development during the Postwar Period" in Scalapino, pp. 51–52. See also Maruo Itaru and Mura Tsuneo, *Bunretsu Kokka ni okeru Keizai Hatten no Futatsuno Ryukei* (Two Patterns of Economic Development in the Divided Nations) (Tokyo, 1962), pp. 49–52.

trusion of the state into the private sector of the economy, the program was "in general characterized by its moderation." [40] In short, the North Korean regime took a great stride toward the foundation of a socialistic state.

THE SITUATION IN THE SOUTH

While the Soviet authority intensified its policy of communizing North Korea, the Americans in the South took steps to encourage democratization by establishing an effective Korean administration under the military government,[41] and by stamping out what they felt were irresponsible leftist political movements.

We have noted that Hodge was actively engaged in fostering a third political grouping to oppose both the Communist elements and the rightist Rhee-Kim forces. This was the Coalition Committee under Kimm Kiu-sic. On October 13, 1946, he announced the creation of the Interim Legislative Assembly (Nam Chosŏn Kwado Ippŏp Ŭiwŏn), which was to be a branch of the proposed South Korean Interim Government (Nam Chosŏn Kwado Chŏngbu), the name to be given to the Korean elements of the military government now that the actual administration had passed from American to Korean personnel. The Assembly would supersede the Representative Democratic Council of South Korea.[42] Hodge hoped that this body would provide an opportunity for indigenous leaders to obtain practical experience in handling legislative matters; it would also provide the military government with a sounding board for Korean public opinion.

Representation in the assembly was to be on the basis of population. There were to be 90 members, of whom 45 were

---

[40] *North Korea: A Case Study in the Techniques of Takeover*, p. 16. For an official North Korean source see *Chosŏn Rodongtang Yŏksa Kyojae*, pp. 158–170.

[41] Pak Mun-ok, *Han'guk Chŏnbu Ron* (Korean Government) (Seoul, 1963), pp. 320–332.

[42] Ordinance No. 118. See USAFIK, *Official Gazette 1945–46*.

to be elected by the people and 45 appointed by the military government.[43] (Kimm recommended that his Committee should elect half the members of the body with the approval of the military governor, and that his delegates should be sent to the provinces to supervise elections.)[44] The Assembly would have the power to enact ordinances on matters affecting general welfare and on such other matters as might be referred to it by the military governor.[45] Everything, however, was subject to the ultimate veto of General Hodge.

When the first election in South Korea since the Japanese annexation was held that month, it became apparent that—contrary to Hodge's expectations—the rightist forces led by Rhee and Kim would overwhelmingly dominate the Assembly. They won 31 of the 45 seats and could also count on support from several independents.[46] Critics charged that the election was "undemocratic and superficial." Kimm Kiusic requested that the results be invalidated. Hodge actually annulled the election of six members (on the charge of election irregularities) and appointed most of the other 45 members to the Assembly from a list of nominees furnished by the Coalition Committee.[47]

The creation of the Legislative Assembly was interpreted

[43] For the function and power of the Assembly see *Summation,* No. 13 (October, 1946), pp. 13–15.

[44] *Summation,* No. 13 (October, 1946), pp. 16–18.

[45] *Summation,* No. 13 (October, 1946), p. 15. For the operation of the Assembly, see Pak Mun-ok, pp. 333–339.

[46] *Summation, op. cit.* See also Yi Ki-ha, *Han'guk Ch'ŏngtang Baltal Sa* (History of the Development of Korean Political Parties) (Seoul, 1961), pp. 178–183.

[47] The composition of the Assembly in September, 1947 was as follows (based on *Summation,* September, 1947, pp. 115–116):

	Elected	Appointed	Total
Right	38	17	55
Moderate	1	15	16
Left	2	12	14
Vacancies	4	1	5
	45	45	90

by many Korean leaders to mean that an "independent" and separate South Korea might evolve. On this basis, the leftist forces, including the Communist Party, openly opposed the election. They accused the American command of carrying out a plan to further divide the country; and the military government began to take measures to restrict their political activities.

The outright suppression of the Communist Party marked an important shift in American occupation policy. In September, 1946, Hodge had closed three left-wing newspapers and arrested many prominent Communist leaders, including the party chiefs.[48] Three weeks after the order for the arrest of Pak Hŏn-yŏng, Yi Kang-guk, and Yi Chu-ha, widespread strikes and riots erupted throughout South Korea. Riots in Taegu and Chŏlla Namdo were very serious; thousands of Communists were arrested and 1,500 of them were prosecuted.[49] This suppression greatly weakened the leftist forces. Russia called South Korea an "unprecedentedly murderous police state."

On the other side, Rhee and the rightists were greatly disturbed by Hodge's appointments to the Assembly. Rhee charged that "the General did not intend to permit him to seize power." Rhee announced that his future policy would be one of open opposition. Hodge retorted that the United States could never be turned aside from its chosen policy by threats and warned Rhee that he must cooperate or "be de-

---

[48] For the suppression of communism, *Korea Today,* pp. 84–88. Pak Hŏn-yŏn, Yi Kang-guk, and Yi Chu-ha were listed as wanted by the police for activities "prejudicial to law and order." *Summation,* No. 12, p. 15.

[49] *Summation,* No. 13 (October, 1946), p. 23; and No. 14 (Nov., 1946), p. 24. The disorders that swept South Korea during October continued in early November with attacks against police and administrative buildings. Some writers attribute these disorders to the brutality of Korean police. For the Communist point of view, see Kim Hi-il, *Mije ŭi Chosŏn Ch'imyak Sa* (History of the Invasion of American Imperialism in Korea) (Pyongyang, 1962), pp. 56–69.

stroyed."[50] Thus, at a time when the close cooperation of these two leaders was most needed, they became, in a practical sense, enemies. The sad truth was that the Assembly could not function as Hodge had expected without the cooperation of this strong rightist force: Kimm was indeed popular, but his power could not match Rhee's.

Sorely disappointed in Hodge's policy, Rhee went to Washington in December, 1946, to present his case personally to the American government. There he proposed that an interim government should be elected for South Korea, to serve until the two halves of Korea could be reunited and a general election held thereafter; and without disturbing direct Russian-American consultation on Korea, this interim government should be admitted to the United Nations and allowed to negotiate directly with Russia and the United States.[51] This proposal was tantamount to suggesting the establishment of a separate government in the South, since there was little hope of settling the problems with the Soviet Union.

General Hodge charged that "either through lack of knowledge of facts or through malicious intent to deceive the Korean people, certain elements are creating the impression that the United States now favors and is actively working toward a separate government in Southern Korea."[52] He made it clear that these assumptions were contrary to the announced policies of the United States. Later this statement was endorsed by the Under Secretary of State.[53]

---

[50] Oliver, *Syngman Rhee*, pp. 228–229.

[51] See Dr. Rhee's six point program, *Ibid.*, p. 232. Already on November 1, 1946, the Korean Representative Democratic Council had appealed to the United Nations for the immediate independence of Korea with simultaneous withdrawal of the two occupation forces. See the official appeal in Harold R. Isaacs, *New Cycle in Asia* (New York, 1947), pp. 91–94.

[52] *Department of State Bulletin*, January 19, 1947, p. 128. See also *Summation*, January, 1947, p. 12.

[53] *Department of State Bulletin*, January 19, 1947, *loc. cit.*

When Hodge publicly stated that a four-power trusteeship might be the only feasible means of unifying Korea, adding that "neither you nor I can change a word of the Moscow Decision,"[54] the anger of the anti-trusteeship forces reached a peak. When the Interim Legislative Assembly opened with Kimm Kiu-sic as its Chairman, 38 members of the right wing boycotted it.[55] Demonstration followed demonstration. The anger of the rightist groups was so intense and the dangers of disorder so imminent that Hodge issued several stern warning statements in January, 1947. Nevertheless, on January 15, a resolution was passed in the Assembly condemning Hodge's policy and trusteeship in Korea.[56] The situation deteriorated to such an extent that in March an effort was made by the former Chungking Provisional Korean Government to declare itself the *de jure* government of the country. A body of 14 political counselors was named, with Rhee as President and Kim Koo as Vice-President. The military government authorities immediately announced that "the act was illegal and there was little evidence of popular support."[57] Nonetheless, a second wave of widespread left-wing demonstrations to denounce both the military government and the extreme rightist actions occurred. The arrest of more than 2,000 Communists followed.

Hodge's efforts to foster the third force had only worsened the situation in South Korea. He regarded the resolution of condemnation passed by the Assembly as an act of opposi-

---

[54] *Summation,* No. 18 (March, 1946), p. 16. In January, Hodge reported to Truman that Korea might in fact erupt in civil war unless American-Russian cooperation brought about some solution to the nation's problems. *Years of Trial and Hope,* p. 322.

[55] *Summation,* No. 15 (December, 1946), p. 14.

[56] The full text of the resolution is in *Summation,* No. 16 (January, 1947), pp. 22–23.

[57] *Summation,* No. 18 (March, 1947), pp. 14–16. For a brief survey of American military government, see W. D. Reeve, *The Republic of Korea* (London, 1963), pp. 23–29; Clyde C. Mitchell, *Korea: Second Failure in Asia* (Washington, 1951).

tion to himself and to American policy, rather than as an expression of anti-trusteeship sentiment. The body he had created to recruit supporters and to strengthen the third force had turned against him, and had become an open forum to embarrass the military government. It was reported early in 1947 that he had agreed to convene the Joint Commission again only if those individuals, parties, and social organization which, after signing the declaration contained in Communiqué No. 5, foment or instigate active opposition to the work of the Joint Commission or to either of the Allied Powers or the fulfillment of the Moscow Decision shall be excluded from further consultation with the Joint Commission. If the Joint Commission were to meet again in the future, it would clearly receive little support from the Assembly.

It was now apparent that the implementation of the Moscow Decision would be almost impossible without the close cooperation of the Rhee-Kim forces. It had become clear that if Hodge weakened the right by alienating these forces from the military government, the leftists would eventually dominate South Korea. If Hodge, contrary to his instructions, had tried to strengthen these forces while negotiating another means of achieving unification with the Soviet Command, it might have been possible to reach some agreement on unification. Had the rightist groups been strong enough to match the left, and had the Soviet Union agreed to have country-wide elections, a unified Korean government still friendly to the West might have been possible.

6

The Search for an Impossible Compromise

On the day following the adjournment of the Joint Commission and again on June 15, 1946, General Hodge wrote letters to General Chistiakov seeking a resumption of negotiations between the two Commands for the unification of Korea. He asked the Soviet general to meet him at a personal conference, at a time and place convenient to Chistiakov, to clear up many issues before the Commission reconvened.[1] These letters, however, were not answered by the Russians until August 6. In the meantime, Chistiakov undoubtedly reported to and received instructions from Moscow.

Chistiakov's letter made it clear that he was ready to send a delegation to Seoul but only on condition that "the American delegation in the Joint Commission [would] uphold the exact fulfillment of the Moscow Decision" and accordingly would consult only with those parties and organizations and their representatives which "without reservation" would support this decision.[2] He also charged that the break in the earlier meeting had been initiated by the American delegation.

---

[1] Letter from Hodge to Chistiakov, U.S. Department of State, *Korea's Independence* (Washington, 1947), p. 21.

[2] Chistiakov to Hodge, *ibid.*, pp. 21–22.

In his August 12 letter to Chistiakov, cited earlier, Hodge firmly declared that the American delegation could not be a party to any "arbitrary, exclusive, or punitive tactics" in dealing with the accredited representatives of the Korean people, except on grounds specifically stated in the Moscow Decision itself and consistent with the world-accepted definition of the word "democratic." He added that the Soviet interpretation of the Moscow Decision was "purely unilateral," and insisted that there was nothing in the Decision that prohibited Koreans from expressing their ideas and desires in the formation of their government.[3]

Hodge's views were strongly endorsed by Under Secretary Acheson. Asserting the desire of the United States to reconvene the Joint Commission, Acheson stated emphatically that "we stand for freedom of speech, of assembly, and of the press; honest criticism is not considered a crime, but is welcomed." [4] Four weeks later, he also said that the Americans "intend to remain in Korea and carry out our duties there until we have achieved the purpose of bringing into being a united, independent Korea." [5] These were the first major policy statements on Korea issued by the State Department since the Moscow Conference. Their obvious aim was to clarify the American stand in the face of the many conflicting rumors about the failure of the Joint Commission, and they appeared to allay somewhat the anxiety of the South Korean leaders.

COMMUNICATIONS BETWEEN CHISTIAKOV AND HODGE

Through sporadic exchanges of lengthy letters,[6] many problems were smoothed out, and gradually Hodge and

[3] Hodge to Chistiakov, August 12, 1946, *ibid.*, pp. 22–23.

[4] *U.S. Department of State Bulletin,* September 8, 1946, p. 462.

[5] *Ibid.*, October 13, 1946, p. 670.

[6] Chistiakov to Hodge, October 26, 1946; Hodge to Chistiakov, November 1, 1946; Chistiakov to Hodge, November 26, 1946; Hodge to Chistiakov, December 24, 1946; Chistiakov to Hodge, February 28, 1947 in *Korea's Independence,* pp. 23–32.

Chistiakov seemed to reach an understanding. Both commanders presented various proposals to serve as a basis for the resumption of the Joint Commission, and those in Chistiakov's letter of November 26 appeared reasonable to the American delegation, provided that a few points were clarified. The Soviet proposals read:

> (1) The Joint Commission must consult those democratic parties and organizations which uphold fully the Moscow Decision on Korea.
>
> (2) Parties or social organizations invited for consultation with the Joint Commission must not nominate for consultation those representatives who have compromised themselves by actively voicing opposition to the Moscow Decision.
>
> (3) Parties and social organizations invited for consultation with the Joint Commission must not and will not voice opposition nor will they incite others to voice opposition to the Moscow Decision and the work of the Joint Commission. If such be the case such parties and social organizations, by mutual agreement of both delegations, will be excluded from further consultation with the Joint Commission.

Although the Russians' previous position remained basically unchanged, these points appeared to offer consultation to all democratic groups that would pledge future cooperation with the Joint Commission. Therefore, in his letter of December 24, Hodge suggested that the Commission be reconvened on the basis of these proposals with a few modifications, provided they guaranteed complete freedom of expression to Korean political parties, social organizations, and individuals. The proposed modifications were:

> (1) The signing of Communiqué No. 5 to support the Moscow Decision and the work of the Commission "be accepted as a declaration of good faith" entitling the signatory to initial consultation by the Commission.
>
> (2) Each party has the right to determine the representatives it desires; "mutual agreement" between the two dele-

gations based on "good reason" alone could require the party to name a substitute representative.

(3) A party or an individual be eliminated from consultation with the Commission only by mutual agreement and only on the ground of fomenting or instigating active opposition to the work of the Joint Commission, the fulfillment of the Moscow Decision, or one of the two powers.

Thus, the Americans seemed to feel that signing Communiqué No. 5 was sufficient evidence of willingness to join in carrying out the work of the Commission. Furthermore, it appeared that they would not agree to any suggestion that would basically change their position on the issue of free expression.

These proposals could not be implemented, however, if Korean leaders were going to continue to voice active opposition to the trusteeship. Thus, according to the modifications, once the Soviet delegation refused to consult with those who instigated "active opposition" to the trusteeship, they would be supplanted by others upon whom the two parties would agree. Further, in his letter of February 28, 1947, Chistiakov said that all subsequent actions of the parties and organizations signing Communiqué No. 5 (and consequently agreeing to fully uphold the Moscow Decision) had to be consistent with that pledge: mere expressions of good intentions seemed insignificant to the Soviet delegation. This meant that the Russians would bar from consultation all groups who in action opposed the trusteeship.

Hodge sought to distinguish between those who fomented active opposition to the Joint Commission, to the Allied Powers or to their implementation of the Moscow Agreement, and those who earnestly opposed only the principle of trusteeship. Whereas he insisted on the right of freedom of expression for Koreans regarding the implementation of the Agreement, he condemned those who instigated active opposition and obstructive tactics against the Allies. However, the Russian reply seemed to reject this distinction, and the two sides found no grounds for compromise. The Joint Commission remained adjourned.

COMMUNICATIONS BETWEEN MARSHALL AND MOLOTOV

From the beginning of Korea's occupation, it should have been clear that ultimate decisions would have to be made by the American and Russian governments, and talks would have to be held at the governmental level. However, Washington had long refrained from directly approaching Moscow, probably in hopes of keeping the Korean problem localized to the peninsula. Yet this policy merely prolonged the endless talk, without tangible results. Major General Arnold, Chief of the American delegation to the first convocation of the Joint Commission, complained to Washington that "there was no hope" of accomplishing unification by negotiations on the occupation authority level, and urged that "if anything is done, it must be on a higher level." [7]

General MacArthur also urged that "measures [should] be taken immediately to break the U.S.-Russian deadlock in Korea by diplomatic means." [8] When Hodge was called to Washington for consultation in the latter part of February, 1947, he likewise recommended to President Truman that the governments of the United States and Russia attempt to find a joint solution to Korean problems. He warned that the Russians were organizing an army of 500,000 men in North Korea, apparently for the purpose of launching an attack on the South. He also warned that Rhee would use extreme rightist groups to sabotage the work of the Commission.[9] As noted earlier, it seemed to him that civil war was imminent if the two governments did not take immediate measures for the unification of Korea. On basis of the reports from Hodge

[7] *New York Times*, October 11, 1946.

[8] Harry S. Truman, *Years of Trial and Hope* (New York, 1956), p. 323.

[9] *Ibid.*

and MacArthur, Truman approved Secretary Marshall's plan for one more effort to make the Joint Commission effective.

On April 8, 1947, Marshall addressed a letter to Foreign Minister Molotov proposing that both governments instruct their military commanders in Korea to reconvene the Joint Commission "as soon as possible" on a basis of respect for the democratic right of freedom of opinion. He also suggested that a mutually acceptable date during the summer of 1947 be fixed "for a review by the two governments of the progress made to that date by the Joint Commission." [10]

In his lengthy reply of April 19, Molotov strongly defended the position of the Soviet delegation on the Commission and accused the United States of fostering anti-democratic elements in Korea. Nevertheless, he agreed that the Commission should resume work in Seoul on the basis of "an exact execution of the Moscow Agreement on Korea." He also suggested that in July or August the Commission should present the results of its efforts on the matter of a provisional democratic Korean government. He was not explicit, however, about a formula for choosing Korean organizations for consultation.[11]

In a subsequent exchange of letters,[12] Molotov and Marshall sought to reach an agreement on this matter. Molotov finally agreed to reconvene the Commission on the basis of the proposal and modifications presented in Hodge's December 24 letter to Chistiakov, and Marshall acknowledged this agreement.[13] Thus, on May 21, 1947, the Joint Commission meetings were resumed.

There is no full explanation of why the Russians changed their minds. However, their willingness to meet was undoubtedly in part attributable to American insistence that further delay in negotiations left the United States no other choice

---

[10] *Department of State Bulletin,* April 20, 1947, p. 716.

[11] *Korea's Independence*, pp. 35–37.

[12] Marshall to Molotov, May 2, 1947; Molotov to Marshall, May 7, 1947; Marshall to Molotov, May 12, 1947, *ibid.*, pp. 38–41.

[13] *Department of State Bulletin,* May 18, 1947, p. 995.

than to greatly increase her economic aid to South Korea and to establish a separate South Korean government.[14] Molotov's May 7 letter to Marshall seemed to point to fear of such unilateral action. Their willingness may also have been based on the fact that Hodge's modifications actually did not have much substance if the Korean leaders were determined to continue their opposition to trusteeship. And, from the recent development of animosity between Hodge and the Rhee-Kim groups, it seems the Russians may also have believed that the leftist forces in Korea would be strong enough—because of South Korean disappointment with military government policies—to upset the strength of the rightists by the time a general election could be held.

SECOND TRIAL OF THE JOINT U.S.–SOVIET COMMISSION

General Hodge called for the cooperation of all Koreans with the Joint Commission in order to make the forthcoming session a success. But the Rhee-Kim forces stated that they would not join in the activities of the Joint Commission until the meaning of "trusteeship" and "democracy" as used by the Commission became clear. On the other hand, the National Independence Federation (Minjok Chaju Yŏnmaeng) which had been newly organized by Kimm Kiu-sic and moderate rightist leaders, as well as all the leftist parties affiliated with the National Democratic Front, declared their support of the Joint Commission activities.[15] Kimm actively urged all patriots to cooperate with the Commission.

Into this atmosphere of division came the five Soviet delegates to Seoul with a staff of 65 persons. The Russian delega-

---

[14] *Ibid.*

[15] Kim Chin-hak and Han Ch'ŏl-yŏng, *Chehŏn Kukhoe Sa* (History of the Constituent Assembly) (Seoul, 1956), pp. 62–69. See also Gaimusho (Japanese Ministry of Foreign Affairs), *Sengoni okeru Chōsen no Seiji Jōsei* (Korean Politics in the Postwar Era) (Tokyo, 1948), pp. 61–67. Early in June the Han'guk Democratic Party, one of the strongholds of the anti-trusteeship groups, decided to participate in the deliberations of the Joint Commission.

tion was headed by General Shtykov, the American by Major General A. E. Brown. The first meeting of the second convention of the Joint Commission took place on May 21, 1947, in the Dŏk Su Palace and, like that of the first convention, was devoted entirely to formal opening ceremonies.

In the first business meeting on May 22, it was decided that the Joint Commission would again consist of five members from each delegation, that chairmanship would alternate weekly, and that the meetings of the Commission would be closed except by mutual agreement for open sessions.[16]

It was also agreed that in the first stage of its work the Commission would limit itself to the preparation of a plan for the formation of a Provisional Democratic Government in Korea. To carry forward this work, three sub-commissions were established. Sub-Commission No. 1 would concern itself with the solution of all problems concerning consultation with the democratic parties and social organizations; Sub-Commission No. 2 would work out the type and structure of the provisional government, the provisional charter, and the development of a political platform; and Sub-Commission No. 3 would deal with methods of selecting members of the government and its administration, and also with the transfer of authority to the government. The sub-commissions started their work on May 26.[17] In the preliminary negotiations each side modified its stand somewhat and they worked together smoothly in a friendly atmosphere.

On June 12, Joint Communiqué No. 1 was issued. It stated that a decision had been reached by the Commission regarding the method of consultation. The Commission offered a questionnaire on the structure and principles of the proposed government to determine the views of the Korean people on its Charter and platform.

---

[16] USAFIK (United States Armed Forces in Korea), *Summation of U.S. Army Military Government Activities in Korea,* No. 20 (May, 1947), p. 19. Hereafter cited as *Summation.*

[17] For detailed information, see *ibid.,* pp. 19–22.

In the most controversial problems, the communiqué stated, the Joint Commission shall be guided by the conditions stated in the letter of the Minister of Foreign Affairs of the U.S.S.R., V. M. Molotov, of May 7, 1947, and accepted by the Secretary of State of the U.S.A.[18] Accordingly, the American delegation gave way to the Russian insistence that Koreans who actively opposed the Moscow Decision should not be consulted, even though this might be interpreted as a limitation upon "freedom of opinion." The Russians, on the other hand, accepted for consultation many Korean parties and social groups that had earlier opposed the Decision, provided they would declare their support by "signing the declaration in Communiqué No. 5" and would refrain from "fomenting or instigating active opposition" to the work of the Joint Commission. It was a reasonable compromise if Hodge was able to recruit the Korean groups led by Rhee-Kim and thus match the leftist forces in numbers. However, it was also a very dangerous compromise, one which gave great advantage to the Soviet Union, if Hodge failed to gain the cooperation of the rightist groups. Not only did Hodge fail—the compromise even increased the rightist antagonism.

Applications for consultation had to be submitted by June 23, and answers to the questionnaire by July 1. Both would be submitted to the Joint Commission at Seoul or Pyongyang and meetings of applicants were to be held in both places; oral consultation would begin July 5. The Chief Commissioner of the Soviet delegation was to preside over the meeting in Seoul, while the Chief Commissioner of the American delegation would preside in Pyongyang.[19]

The committees for consultation were set up in the capi-

---

[18] The communiqué contained a document entitled, "The Method of Consultation with Korean Democratic Parties and Social Organizations in Northern and Southern Korea." See the text in *Summation,* No. 21 (June, 1947), pp. 16–26.

[19] The full text of the Commission's Decision No. 12 is in *Korea's Independence,* pp. 41–45. The date of oral consultation was later changed to July 7, *Summation,* No. 21 (June, 1947), p. 26.

tals of the two zones. Thirty-eight organizations in North Korea and 425 in South Korea submitted applications. Although this seemed to be an auspicious start, disaster soon followed because the old differences with regard to consultations arose. In the American view, the Soviet delegation reverted to the position it had assumed in the 1946 Joint Commission. These are the basic issues which were involved in the subsequent meetings.

The Soviet Position

Parties and organizations falling within the following categories should not be included in the list of initial consultations:

(1) Those not classified by the Russians as social organizations.

(2) District and other "purely local and insignificant organizations which do not have zonal character," and democratic parties and social organizations claiming under 10,000 members.

(3) Those groups which had been created specifically to oppose the Moscow Decision, especially members of the Anti-Trusteeship Committee [20] and similar organizations; such parties would be acceptable only if they publicly withdrew from membership in the Anti-Trusteeship Committee and ceased to fight the Decision and the Joint Commission.

(4) Those organizations whose existence or membership aroused suspicion, such as the so-called Korean Engineers and Architects League which claimed a total membership of 1,220,000, an impossible figure since all Korea has fewer than 1,000,000 workers.

(5) Those groups not accepted by either or both delegations.

The Soviet delegation specifically contended that the total number of members of parties and organizations of South Korea filing for consultation was 52,000,000. This number

[20] This Committee was first organized in January, 1946, and reorganized in June; it became very active in May, 1947. Fifteen rightist parties were affiliated with it.

was obviously suspicious since this would mean that every adult Korean, both male and female, belonged to five organizations—an unlikely possibility.[21]

The American Position

(1) The Moscow Decision did not define the term "social organization" and the Soviet delegation refused the American request for a definition by the Joint Commission.

(2) District and other purely local organizations were not barred by any provision of the previous agreement; in order to eliminate small organizations, the U.S. offered to limit oral consultation to groups with membership in excess of 1,000 or any other reasonable figure.

(3) Parties that were members of the Anti-Trusteeship Committee and affiliated organizations were "clearly eligible for initial consultation under the Marshall-Molotov agreement" since they signed the declaration contained in the Joint Commission's Decision No. 12 and also submitted a full statement reaffirming their desire to cooperate with the Commission under the terms of the Moscow Agreement.[22]

(4) These parties should remain eligible unless and until they were by mutual agreement excluded after indictment for trying to foment or instigate active opposition to work of the Joint Commission or the Moscow Agreement.

(5) The arbitrary distinction drawn by the Soviet delegation between "eligibility for consultation" and "admission for consultation" would nullify the agreement reached by the two foreign ministers and by the Commission.

The American delegation insisted that the Soviet delegation was attempting to establish an arbitrary "veto power" over

---

[21] The above information is based on the text of the declaration of the Chief Commissioner, Soviet delegation, at a press conference on July 21. *Summation,* No. 22 (July, 1947), pp. 23–27. See also *Seoul Shinmun,* July 22, 1947; and Kim Hi-il, *Mije ŭi Chosŏn Ch'imyak Sa* (History of the Invasion of American Imperialism in Korea) (Pyongyang, 1962), pp. 66–67.

[22] See the letter, submitted to the Commission by members of the Anti-Trusteeship Committee, signed by Yi Yun-yŏng, Vice-Chairman of the United Council. *Korea's Independence,* pp. 49–50.

the consultation that was contrary to the first paragraph of the agreement accepted by its foreign ministers.[23]

Disagreement created a deadlock on July 12, when the Russian delegation proposed a drastic cut in the number of groups to be consulted in South Korea. The Soviet plan would omit most of the rightists who were affiliated with the Anti-Trusteeship Committee and thereby reduce the original 425 applicants to 118. According to records available to the American delegation, Russia classified the groups as set forth in Table 1.

TABLE 1

RUSSIAN CLASSIFICATION OF POLITICAL GROUPS[a] IN SOUTH KOREA

Classification	Parties included	Number of members[b]
A. Rightist	44	12,483
B. Moderate right	18	4,029
(Subtotal: A and B)	(62)	(16,512)
C. Moderates	9	2,882
(Subtotal: A, B, and C)	(71)	(19,394)
D. Moderate left	6	4,609
E. National Democratic Front	41	14,450
(Subtotal: D and E)	(47)	(19,059)
Grand totals	118	38,453

[a] Only parties and social organizations having a claimed membership of at least 10,000 members were included.

[b] Figures are in thousands (000 omitted).

If to tabulations in Table 1 there are added the 38 North Korean (NDF) groups with membership in excess of 10,000,

[23] Information on the American position is based on the text of the statement by the chief of the American delegation on July 15 and 31. *Summation*, No. 22 (July, 1947), pp. 20–23 and 27–31.

the classification of parties and social organizations of all Korea would be as set forth in Table 2.[24]

TABLE 2

RUSSIAN CLASSIFICATION OF POLITICAL GROUPS [a] IN NORTH AND SOUTH KOREA

Classification	Parties included	Number of members [b]
A. Rightist	44	12,483
B. Moderate right	18	4,029
(Subtotal: A and B)	(62)	(16,512)
C. Moderates	9	2,882
(Subtotal: A, B, and C)	(71)	(19,394)
D. Moderate left	6	4,609
E. National Democratic Front	79	27,709
(Subtotal: D and E)	(85)	(32,318)
Grand totals	156	51,712

[a] Only parties and social organizations having a claimed membership of at least 10,000 members were included.
[b] Figures are in thousands (000 omitted).

The tabulation in Table 2 reveals clearly the effects of the Soviet proposal. Even if the moderate groups were lumped

[24] Figures are based upon the statement made by the U.S. Chief Commissioner on July 31, 1947. *Summation,* No. 22 (July, 1947), pp. 27–31. In North Korea the only applicants were members of the National Democratic Front. On July 12, the Soviet delegation proposed the elimination of 27 parties of South Korea, 3 for fraud, and 24 others which represented large rightist groups. The 24 parties eliminated had a claimed membership of over 15,000,000 which is over half the total members claimed by South Korean rightists. Eventually, the Soviet list showed only 118 parties and social organizations for South Korea, eliminating more rightist organizations. The adult population of South Korea at this time was approximately 9,500,000; of North Korea, 4,500,000. Therefore, in both cases the membership showed much overlapping and was greatly exaggerated. The membership claims, if true, would indicate that in South Korea each adult, regardless of sex and age, held membership in five groups; and in North Korea, each belonged to more than three groups.

together with the right (though, in fact, they were closer to the left), the situation in South Korea would be 71 "rightist" organizations with a total membership of 19.4 million, as compared with 47 leftist groups with 19.1 million. By adding the 38 parties and organizations of North Korea, the nation-wide situation would be the recognition of 85 leftist groups having a total membership of 32.3 million, while the total number of "rightists" would remain the same as in South Korea—19.4 million. By the Russian proposed standards, then, the approved leftist organizations would have a total membership almost twice that of the approved rightist groups. Further advantage would be gained from the fact that the leftists were generally well disciplined and willing to follow the Communist line, whereas the rightists (including the moderates) were notoriously intransigent and continuously plagued by schisms and factionalism. Nonetheless, since only about one-third of the total Korean population was in the North, it was clear that Communist objectives were to try to reduce as far as possible the representation from the South.

The American delegation concluded that adoption of the Soviet proposal would inevitably lead to a communist-dominated Korea.[25] Accordingly, General Brown became inflexible in his opposition to the Russian demands, and the Soviets were not willing to compromise. We can discern two basic questions affecting the attitudes of the two delegations. Might one delegation unilaterally exercise veto power and exclude from consultation any party or social organization that it did not approve? According to the Americans, the Soviets wished to "exercise such veto power," [26] and they maintained that this was an arbitrary position contrary to the agreement of the foreign ministers. Secondly, what should be the Commission's attitude toward a party or social organi-

---

[25] From the statement of General Brown on July 31, 1947, *ibid.*

[26] From the statement of General Brown on July 15, 1947. *Department of State Bulletin,* August 10, 1947, p. 297.

zation affiliated with the so-called Anti-Trusteeship Committee? The Soviet wanted to exclude these groups from consultation. But the U.S. held that no party or social organization would be assumed guilty until it was shown to have incited and fomented active opposition to the Joint Commission, the Moscow Decision, or either of the Allies. These two questions could not be resolved so long as each of the occupying powers demanded a Korea favorable to itself.

The American delegation first attempted to break the deadlock by suggesting that the Russian and American authorities consult separately with the Korean parties in their respective zones. This proposal was summarily rejected by the Soviet delegation at the July 29 meeting. The next American move, on August 1, was an offer to consult, on behalf of the whole Commission, with those parties to which the Soviet delegation objected. This was likewise rejected by the Russians. The Americans then put forward a third proposal. This was that oral consultations be dispensed with, and that written questionnaires completed by the applicant parties be accepted as consultation under the terms of the Moscow Agreement. It also recommended that the Commission proceed to set up the framework of a provisional government for a united Korea, and that a general election for the membership of the national legislature be held immediately under "international supervision." [27]

Meanwhile, Secretary Marshall had sent a letter to Molotov proposing, to avoid further delay, that the Joint Commission should report the results of its deliberations by August 21 so that each government might promptly consider what further steps could be taken to achieve the aims of the Moscow Agreement.[28] These various moves by the American delegation and by Marshall met with no apparent Russian response. The Commission continued its meetings, but

---

[27] The text of the proposal appeared in Brown's statement on August 23, 1947, *Summation,* No. 23 (August, 1947), pp. 182–185.

[28] The text of the letter is in *Korea's Independence,* pp. 50–51.

progress ceased. Bickering and recriminations held the stage: the negotiations seemed more and more an exercise in futility.

As the situation within the Commission deteriorated, the American command in South Korea seemingly lost its patience—or its head. Heretofore, a ban on mass demonstrations against the Moscow Decision had been strictly enforced. This ban was now rescinded. The effect, in the charged atmosphere prevailing, amounted to an invitation for the rightist groups to attack the Soviet openly. Large-scale rightist demonstrations promptly broke out, and there was even a physical attack on members of the Soviet delegation in Seoul on July 26.

Moreover, the American military government began an active campaign against active leftists. More than 100 "revolutionary ringleaders" were arrested in Seoul during the middle part of August, and many more were taken into custody in the provinces. This anti-communist campaign, as could well be expected, resulted in even more heated recriminations between the delegations in the Commission.[29] General Shtykov charged that "such a situation is being created, it seems, with the aim of undermining the work of the Joint Commission."

From the American point of view, the negotiations within the Commission undoubtedly seemed frustrating. It may also have appeared desirable to encourage and strengthen the rightist parties—who formed the only local support for the American position. Nevertheless, the American actions were unfortunate in their effect. The ill-timed arrest of the leftists actually hastened the end of the Joint Commission.

---

[29] See the statements of Shtykov made on August 2, 9, 14, 20, and 28 and answers made by Brown on August 7, 9, and 25. Full texts appear in USAFIK, *South Korean Interim Government Activities,* No. 1 (August, 1947), pp. 163–193. USAFIK *Summation* changed its name to "South Korean Interim Government Activities" after August. Hereafter it is cited as *Interim Activities.*

On August 28, Shtykov declared that the last American proposal not only appeared unsatisfactory to the Soviet delegation, but also was made with a purely propagandistic purpose.[30] He presented a counter-proposal that agreed to dispense with oral consultation of parties, but advocated the creation of a "provisional assembly" based on equal representation from the North and South of those parties that "fully support the Moscow Agreement."[31] This unreasonable Soviet offer was bound to be unacceptable to the American delegation: the Russians wanted no internationally supervised election in their zones, whereas the Americans, having two-thirds of the population in their zone, would not accept the idea of equal representation. Moreover, the Soviet offer represented no retreat from their proposed exclusion of the important rightist parties. There appeared to be no more room to negotiate, since all feasible avenues for compromise were blocked by Soviet intransigence.

As for Marshall's request for a joint report, Molotov replied that the Soviet Government had no objection to the issuance of such a report, but complained that the recent arrests of many leftists was hampering the work of the Commission.[32] Unable to come to an agreement, the two delegations announced that their divergence of views prevented the making of a joint report.[33]

LOVETT PROPOSAL

The complete deadlock in the Joint Commission eloquently testified that Korean issues could not be solved by negotiations between the two commands, and that such issues again needed to be considered at the governmental level. In

---

[30] Statement of Shtykov on August 28, *ibid.*, pp. 190–193.
[31] *Ibid.*
[32] Molotov to Marshall, August 23, 1947. *Department of State Bulletin*, September 7, 1947, p. 475.
[33] Letter from Acting Secretary of State Lovett to Molotov, August 26, 1947. *Ibid.* (September 7, 1947), p. 474.

hope of finding a way to break the impasse, Acting Secretary of State Lovett dispatched a new proposal on August 26 to the Foreign Ministries of the Soviet Union, the United Kingdom, and China. This suggested that the four powers adhering to the Moscow Agreement meet to consider how that Agreement may be speedily carried out. The new proposal set forth a substitute for the Moscow plan, the core of which was the idea of holding general elections in the zones under the guidance of the United Nations. The U.S. paper read:[34]

> (1) In both the U.S.S.R. and U.S. zones of Korea there shall be held early elections to choose wholly representative provisional legislatures for each zone. Voting shall be by secret, multi-party ballot on a basis of universal suffrage and elections shall be held in accordance with the laws adopted by the present Korean legislatures in each zone.
>
> (2) These provisional zonal legislatures shall choose representatives in numbers which reflect the proportion between the populations of the two zones, these representatives to constitute a national provisional legislature. This legislature shall meet at Seoul to establish a provisional government for a united Korea.
>
> (3) The resulting Provisional Government of a united Korea shall meet in Korea with representatives of the Four Powers adhering to the Moscow Agreement on Korea to discuss with them what aid and assistance is needed in order to place Korean independence on a firm economic and political foundation and on what terms this aid and assistance is to be given.
>
> (4) During all the above stages the United Nations shall be invited to have observers present so that the world and the Korean people may be assured of the wholly representative and completely independent character of the actions taken.
>
> (5) The Korean Provisional Government and the Powers concerned shall agree upon a date by which all occupation forces in Korea will be withdrawn.
>
> (6) The provisional legislatures in each zone shall be encouraged to draft provisional constitutions which can later

[34] United States Seven Points Proposals Regarding Korea. See *ibid.*, or *Korea's Independence*, p. 56.

be used as a basis for the adoption by the national provisional legislature of a constitution for all of Korea.

(7) Until such time as a united, independent Korea is established, public and private Korean agencies in each zone shall be brought into contact with international agencies established by or under the United Nations and the presence of Korean observers at official international conferences shall be encouraged in appropriate cases.

The American proposal was accepted by the United Kingdom and China, but not by the Soviet Union. The latter stated that such a conference would be outside the scope of the Moscow Agreement, and that the Americans had not exhausted all possibilities for realizing that Agreement within the framework of the Joint Commission. Molotov told the United States that the impasse "is primarily the result of the position adopted by the American delegation" in the Joint Commission.[35] He further expressed his disapproval of the unilateral action taken by the Acting Secretary of State in dispatching invitations to the governments of Great Britain and China to participate in the discussions.

The Russian refusal made the proposed four-power Washington Conference useless; the unification of Korea now seemed far more remote than ever before. The American government, therefore, resolved to submit the Korean problem to the United Nations in September, 1947. In doing so, a new chapter was begun in the unhappy story of American postwar policy in Korea.

In retrospect, the failure of the Joint U.S.-Soviet Commission was not surprising because the Commission had tried from the beginning to achieve the impossible.[36] The aims of the two nations were diametrically opposed. The United States wanted to establish a united, democratic country

---

[35] Molotov to the Acting Secretary of State, September 4, 1947. *Department of State Bulletin*, September 28, 1947, p. 623.

[36] Benjamin Weems, "Behind the Korean Election," *Far Eastern Survey*, June 23, 1948, p. 144. Weems was then a member of the American staff in the Joint Commission.

whereas the Soviet Union was eager to set up a satellite in Asia.

The words "democracy," "reactionary," and "friendly" have different meanings in the two countries: had they not, it would have been less difficult to reach some agreements in the Joint Commission. The failure of negotiations, however, was due more basically to the reluctance of either nation to see the tiny peninsula dominated by the opposing power.

General Shtykov in the 1946 Joint Commission meeting unequivocally stated that the Soviet Union wished to see Korea become a "friendly nation so that in the future it will not become a base for an attack on the Soviet Union."[37] The United States, meanwhile, was equally determined to create a Korean government friendly to the West, or which —at the very least—would help to contain the expansion of communism. In a sense, both struggled to create a nation to serve their own national interests. Neither wished to give up its predominant role over half of the country in exchange for a united Korea that might end up in the hostile camp.

Although the American delegation wanted a government truly representative of the people—which, as America saw it, would mean a government oriented toward democracy in the Western sense of the word—concern for Koreans was actually secondary. Thus General Hodge suppressed the most influential forces in the nation because their aims conflicted with those of the military government. He later changed his policy to reconciliation of these anti-trusteeship groups, not because he felt that they represented the dominant will of the people, but because the new policy would better serve American interests. However, frequent switches of support from one group to another in accordance with a near-sighted view of national interest creates inconsistencies which, in turn, spawn political enemies. Hodge's unsuccess-

[37] *Source Materials on Korean Politics and Ideology*, comp. Donald G. Tewksbury (New York, 1950), pp. 77–78.

ful efforts to create a third force are an example of the result of such policies.

In the field of foreign affairs, national interest is considered the prime criterion for evaluating a situation, for determining the relative priorities of different goals, and for establishing courses of action.[38] By the time of the second conference of the Joint Commission, the possibility of reconciling the national interests of the two powers was small. The hope for "one world" evaporated soon after the end of World War II. By March, 1947, the American mood had changed drastically as events impressed both officials and the public with the futility of attempted cooperation with the Soviet Union. Perhaps it was inevitable, as John Foster Dulles later said, that the wartime coalition would break up after victory as had other grand alliances throughout history.[39]

In the spring of 1947, the foreign policy of the United States decisively changed direction. Instead of accommodation, George Kennan's "containment policy" was adopted. The country now began to develop economic commitments, defense treaties, and alliances. This shift first materialized in the dramatic enunciation of the Truman Doctrine on March 12, 1947. A "revolutionary land mark" in American foreign policy,[40] it made it clear that the United States intended to resist aggression by the Soviet Union. Then came Secretary Marshall's famed European Reconstruction Proposal, first set forth at Harvard.[41] Russia viewed these new policies not

---

[38] Charles O. Lerche, *Foreign Policy of the American People* (New York, 1958), p. 6. See also Hans J. Morgenthau, *In Defense of the National Interest* (New York, 1951).

[39] *The United States in World Affairs: 1945–47*, ed. John C. Campbell (New York, 1947), p. vii.

[40] William G. Carleton, *The Revolution in American Foreign Policy* (New York, 1957), p. 53.

[41] A full account of the origin and operation of the Marshall Plan is in Harry B. Price, *The Marshall Plan and Its Meaning* (Ithaca, 1955).

only as barriers to the spread of communism, but also as serious threats to herself.

The reaction was immediately apparent in Korea. Russia suddenly changed the conciliatory policy she had shown in the correspondence between Molotov and Marshall. It was exactly one month after the announcement of the Marshall Plan that the Soviet delegation to the Joint Conference suddenly reverted to its earlier position of non-consultation with the Anti-Trusteeship Committee. This is what led to the total impasse on Korea.

The failure of the Joint Commission is also an example of the insurmountable diplomatic difficulties in an era of bipolarization. After World War II, the reduction in the number of states able to play a major role in international politics seriously affected diplomatic flexibility, partly because of the disappearance of an effective balancer.[42] Thus, no nation was in a position to provide its good offices to break this Korean deadlock between the United States and the Soviet Union.

Undoubtedly, Russia did the most to contribute to the diplomatic impasse in Korea. Her policy of making the 38th parallel an unbreachable barrier was certainly the first and most decisive step on the path leading to the permanent division of the country. The ruthlessness of her occupation, the establishment of an unrepresentative government, and the playing of semantic games in the Joint Commission were governed by neither the spirit nor the letter of the wartime and postwar agreements between the Powers. The style with which Russia stole one half of Korea from the Koreans, and also from the rest of the world, sought to—and, in fact, did—deceive some as to her real intentions in Asia. The aggression that came later was to dispel such illusions.

---

[42] Hans J. Morgenthau, *Politics Among Nations: the Struggle for Power and Peace* (New York, 1955), pp. 322–362.

Part III

Era of Containment Policy

7

United States Policy in the United Nations

After the enunciation of the Truman Doctrine, it became apparent that America was unwilling to make further concessions merely for the sake of peace and the maintenance of great power unity. The United States now turned to a policy of "supporting free people who are resisting attempted subjugation by armed minorities or by outside pressures."[1] American policy was based on the thesis that "the main element of any United States policy toward the Soviet Union must be that of a long-term, patient, but firm and vigilant containment of Russian expansive tendencies."[2] In view of this overall change of United States policy toward the Soviet Union, Molotov's rejection of Lovett's seven-point Korean proposal was not surprising. The Joint Commission, created during the American-Soviet cooperative period, was doomed to failure in the wake of this change of overall U.S. policy, whatever may have been the wishes of the Korean people. This breakdown of the Joint Commission's efforts marked

[1] See the message of President Truman, delivered before a joint session of Congress on March 12, 1947. *Department of State Bulletin*, March 23, 1947, pp. 534–537.

[2] George F. Kennan, *American Diplomacy 1900–1950* (Chicago, 1951), p. 117. This article first appeared in the July 1947 issue of *Foreign Affairs* under the anonymous name "X." Kennan had already sent a similar long warning to the State Department from Moscow in February, 1946.

the end of many attempts to solve the Korean problem through direct negotiations, at the diplomatic or occupational command levels, between the United States and the Soviet Union.

REASON FOR THE APPEAL TO THE UNITED NATIONS

Since direct negotiations had failed to produce agreement, the United Nations seemed to America to be the only remaining avenue for the reunification of Korea. After receiving Molotov's refusal of the Lovett proposal, the State Department informed the Russian government on September 17, 1947,[3] that the United States intended to refer the entire problem to the forthcoming session of the General Assembly of the United Nations, since "bilateral negotiations have not advanced Korean independence" and "the Soviet government does not agree to discussions among the powers adhering to the Moscow Agreement." [4] The American note was delivered in Moscow only a few hours before Secretary Marshall announced the American decision in the course of an address to the General Assembly in New York.[5]

The request that "the problem of the independence of Korea" [6] be included on the agenda of the second session of the General Assembly was almost a complete surprise. In the course of general debate at the 82nd plenary meeting of the Assembly, Marshall explained the reasons that led to the request:

> It appears evident that further attempts to solve the Korean problem by means of bilateral negotiations will only serve to delay the establishment of an independent, united Korea.

---

[3] U.S. Department of State, *Korea's Independence* (Washington, 1947), pp. 10–11 and Appendix 12.

[4] Council on Foreign Relations, *Documents on American Foreign Relations* (New York, 1947), p. 119.

[5] *Survey of International Relations, 1947–48,* ed. Peter Calvocoressi (London, 1952), p. 315.

[6] U.N. Document, *A/BUR/85.*

> It is, therefore, the intention of the United States government to present the problem of Korean independence to this session of the General Assembly. Although we shall be prepared to submit suggestions as to how the early attainment of Korean independence might be effected, we believe that this is a matter which now requires the impartial judgment of the other members. We do not wish to have the inability of two powers to reach agreement delay any further the urgent and rightful claims of the Korean people to independence.[7]

In thus submitting the question, did American policy makers really believe that the United Nations could solve the problem? What were the motives behind transferring it to the international body?

It was the judgment of the Joint Chiefs of Staff that from the point of view of military security, "the United States has little strategic interest in maintaining the present troops and bases in Korea." [8] They felt that in the event of hostilities in the Far East, American forces in Korea would be "a military liability" and could not be maintained there without substantial reinforcement prior to the initiation of hostilities. They also agreed that the United States would most probably bypass the peninsula in the event of major Asian war. Neutralization of all hostile bases and forces in Korea by air action was seen to be "more feasible and less costly than large-scale ground operations." Finally, shortages of military manpower in many areas of American responsibility throughout the world necessitated the use of manpower in accordance with relative military priorities. They agreed that "in the light of the present severe shortages of manpower, the corps of two

---

[7] U.N. Document, *A/315.* Leland M. Goodrich, *Korea: A Study of United States Policy in the United Nations* (New York, 1956) is an excellent study of United States policy in the United Nations.

[8] Memorandum to the Secretary of State, September 25, 1947. See Harry S. Truman, *Years of Trial and Hope* (New York, 1956), pp. 325–326. At the time the J.C.S. consisted of Admiral Leahy, General Eisenhower, Admiral Nimitz, and General Spaatz.

divisions, totaling some 45,000 men, now maintained in South Korea could well be used elsewhere."

The United States also had financial problems in supporting its position in Korea and in maintaining the military government. From the beginning of the occupation through July, 1948, she had spent or obligated over 250 million dollars for economic assistance to South Korea.[9] The 1947 War Department aid appropriation for South Korea alone was over 70 million dollars, most of which went for such essential items as food, fertilizer, and agricultural supplies.[10] The United States had considered launching an economic rehabilitation plan for South Korea as early as March, 1947; but, pending the outcome of the second meeting of the U.S.-Soviet Joint Commission, the State Department withdrew its half billion dollar proposal. One factor was that the money-conscious Republican Congress was reluctant to provide more funds. Funds for economic rehabilitation were further delayed many months while the Korean question was being dealt with by the United Nations.

After World War II, South Korean economic separation from the North, and the removal of Japanese technicians, resulted in the disorganization of production, loss of technical and managerial skills, interruption of trade, and, finally, complete collapse of the Korean economy. Mr. Pauley, the President's personal representative on an economic fact-finding mission in 1946, had already reported that in order for Korea to be ready to go ahead industrially, the iron barrier at the 38th parallel must be dissolved and free commerce be established between the two parts of Korea.[11] American authorities in this field felt that "continued lack of

---

[9] U.S. Department of State, *Korea: 1945 to 1948,* Far Eastern series 28, released October, 1948, p. 39. This is a report on political developments and economic resources with selected documents.

[10] *Department of State Bulletin,* May 18, 1947, p. 962. This was a comparatively small amount compared with $186 million for Japan in the same period.

[11] *Department of State Bulletin,* August 4, 1946, p. 233.

progress toward a free and independent Korea, unless offset by an elaborate program of economic, political, and cultural rehabilitation, in all probability [would] result in such conditions, including violent disorder, as to make the position of the United States occupation forces untenable."[12] This opinion was also supported by General Wedemeyer, who headed a fact-finding mission to China and Korea in the summer of 1947. After meeting in Seoul with leaders representing a wide range of political viewpoints, the General reported to the President that it was not feasible to make South Korea self-sustaining, and that "if the United States elects to remain in South Korea, support of that area should be only on a relief basis."[13]

In addition to tactical military and financial considerations, another motive for the transfer to the United Nations was the extreme restiveness of the Korean people after the failure of the Joint Commission. The difficulties in maintaining either political or economic stability were manifoldly increased by the negative attitude of the military government toward any temporary Korean self-government. It was considered preferable that major political and economic decisions should be left for a united Korea to make for itself. At the same time, the strong suppressive measures against both the extreme left and right groups isolated the American command from any groups they could rely upon politically. The feud between Hodge and the Rhee-Kim faction, plus the frequent leftist revolts, created seemingly hopeless chaos. The leftists started rumors that the United States was building military bases in Korea and was shipping grain to Japan,[14] and these rumors fed the growing anti-American

---

[12] Report of the Joint Chiefs of Staff, *Years of Trial and Hope*, pp. 325–326.

[13] *Korea: Report to the President Submitted by Lt. Gen. A. C. Wedemeyer, September, 1947*, printed for the Committee on Armed Services, U.S. Senate (Washington, 1951), p. 6. See also Albert C. Wedemeyer, *Wedemeyer Reports* (New York, 1958), pp. 463–479.

[14] USAFIK (United States Armed Forces in Korea), *Summation of*

sentiment. Hodge once confided to General Clark that "if he were a civilian, free of military or government orders, he wouldn't stay on his job for a million dollars a year." [15]

What annoyed the Americans most was the North Korean development. The contrast with the South was really striking. The occupation authorities of the Soviet Union systematically carried out plans made well in advance. The Soviet-supported regime was entrusted with the task of organizing a militia, of winning the sympathies of the peasantry by land reform, and of purging pro-Japanese elements.[16] The regime set up by the Russians gave the impression, erroneous or not, that Korean leaders possessed more than nominal authority in the administration of their homeland.

Thus, in the presence of all these problems, the United States government faced the question of how to withdraw from an embarrassing situation without losing prestige in Korea and the rest of the world. The Joint Chiefs of Staff had already concluded that withdrawal of American forces from Korea would not impair the military position of the Far East Command unless, as a result, "the Soviets [would] establish military strength in South Korea capable of mounting an assault upon Japan." [17] However, unconditional withdrawal, leaving South Korea to be overrun by the Russian-trained North Korean army, would not only be a blow to American prestige, but would also contradict the Truman containment policy. It would appear highly inconsistent to retreat in Asia while resisting the Communists in Europe and the Middle East. Only if the United States established a

---

U.S. Army Military Government Activities in Korea, No. 14 (November, 1946), p. 15.

15 Mark W. Clark, *From the Danube to the Yalu* (New York, 1954), p. 15.

16 For one of the best analyses for this period, see U.S. Department of State, *North Korea: A Case Study in the Techniques of Takeover* (Washington, 1961); see also *North Korea Today,* ed. Robert A. Scalapino (New York, 1963), pp. 17–19.

17 *Years of Trial and Hope, loc. cit.*

strong anti-Communist government in Korea before withdrawing its forces would the retreat seem less obvious. General Wedemeyer recommended to Truman, therefore, that America should assist the South Koreans in the building and training of a native defense force before our U.S. troops were withdrawn.[18]

General Hodge was also very much interested, from the beginning of the occupation, in establishing a Korean army, not only to relieve American troops of many details in handling Korean security, but also to prepare for a future Korean government.[19] When the Department of the Army requested General MacArthur's view on the subject, he turned to Hodge. The latter replied that a South Korean army of six divisions, complete with headquarters and service troops, could, if equipped and trained by the United States, be readied within one year. But MacArthur then believed that the establishment of such an army should be deferred until the course to be designated by the United Nations was clear.[20] It is notable, however, that the organization of a Korean army was actively discussed at this time. Though Syngman Rhee's proposal of December, 1946, for an independent South Korea that could contain Communist expansion had been given a cold shoulder,[21] the United States now, only one year later, turned to exactly what he had proposed.

It is doubtful that the planners of American policy genu-

---

18 *Wedemeyer Reports,* pp. 477–479.

19 U.S. Department of the Army, "History of the American Military Advisory Groups in Korea," MS, pt. 1, p. 29. Hereafter cited as *KMAG History.* This manuscript was later published with the title *Military Advisors in Korea: KMAG in Peace and War* (Washington, 1962).

20 *Ibid.*

21 Robert T. Oliver, *Syngman Rhee: The Man Behind the Myth* (New York, 1954), p. 232. Rhee's major points were: (1) establishment of a South Korean government; (2) admission of this government to the United Nations; and (3) retention of U.S. troops in Korea until the withdrawal of Russian forces from the North. For another point of view, see Richard C. Allen, *Korea's Syngman Rhee: An Unauthorized Portrait* (Tokyo, 1960), pp. 88–89.

inely hoped to attain a unified, democratic Korean government through the United Nations. The Soviet Union was certainly expected to veto American moves in the Security Council: the Russian representative had already expressed strong objections to the United States policy. Furthermore, the functions and powers of the General Assembly of the United Nations were limited to investigation, discussion, and recommendation.[22] Under the Charter, recommendations have no legal binding force, though they may exert moral pressure upon the members who oppose them.[23] Consequently, the United States probably only sought to transfer to the world body and its members some of the responsibility that she had hitherto assumed alone. Other purposes may have been: (1) the desire to win international sympathy by dramatizing the uncooperative Soviet attitude; (2) the need to give moral support to those South Koreans who were struggling against Communist domination; and (3) the need to maintain the precarious balance of power in the Far East by containing Soviet expansion.

The record of the United Nations reveals that the General Assembly has, in most cases, adopted the resolutions that have been approved or introduced by the United States. During its first nine sessions, only three resolutions on major political questions were adopted over a negative American vote.[24] Additionally, a favorable Assembly vote would embarrass Russia, and assist the United States to establish a strong anti-communist government in South Korea with the resultant support of the international organization.[25]

---

[22] See Articles 10–17 of the United Nations Charter. Leland M. Goodrich and Edward Hambro, *Charter of the United Nations: Commentary and Documents* (Boston, 1949), pp. 150–198.

[23] Amry Vandenbosch and Willard N. Hogan, *The United Nations* (New York, 1952), pp. 111–123.

[24] Robert E. Riggs, *Politics in the United Nations: A Study of United States Influence in the General Assembly* (Urbana, 1958), p. 163.

[25] This view was suggested by Professor Goodrich in *Korea: A Study of U.S. Policy in the United Nations,* pp. 40–41.

THE UNITED NATIONS LOOKS AT THE KOREAN QUESTION

The immediate reaction of the Soviet Union to the inclusion of "The Problem of the Independence of Korea" in the agenda was made public through the statement of Andrei Vyshinsky at the 84th plenary meeting. He charged that Marshall's proposal was a direct violation of the Moscow Agreement and an attempt to cover up America's unilateral and entirely unjustified action, asserting that the Russian government would not agree to such a violation.[26] But despite his furious opposition, the General Assembly voted on September 23, 1947, to place the Korean question before its First Committee for consideration and report.

During the course of debate in both the General and First Committees, the Soviet delegate used distinctly different but interrelated tactics. One was to debate the legality of the American proposal. The other, aimed at regaining the diplomatic initiative, was to propose the immediate withdrawal of occupation forces from both zones. After it became evident that these two moves were not effective, Vyshinsky sought to find some pretext to justify his position. That purpose was served by the issue of the participation of Korean representatives in the General Assembly debates. A detailed discussion of the Russian tactics follows.

1. *Legality of the United States Proposal*

The Soviet delegation initially contended in the General Committee that the United States should assume the blame for the situation that had arisen in the Joint Commission, as it was the United States which had refused to fulfill the obligation that had been assumed under the Moscow Agreement.[27] Therefore, if the American government was dissat-

[26] U.N. *Official Document, Verbatim Record, Second Session,* 1947, the Plenary Meeting, Vol. 1, p. 91.

[27] Statement by Vyshinsky at the 90th and 91st plenary meetings of

isfied with the results of the Commission, the procedure should be to place the question before the governments of the other three powers concerned, namely the Soviet Union, the United Kingdom, and China. The Russians claimed that, even though Articles 10 and 11 of the U.N. Charter gave the General Assembly ample power to discuss any questions relating to the maintenance of international peace and security, it was clear from paragraph 2 of Article 35 that questions like that raised on Korea could not—because of the existence of an international agreement—be a matter for Assembly review.[28] It further cited Article 107,[29] which limits the power of the United Nations in matters which resulted directly from the war. The six members of the Soviet bloc shared this opinion and argued that the primary task of the United Nations is to maintain international peace and security, and that it should not deal with the disposition of territories formerly occupied by an enemy state.[30]

The United States countered that one of the most fundamental principles upon which the United Nations was founded is expressed in the second paragraph of Article 1 of the Charter. She urged her fellow delegates to keep their sights "lifted to these high points, and not to undertake . . . to discuss things on a legalistic basis, or in any other way that will bar the United Nations from performing at least the function of discussing a proposition that concerns a small country which is a victim of conditions."[31] It was argued that Article 107 did not apply to the question raised,

---

the General Assembly, U.N. *Official Document, Verbatim Record, Second Session,* 1947, the Plenary Meeting, Vol. 1, p. 276.

[28] *Ibid.*

[29] Article 107 of the Charter reads: "Nothing in the present Charter shall invalidate or preclude action, in relation to any state which during the Second World War had been an enemy of any signatory to the present Charter, taken or authorized as a result of that war by the governments."

[30] U.N. Document, *A/C.I/195* and *218.*

[31] U.N. *Official Document, Verbatim Record, Second Session,* 1947, the Plenary Meeting, Vol. 1, p. 286.

as Korea was not an enemy state. Article 14 was also invoked to justify consideration by the General Assembly.

Mr. Evatt, the delegate from Australia, asserted that Articles 11 (2)[32] and 14 permitted the Assembly to consider the question, and that Article 107 did not preclude consideration, as the General Assembly had the necessary competence to recommend, if not to carry out, measures.[33] Since the Allied Powers had been unable to conclude peace treaties speedily, it fell to the United Nations to deal with the question. "Nevertheless," he asserted, "such questions should only be brought before the General Assembly as a last resort, because its function was not to intervene in the preparation of peace treaties, but to see that peace was maintained once the treaties had been signed." [34]

The General Assembly is empowered by Article 14 to recommend measures for the peaceful adjustment of any situation which results from dissatisfaction with a treaty, or from otherwise-caused conflict of interests, when such dissatisfaction is deemed likely to impair either the general welfare or friendly relations among nations. The specific reference to the Charter makes it clear that under this Article the Assembly may deal with any alleged violation of principles, such as that of "equal rights and self-determination of peoples." [35] Hans Kelsen has pointed out that since Korea was not an

---

[32] Article 11 (2) reads: "The General Assembly may discuss any questions relating to the maintenance of international peace and security brought before it by any member of the United Nations, or by the Security Council, or by a state which is not a member of the United Nations in accordance with Article 35, paragraph 2, and except as provided in Article 12, may make recommendations with regard to any such question to the state or states concerned or to the Security Council or to both. Any such question on which action is necessary shall be referred to the Security Council by the General Assembly either before or after discussion."

[33] U.N. Document, *A/C.I/SR. 87.*

[34] See *Cases on United Nations Law,* ed. Louis B. Sohn (Brooklyn, 1956), p. 507.

[35] Goodrich and Hambro, *Charter of the United Nations,* p. 179.

enemy state, it is doubtful whether Article 107 applied at all. "But even if Korea was considered to be part of the territory of a former enemy state," he writes, "it could hardly be argued that Article 107 excludes the competence of the General Assembly to discuss the problem of the independence of Korea and make recommendations in this respect, provided that this problem is a question within the scope of the Charter."[36]

Since the Charter states that the purpose of the United Nations is to maintain and restore international peace and security by preventive and repressive measures (Preamble, Articles 1 and 2), there is hardly any international matter which the Assembly is not empowered to discuss, provided it does not violate domestic jurisdiction as provided in Article 2 (7).

The position taken by the General Assembly was that Article 107 was permissive, and did not bar action by the international body.[37] In the General Committee, the representatives of Poland and Russia opposed the inclusion of the Korean question in the agenda, while the representatives of China, Syria, and the United Kingdom supported the request of the American delegation. By a vote of 12 to 2, the General Committee recommended inclusion, and the General Assembly considered the recommendation on September 23. In turn, the General Assembly decided by a vote of 41 to 6, with 7 abstentions (one delegation being absent), to adopt the recommendation, and referred the Korean question to the First Committee for consideration and report.[38]

---

36 Hans Kelsen, *The Law of the United Nations: A Critical Analysis of Its Fundamental Problems* (New York, 1950), p. 199.

37 U.N. Document, *A/C.I/SR. 87* and *A/C.I/SR. 88*.

38 *Opposed:* Byelorussia Soviet Republic, Czechoslovakia, Poland, Ukrainian Soviet Republic, Union of Soviet Socialist Republics, Yugoslavia. *Abstained:* Afghanistan, Egypt, Ethiopia, Iraq, Lebanon, Saudi Arabia, Syria. *Absent:* Bolivia. U.N. *Official Document, Verbatim Record, Second Session,* 1947, the Plenary Meeting, Vol. 1, p. 299.

2. *Withdrawal of the Occupation Forces*

After this overwhelming defeat, the Soviet Union showed little interest in legal technicalities. In the First Committee debate their arguments were mainly based upon two issues: the immediate simultaneous withdrawal of the occupation forces from the two zones, and the participation of Korean representatives in the General Assembly's debate. They announced to the First Committee that they would participate in the discussion, even though they considered the situation a "regretful affair." Russia then submitted a counterproposal in order to regain diplomatic initiative in the Korean issue.

On September 26, three days after the General Assembly vote, the Russian delegation to the Joint U.S.-Soviet Commission in Seoul offered a substitute proposal, recommending that all foreign occupation troops in Korea be withdrawn simultaneously at the beginning of 1948, thus permitting the Koreans to organize their own government without outside interference.[39] The American delegation to the Commission contended that such a proposal was outside the authority delegated to the Commission.[40] Consequently Molotov amplified the proposal in a letter to Marshall (October 9, 1947), charging that the Americans did not wish to continue the work of the Commission and pressing for a reply.[41]

This Soviet proposal was designed to embarrass both the American military government and the Korean rightist groups, since it appeared to be a popular solution to the entire question. For Rhee, it was a real surprise. The right had long advocated evacuating foreign troops, as well as abandoning trusteeship plans, so that they might themselves unify the nation. The rightists were now forced either to

---

[39] *New York Times,* September 27, 1947; *Soviet News,* October 2, 1947.

[40] *Korea: 1945 to 1948,* p. 6.

[41] *Ibid.,* pp. 48–49.

stand firmly by their own word, or to face a situation in which South Korea would almost certainly be overwhelmed by the well-trained North Korean army working with the leftist elements of South Korea.

The Americans were well aware that withdrawal of American forces at this stage would mean the end of hopes for a Western-oriented, democratic South Korea. Even though the Joint Chiefs of Staff had previously recommended the withdrawal of troops, they did not mean that the United States should allow the creation of another Soviet satellite state. As Hodge had reported, it would take at least one year to build the six divisions of the South Korean army. The United States needed time. In this, America and Rhee were in complete agreement.

As a realist, Rhee abruptly changed his appeal for the withdrawal of foreign troops. He declared that while Russian troops should be withdrawn immediately, either the North Korean army should be disarmed, or else the American forces should remain until they had trained and equipped an adequate South Korean army.[42] The rightist newspapers charged that premature withdrawal of American forces would mean certain civil war in Korea, and that South Korea would "be promptly overrun by well-trained and well-equipped Communist forces." Meanwhile, the left-wing papers asserted that the Soviet proposal freed the Korean people from international strategy and gave them an opportunity to establish their own democratic government.[43] A poll made by the Korean Public Opinion Association shows that Russia succeeded in temporarily gaining favor for herself by this diplomatic gesture. The poll indicated that 57 percent of the participants favored the Soviet proposal.[44]

---

[42] *New York Times,* September 28 and October 1, 1947.

[43] *Ibid.* For the opinions of the left and the right, see *Dong-A Ilbo,* September 27 through October 1, 1947.

[44] Most Koreans also did not believe that the United Nations would

In order to counter this Russian strategy, the American representative on October 17 submitted a draft resolution in the First Committee of the General Assembly. It proposed that elections be held by the occupying powers in their respective zones not later than March 31, 1948; and that the election be supervised by a United Nations Temporary Commission reporting to the General Assembly. Those elected would constitute a National Assembly for Korea, which in turn should form a government that would establish its own security force before the withdrawal of occupation forces in accordance with an arrangement between the National Government and the occupying power. Representation in the National Assembly should be on the basis of population; South Korea would thus be assured roughly two-thirds of the total number of representatives. The United States draft resolution conspicuously stated as its purpose "that the national independence of Korea should be reestablished and all occupying forces should be withdrawn from Korea at the earliest practicable date." [45]

The next day, Acting Secretary of State Lovett replied to Molotov and elucidated the American position. He stated that "in the opinion of the United States Government the question of withdrawal of occupation forces from Korea must be considered an integral part of the solution of that problem" [46]—that problem being the establishment of the independent unified government.

The First Committee began considering the Korean question at its 87th meeting on October 28, 1947. Opening the debate, John Foster Dulles, as the American representative, reviewed again the events that had led up to the Korean

---

succeed in achieving unification of the country. A public opinion poll indicated that 83 percent of the participants voted "no," while 17 percent voted "yes." USAFIK, *South Korean Interim Government Activities,* November, 1947, p. 248. This is the continuation of *Summation* in different title.

[45] U.N. Document, *A/C.I/218.*

[46] *Korea: 1945–1948,* p. 50.

situation and prompted the United States to submit the problem to the General Assembly. He reiterated that his country felt the withdrawal of troops must be considered "as part of the general problem of the establishment of an independent government for the whole of Korea." [47] He emphasized that "the United States was anxious to withdraw its troops from Korea, but withdrawal must be subsequent to the establishment of machinery for effecting the transition from the present state of affairs to the formation of a single government representing the Korean people." [48] Dulles also pointed out that the Soviet proposal was inadequate, since it made no provision for the government that would follow the withdrawal of troops. It would be unrealistic to suppose that without such machinery Korea could, in reality, peacefully become an independent and unified nation. Were the American draft resolution adopted, the Korean people would be able to elect a stable government.

Andrei Gromyko, the Soviet representative, charged that it was the United States that had prevented the creation of a democratic Korean government as provided by the Moscow Agreement.[49] He stated that America sought to direct the blame "from the head of a sick person," as a Russian proverb put it, "to the head of a healthy one." In the opinion of the Soviet delegation, Korea could not establish its government freely until after the complete withdrawal of foreign troops.

Gromyko then submitted his draft resolution, proposing that the General Assembly recommend to the governments of the United States and the Soviet Union the simultaneous withdrawal of their troops from Southern and Northern Korea at the beginning of 1948, thereby affording the Korean people an opportunity to establish their own national

---

[47] U.N. Document, *A/C.I/195* and *A/C.I/218.*

[48] U.N. Document, *Official Record, First Committee of the General Assembly, Second Session,* 1947, pp. 248–250.

[49] *Ibid.,* pp. 251–252.

government.[50] This, he said, would provide the wisest and simplest settlement and would exclude the possibility of any outside influence. He also proposed that representatives of the Korean people be invited to participate in the consideration of the question.[51]

The Russian draft resolution was rejected in the First Committee by a vote of 20 to 6, with 7 abstentions. At the plenary session of the General Assembly on November 14, this resolution was again rejected, 34 to 7, with 16 abstentions.

3. *Participation of Korean Representatives*

At the 87th meeting of the First Committee, the Russians orally proposed that, since the Korean question could not be fairly resolved without the participation of the indigenous population, the First Committee should invite elected representatives of the Korean people from the North and South.[52] The issue of Korean representation caused heated discussions between the Soviet bloc and the Western nations both in this Committee and in the plenary meetings of the General Assembly. Of course, the idea of having Koreans take part in determining their future could not easily be attacked. There was a precedent in the United Nations: in the Palestine question, the General Assembly had by a large majority decided to hear non-governmental representatives of that country. Virtually all speakers in the subsequent discussions in the Political Committee predictably agreed that Koreans should participate in any United Nations consideration of their problems.

In the 89th meeting of the First Committee, Gromyko

---

[50] U.N. Document, *A/C.1/229.*

[51] *Ibid.* These proposals were advanced orally by Gromyko at the 87th meeting of the First Committee, and then submitted in writing at the 89th meeting.

[52] *Ibid.*

again emphasized that the Soviet Union considered the question of participation one of the main issues which should be studied carefully. He pointed out that the United Nations had already recognized that, when dealing with questions involving nonmember states, representatives of their people should be heard. The Korean problem, he asserted, was similar to the Palestine question in that respect; thus he could not understand why it was impossible to hear Korean representatives.[53]

Dulles answered this logic with great diplomatic skill. He conceded that his delegation was completely agreed that consultation with true representatives of the Korean people was necessary. Then he argued that the Russians had not indicated any method of finding true representatives, and pointed out that both countries had earlier been unable to agree on "true representatives" in the Joint Commission. In view of the fact that some 500 political and social organizations had so far claimed to represent some part of the Korean populace, it would be impossible for the General Assembly or the First Committee to solve the problem in New York.[54]

Therefore, while accepting the principle of the proposal, Dulles submitted an amendment to the second Soviet draft resolution, suggesting that a United Nations Temporary Commission on the Korean question be established to facilitate and expedite the participation question and to assure that Korean representatives were in fact duly elected by the people, and not appointed by the military authorities in Korea. He stated further that the Commission ought "to be present in Korea with the right to travel, observe, and consult throughout Korea,"[55] emphasizing once more that it was impossible to decide in the First Committee who truly represented Korea. The delegates of China, the United King-

[53] U.N. Document, *A/C.I/195* and *A/C.I/218.*

[54] U.N. *Official Record, First Committee of the General Assembly, Second Session,* 1947, pp. 260–261.

[55] U.N. Document, *A/C.I/230.*

dom, Australia, Haiti, Belgium, the Dominican Republic, and El Salvador supported the United States amendment.[56]

Gromyko, of course, opposed it, asserting that it tried to introduce into the procedural discussion a question of substance. It was the view of the Soviet delegation that the question, including the suggestion of a commission, should be decided upon in the presence of Korean representatives. In his view, the United States amendment was not properly an amendment at all, but the original American proposal in modified form, and should be dealt with only after the procedural question had been considered.[57] He then asked the United States to withdraw the amendment.

Vladimir Popovic, delegate of Yugoslavia, also contended that the American amendment would lead to the postponement of Korean unification. A dangerous precedent would be set, he maintained, by having a United Nations Commission participate in elections which were the right of the Korean people alone.[58] Mr. Evatt of Australia, on the other hand, contended that it was unnecessary for Koreans to be present at United Nations discussions, since they would naturally agree with the objective of a free, independent, and unified state. Then he asserted that the American proposal would set up the desirable machinery.

After a long wrangle over procedure, the First Committee on October 30 approved the American amendment and rejected the original draft proposal of the Soviets. When the Committee rejected the Soviet proposal by a vote of 35 to 6 with 10 abstentions, Gromyko stated that if a United Nations Temporary Commission on Korea were set up after the General Assembly had considered the question without Korean representatives, Russia would not participate in the work of the Commission. He then suggested that the First

[56] *Yearbook of the United Nations*, 1947, p. 84.

[57] U.N. Document, *A/C.I/195* and *A/C.I/218*.

[58] U.N. *Official Record, First Committee of the General Assembly, Second Session*, 1947, pp. 275–279.

Committee postpone further consideration of the Korean question, but was overwhelmingly defeated.[59]

RESOLUTION OF THE GENERAL ASSEMBLY

At the 92nd meeting of the First Committee on November 4, Dulles introduced the American revised draft resolution,[60] taking into account the resolution adopted by the First Committee at its 91st meeting, and incorporating procedural suggestions made by several delegations, particularly India's. The resolution now included the Chinese and Indian motions that elections might be held on a national, not necessarily a zonal, basis. It also stated that elections should take place not later than March 31, 1948.

On November 5, the Political Committee finally adopted the American resolution as a whole, by a vote of 46 to 0, with 4 abstentions. The representatives of Russia, the Ukraine, Poland, Byelorussia, Czechoslovakia, and Yugoslavia did not take part in the voting because they felt that the absence of Korean representatives was a contravention of the provisions of the Charter and the right of self-determination of peoples.[61]

Immediately after this, Dulles suggested that the newly created Temporary Commission be composed of representatives from Australia, Canada, China, El Salvador, France, India, the Philippines, Syria, and the Ukrainian Soviet Socialist Republic. In answer, Mr. Manuilsky, the representative of the Ukraine, declared his refusal to participate because of the representation problem. It would have been better, he suggested, if the Commission were composed of neutral persons, and not mostly of representatives favoring United States policy. Later, Gromyko reiterated his denunciation, charging that the United Nations Commission was

---

[59] Vote: 38 to 6, with 12 abstentions. *Ibid.*, pp. 281–282.

[60] U.N. Document, *A/C.I/218/Rev. 1.*

[61] U.N. *Official Record, First Committee of the General Assembly, Second Session,* 1947, p. 305.

simply a screen to conceal American unilateral activities meant to convert Korea into "an American colony." [62] At the 112th plenary meeting, he resubmitted the Soviet proposal, previously rejected by the First Committee, for simultaneous withdrawal of foreign troops.

On November 14, the General Assembly adopted the American draft resolution (already adopted and recommended by the First Committee) by a vote of 43 to 9, with 6 abstentions. The Soviet bloc did not participate in the voting. The Assembly then rejected the Soviet proposal, 34 to 7, with 6 abstentions. At the same time, it recommended that a Temporary Commission on Korea, consisting of representatives of Australia, Canada, China, El Salvador, France, India, the Philippines, Syria, and the Ukrainian S.S.R., be created to facilitate and expedite fulfilment of the program laid down in the resolution.[63]

The adopted resolution advised that elections be held on the basis of adult suffrage and by secret ballot with a system of proportional representation from the population. The Commission was to supervise the election. Those elected would make up a Constitutional Assembly, which would establish a Korean National Assembly to assume civil and military functions throughout Korea and arrange with the occupying powers the complete withdrawal of their armed forces within 90 days, if possible. Then the Temporary Commission would report its conclusions to the General Assembly and consult with the Interim Committee established by the 1947 Assembly. The resolution called upon members to

---

[62] U.N. *Official Document, Verbatim Record of General Assembly, Second Session,* 1947, the Plenary Meeting, Vol. II, p. 829. Mr. Gromyko also charged that "politically, South Korea is being turned into a center of reaction in Eastern Asia. Territorially, Korea is apparently regarded as a kind of United States base." *Ibid.* See also the similar charge in *Izvestia,* October 2, 1947, from *Soviet Press Translations,* University of Washington, December 15, 1947, pp. 290–291.

[63] U.N. *Official Record, Second Session, General Assembly Resolution 112 (11)*, pp. 16–18.

afford all assistance to the Commission and to refrain from interfering in Korea's internal affairs.

The transfer of the Korean issue to the international forum was a great diplomatic victory for the United States. The General Assembly was used as a suitable instrument for mobilizing political and psychological world opinion. Though the recommendations of the Assembly were not legally binding, they undoubtedly exerted great pressure on the Soviet Union to temper her ambitions.

Soviet diplomacy suffered a complete defeat: the Assembly recommended almost the same actions as those proposed by Lovett in his correspondence with Molotov, differing only in that elections were to be on a national, not zonal, basis. Gromyko was consistently supported only by the six delegations of the Soviet bloc, recruiting just one country—Egypt—in the final vote for its own draft resolution. Dulles, on the other hand, was diplomatically shrewd in gaining cooperation from other countries. He wisely accepted most of the suggestions made by friendly nations so that his resolution would recruit the widest possible support from non-Communist groups. He got most of the Middle Eastern countries to abstain from much of the voting, and secured the votes of Great Britain, France, Canada, Australia, China, and most of the Latin American countries.

The American viewpoint had thus prevailed in the United Nations, but the Russian decision to boycott the Assembly resolution was to make this victory a hollow one. The achievement of the aim of the world body—a unified, independent, democratic Korea—remained remote so long as Russia refused to help implement the resolution. Since American policy makers certainly did not contemplate implementing the program in North Korea by means of armed force, it was quite possible that behind their move there was only, at best, a naive hope that the Kremlin would yield in some way to United Nations pressure. When subsequent Soviet statements made it clear that it would not, the only alternatives appeared to be either an early abandonment of the project, or the continuation of a modified arrangement that would apply to South Korea alone.

In these circumstances, it was highly questionable that the transfer of the Korean issue at this time to the United Nations was especially apt. If there were still some room for discussion at bilateral or four-power levels, and if all possible methods for conciliation were not yet exhausted, it was too early to present the issue to the international body. As one critic said, "the United States could, with some justification, be accused of giving the United Nations a hot potato, of passing to the international organization a responsibility which the latter was far too weak to assume, and which the United States was unwilling to continue to carry." [64] Sadly, this untimely action actually accelerated the establishment of two separate Korean governments, thus perpetuating the division of Korea.

[64] *Korea: A Study of U.S. Policy in the United Nations,* p. 41.

8

The Role of UNTCOK and Unification Efforts by Korean Leaders

The United States had won an important victory in the United Nations by securing passage of its draft resolution for Korean unification despite vehement opposition from the Soviet Union. Yet a major obstacle remained. The resolution had little prospect of realization because the Soviet delegation emphatically declared that Russia would not cooperate with the United Nations Temporary Commission on Korea (UNTCOK). Nevertheless, within two months after the Assembly's decision on November 14, 1947, the Temporary Commission began its work in Seoul.

UNTCOK IN SEOUL

The UNTCOK held its first meeting in Seoul on January 12, 1948, with representatives from Australia, Canada, China, El Salvador, France, India, the Philippines, and Syria; [1] only the Ukrainian representative was not present.

To clarify its mission to the Korean people, the Commission first adopted a resolution that "every opportunity be taken to make it clear that the sphere of this Commission is

[1] For the name of the UNTCOK representatives, see U.N. Document, *A/575*, p. 6.

the whole of Korea and not merely a section of Korea."[2] All agreed that elections must be conducted by the occupation authorities, with UNTCOK limiting its activities to "inquiring, advising, and informing." They realized that it was utterly impossible for themselves alone to exercise responsibility for the elections.[3]

On January 15 Dr. Kumara P. S. Menon of India, the elected Chairman of the Commission, informed the military commander in both zones of his wish to pay them immediate courtesy calls.[4] Hodge politely received him and promised close cooperation, but the letter to the Soviet commander in Pyongyang was not accepted.[5] Gromyko, contacted in the U.N., responded only with a reminder of "the negative attitude taken by the Soviet government" during the second session of the General Assembly toward the establishment of the Commission.[6]

The Soviet Union stood firm on its announced policy of antipathy toward the Commission. This was obviously based on the confidence that without Soviet cooperation, UNTCOK would fail. Russia had everything to gain by boycott. The United States would easily be placed in an embarrassing position should UNTCOK decide to return to the General Assembly, because the Russians' negative attitude would seem to make the resolution meaningless and a general election throughout Korea impossible.

When it became clear that the Commission would not be able to execute its program in North Korea,[7] sharp differ-

---

[2] For an excellent analysis of the works of the Commission in Korea, see Leon Gordenker, *The United Nations and the Peaceful Unification of Korea* (Hague, 1959).

[3] U.N. Document, *A/575, add. 1,* pp. 37–39.

[4] U.N. Document, *A/575, add. 1,* p. 6.

[5] First part of the Report of the United Nations Temporary Commission on Korea, 1948, Vol. 11-Annex 1-VIII, U.N. Document, *A/575 add. 1,* p. 8.

[6] U.N. Document, *A/AC.18/23.*

[7] U.N. *Official Record, First Committee of the General Assembly, Second Session,* 1947, p. 335.

ences arose among members as to the best course to follow. The representatives of China, the Philippines, and El Salvador thought it would be better to hold an election in the area accessible to the Commission and establish a separate and independent State in South Korea;[8] whereas the representatives of Australia, Canada, India, and Syria believed such a step might harden and perpetuate the existing antagonism and eventually result in the permanent division of the country.[9] Mr. Jean Paul-Boncour, the French representative, though uncommitted, generally supported the former group. In principle, however, all members of UNTCOK agreed that "they must go on functioning as long as there is a shred of hope" that a unified government of Korea could be established with general goodwill. They also agreed that a separate government in South Korea could not be a national government as defined in the resolution of the General Assembly.

On February 6, the Commisson finally resolved to consult with the Interim Committee of the General Assembly. They agreed to send Menon and Dr. Victor Hoo, Secretary General of the Commission, with the following questions:

> (1) Is it open to or incumbent upon the Commission, under the terms of the General Assembly resolution of November 14, 1947, and in the light of development in the situation with respect to Korea since that date, to implement the programme as outlined in resolution II in that part of Korea which is occupied by the armed forces of the United States of America?
>
> (2) If not, (a) should the Commission observe the election of Korean representatives to take part in the consideration of the Korean question, as outlined in resolution I of 14 November, 1947, provided that it had determined that elections can be held in a free atmosphere? and (b) should the Commission consider such other measures as may be possi-

[8] For a summary of views, see Menon's report to the Interim Committee, U.N. Document, *A/AC. 18/28*, pp. 69–72.

[9] *Ibid.*

ble and advisable with a view to the attainment of its objectives? [10]

RESOLUTION OF THE LITTLE ASSEMBLY

According to the Soviet Union, the action of UNTCOK was that of "an illegal Commission seeking instructions from an illegal Committee." [11] The creation of the Little Assembly (Interim Committee) as a subsidiary organ of the General Assembly under Article 22 of the U.N. Charter was viewed by the Soviet delegation as an attempt to circumvent the Security Council, to derogate from the Council's power and thus to nullify the unanimity rule.[12] Thus, when the report of the Commission was brought up in the Little Assembly, the United States was placed in a delicate position, both because this body had been established at the second session of the Assembly against the strong opposition of the Soviet bloc, and because certain friendly nations, such as Canada and Australia, had expressed their disagreement with the American position on the establishment of a separate government in South Korea.

As the United States saw it, if the Interim Committee did not consult with the Commission, there would not only be a major American setback in the world forum, but there would also inevitably be created a power vacuum in this traditionally shadowy area of Asia. Furthermore, if the United States failed to receive U.N. support, she had to choose either an undesirable prolongation of the military occupation or abandon her commitment entirely, allowing the Soviet Union to fill the vacuum. This would, in effect, permit Soviet-inspired communism to take over the whole country. In this situation, America felt it was imperative to transfer her share of responsibility in Korea to the international organization.

[10] U.N. Document, *A/AC. 18/27.*

[11] *Survey of International Affairs: 1947–48,* ed. Peter Calvocoressi (London, 1952), p. 319.

[12] See the statements by Vyshinsky on October 14 and November 6, 1947, U.N. Document, *A/C.1/SR.74,* pp. 133–137.

For the United Nations, the adoption of UNTCOK's suggestions by the Interim Committee would mark a turning point in its Korean activities. Since the Soviet Union consistently viewed the Commission as an instrument of American policy, adoption would be viewed as a definite and final choice between the American and Russian approaches to the problem.[13] Additionally, it would also strengthen the impression that the United Nations was acting as a tool of American policy by bearing the burden of supervising the election: such an impression would only perpetuate the division of the country. To go one step further, the United Nations might, as the Australian representative hinted, be placed in "the difficult position of having either to actively support or else to renounce all responsibility for the government it had established in case the North Korean regime resorted to armed aggression for the unification of Korea." [14]

On February 19, the first of six meetings with the Interim Committee was devoted to consideration of the Korean question.[15] Menon presented a detailed survey of the Korean political situation and of the views of the representatives in UNTCOK. He then outlined three alternatives that, in view of the "negative attitude" of the Soviet Union, seemed to be open.

As the first alternative, the Commission could continue with the program outlined in resolution II in South Korea alone: "that is to say, to observe elections, which will necessarily be confined to South Korea; to facilitate the establishment of a government in South Korea, to be recognized as the national government of Korea." The second alternative was to observe elections for the limited purpose mentioned in resolution I, that is, for the purpose of consultation with elected representatives of the people. As a third alternative,

---

[13] Leland M. Goodrich, *Korea: A Study of U.S. Policy in the United Nations* (New York, 1956), p. 49.

[14] U.N. Document, *A/AC. 18/SR.9.*

[15] U.N. Document, *A/583.*

he suggested that the Commission could explore or at least take note of other possibilities of establishing the national independence of Korea, such as a meeting of the leaders of the North and South.[16] Since the General Assembly's resolution had no legal force, these three alternatives appeared to be the only solutions for UNTCOK, even though none of the three methods ensured the unification of Korea.

The position of the United States was eloquently presented by Dr. Philip C. Jessup in the Interim Committee debate. He argued that if existing conditions made general elections for a national government impossible, the United Nations should, nevertheless, hold elections in South Korea alone. He emphatically objected to elections for establishing a "purely consultative body" on the grounds that it would be contrary to the spirit and letter of the Assembly's resolution.[17] He then submitted a draft resolution to this effect.[18]

Many friendly nations, however, did not support this view, maintaining that this action would actually result in permanent division and two hostile governments. The Australian delegation favored holding elections for consultation purpose only,[19] whereas others, such as Mr. Pearson of Canada, opposed holding any election because it could not be brought within the terms of the General Assembly's resolution.[20] Some nations, such as Sweden and Norway, favored calling a special session of the General Assembly, or appealing for new negotiations between the two occupation powers.

Nevertheless, the draft proposal of the United States was supported by 31 nations and opposed by 2, with 11 abstentions; the Soviet bloc boycotted the meeting and did not participate in the voting.[21] This record clearly showed a feeling

[16] U.N. Document, *A/AC. 18/28.*
[17] U.N. Document, *A/AC. 18/SR.6*, p. 6 (February 26, 1948).
[18] U.N. Document, *A/AC. 18/31.*
[19] U.N. Document, *A/AC. 18/SR.9.*
[20] *Ibid.*
[21] *Opposed:* Canada and Australia. *Abstained:* Afghanistan, Colom-

of hesitation among the members of the Little Assembly. They felt it was a mistake to adopt a course which might not only perpetuate the division of Korea, but also eventually endanger world peace. In fact, the two negative votes were cast by members of UNTCOK who formerly favored United States policy; and three Latin American and three Scandinavian countries that customarily voted for American proposals on Korea conspicuously abstained from voting. It was clear that future difficulties could arise in the execution of the resolution by the Commission. Nonetheless, on February 26, 1948, the Little Assembly resolved that: "In its view it is incumbent upon the United Nations Temporary Commission on Korea, under the terms of the General Assembly resolution of November 14, 1947, and in the light of developments in the situation with respect to Korea since that date, to implement the programme as outlined in resolution II, in such parts of Korea as are accessible to the Commission." [22]

DEBATE IN UNTCOK

The members of the Commission held an informal meeting on February 28 at Seoul, with the Chairman and the Canadian representative absent.[23] It was unanimously decided to implement the resolution of the Interim Committee, and a statement was issued that the Commission will observe elections in that part of Korea which is accessible to the Commission, not later than May 10, 1948, and that the elections be held on the basis of adult suffrage and by secret ballot, and in a free atmosphere wherein democratic rights of freedom of speech, press, and assembly would be recog-

---

bia, Denmark, Egypt, Iraq, Norway, Panama, Saudi Arabia, Sweden, Syria and Venezuela.

[22] U.N. Document, *A/583*. Many members of the United Nations did not believe that the Commission had much chance to bring about the unification of Korea. Gordenker, p. 242.

[23] Menon gave his approval of the decision reached at this meeting by telephone on the following day.

nized and respected.[24] In the course of a speech delivered in Seoul, the statement was read by the Chinese representative, Acting Chairman of UNTCOK. On the same day, General Hodge issued a proclamation in which he announced that an election of representatives of the Korean people would be held in South Korea on May 9, 1948, under the supervision of the United Nations Temporary Commission.[25]

The statements of the Chinese representative and Hodge created great turmoil when the Commission convened for its first formal meeting after Menon's return from New York. At the 17th and 18th meetings, the Canadian representative argued that UNTCOK had not yet officially reached a decision concerning the observation of elections; Hodge's statement was therefore illegal and unfounded. The Canadians insisted that the advice of the Interim Committee was not only "unwise," but also "unconstitutional." The Australian representative strongly supported this stand, stating that a vital development—the boycott by all parties in Korea except the extreme rightist groups—had taken place, and that this might have altered the view of the Little Assembly had it materialized earlier. The representatives of China, the Philippines, and El Salvador, on the other hand, strongly supported the Interim Committee's resolution and stood unreservedly for the immediate observation of elections by the Commission. The Indian and French representatives considered that UNTCOK was bound by the resolution of the Little Assembly. Finally, the Syrian delegation doubted the wisdom of observing elections, but as there was no third alternative, he was willing to cooperate on the ground that the situation in the South would be corrected by guarantee-

---

[24] UNTCOK Press Release 33, February 29, 1948. U.N. Document, *A/AC. 19/41.*

[25] *Department of State Bulletin,* March 14, 1948, p. 344. Hodge supplemented this proclamation by releasing another statement on March 4, which explained in further detail the legal basis of the forthcoming election and its procedure.

ing a free election.[26] After several heated discussions, the Commission formally decided on March 12, 1948, by a small majority, to implement the resolution of the Little Assembly.[27]

POLITICAL DEVELOPMENT IN SOUTH KOREA

Sharp divisions and realignments among the political and social groups in South Korea were provoked by the UNTCOK resolution to hold an election in the South alone. Political parties fell roughly into three groups, according to the method each wished to pursue for the unification of the country. The confirmed right and left groups were consistent in their policies, but the middle-of-the-roaders often fluctuated between the left and the right as the situation changed.[28] When the General Assembly decided in November, 1947, to observe the election throughout Korea, the rightists and moderates had unanimously and enthusiastically supported the decision, whereas the leftists challenged the Commission as a "hireling of the dollar of American imperialism." [29] The decision to hold elections only in the South disrupted this pattern.

The major groups supporting an immediate Southern general election were the National Society for Acceleration of Korean Independence under the leadership of Syngman Rhee; the Han'guk Democratic Party led by Kim Sŏng-su; and the Chosŏn Democratic Party, representing refugees

---

[26] See *First Part of the Report of the United Nations Temporary Commission on Korea,* U.N. Document, *A/575/add.5,* pp. 28–29.

[27] See the resolution of the Commission in U.N. Document, *A/AC. 19/48* and *A/AC. 19/49. In favor:* China, El Salvador, India, and the Philippines. *Opposed:* Australia and Canada. *Abstained:* France and Syria.

[28] For an analysis of party movements during this period, see Cornelius Osgood, *The Koreans and Their Culture* (New York, 1951), pp. 304–324, and George M. McCune and Arthur L. Grey, Jr., *Korea Today* (Cambridge, 1950), pp. 89–92.

[29] Interception of Radio Pyongyang, USAFIK, *South Korean Interim Government Activities,* January, 1948, p. 189. Hereafter cited as *Interim Activities.*

from North Korea. These were also supported by various youth organizations. They recognized that a strong government in the South was necessary as a protection from North Korean military power. They argued, too, that the government could be rightly claimed as a "national government" since 35 percent of the North Korean population had migrated into South Korea.[30]

The leftist groups vehemently expressed their opposition to the UNTCOK and separate elections in South Korea, asserting that it was essential for political leaders from both North and South Korea to meet, and then for American and Soviet troops to withdraw.[31] They charged that the separate election was "an attempt by American imperialists to cut through the middle, chop off the arms and legs of our homogeneous nation and tramp down our beautiful land with iron boots of imperialism."[32] The leftists were "firmly united under the flag of the National Democratic Front," led by the South Korean Workers Party (the new name of the Communist party after it merged with several leftist groups in November of 1946). They stirred up sabotage, riots, and strikes, and organized the "South Korean All-Out Strike Committee against the United Nations Commission on Korea," which in turn issued its own "strike declaration." Violence spread through the provinces and sporadic armed conflicts between police and rioters occurred.[33]

Early in 1948, the moderate groups under the leadership

---

[30] See a statement of Chosŏn Democratic Party, *Interim Activities,* December, 1947, p. 161. See also the hearing of Rhee in the U.N. Commission on January 26, 1948 U.N. Document, *A/AC. 19/SC. 2/PV.5;* and Han Tae-su, *Han'guk Chŏngtang Sa* (History of Korean Political Parties) (Seoul, 1961), pp. 97–103.

[31] See the statement of the South Korean Workers Party (Communist Party) on December 11, 1947 in *Interim Activities,* December, 1947, p. 161. See also the hearing of Lyuh Woon-hyung, U.N. Document, *A/AC. 19/SC. 2/PV.9* and Yi Ki-ha, *Han'guk Chŏngtang Baltal Sa* (History of the Development of Korean Political Parties) (Seoul, 1961), pp. 186–192.

[32] Han Tae-su, pp. 99–104.

[33] Report of the National Police in *Interim Activities,* April, 1948,

of Kimm Kiu-sic, Chairman of the South Korean Interim Legislative Assembly, established a loosely knit coalition called the National Independence Federation, which embraced political groups ranging from left to right. As noted earlier, Kimm was strongly supported by the military government in his program for a formation of a "genuinely democratic party."[34] In October, 1947, the Democratic Independence Party (Minju Tongnip Tang), which became the core of the above Federation, had finally been organized under the leadership of Kimm and Ahn Chae-hong, who had been the chief Korean civil administrator in the military government. This party became, in effect, the military government party, receiving American backing despite severe criticism from the other rightist and leftist groups.

Kimm's moderates originally supported both a unified election throughout Korea under the United Nations Commission and a Conference of North and South Korean political leaders. With the changes resulting from the uncooperative Soviet attitude and the subsequent resolution of the Interim Committee to observe elections south of the 38th parallel only, most parties in the National Independence Federation were disenchanted and expressed strong opposition to such elections.[35]

This reversal of opinion was powerfully strengthened by a sudden change in Kim Koo's attitude toward UNTCOK. Kim, Chairman of the Korean Independence Party (Han'guk Tongnip Tang) which had been one of the strongholds of the die-hard rightists, had hitherto cooperated closely with Rhee. His prestige as president of the Korean Provisional Government in Chungking was so enormous that his acts

---

p. 203. Arrests numbered 8,479. See the report of the police in U.N. Document, *A/AC. 19/W.22/Add.5*. Under these circumstances, Chang Dŏk-su, leader of the Han'guk Democratic Party, was assassinated on December 2, 1947.

[34] *Interim Activities*, September, 1947, p. 117.

[35] Hearing of Kimm Kiu-sic in Subcommittee No. 2 of UNTCOK, on January 27, 1948, U.N. Document, *A/AC. 19/SC. 2/PV.8*.

greatly influenced Korea's future political development. Suddenly, in February, 1948, Kim stated that a meeting of prominent leaders from North and South Korea should be held so that the Korean problems might be solved by the Koreans themselves.[36] With the followers of Kimm, he shared the belief that the election proposed by UNTCOK and supported by Rhee's rightists would act to perpetuate the division of Korea, rather than lead to its ultimate unification.[37] In this atmosphere, Kimm and Kim Koo initiated a proposal for a joint conference of political leaders from North and South Korea.[38] Though this proposal was similar to those of the leftists, there was no doubt about their sincerity and genuine hope for unification through the Koreans themselves, without outside interference.

Naturally, the Kimm–Kim Koo statement caused a great split among the rightist parties. The National Society for Acceleration of Korean Independence, the Han'guk Democratic Party, and the Chosŏn Democratic Party publicly expressed their complete disapproval, even suggesting that the two leaders had sold out to the Communists. General Hodge once again faced a most awkward situation: Kimm, his strong supporter, had turned against him by condemning the United Nations Commission and, on the pretext of ill health, had resigned from the chairmanship of the Interim Legislative Assembly which was the General's creation.

THE NORTH–SOUTH LEADERS' CONFERENCE FOR KOREAN UNIFICATION

As early as December, 1947, certain South Korean leaders such as Kimm Kiu-sic, Kim Koo, Cho So-ang, and Lyuh

---

[36] Hearing of Kim Koo, U.N. Document, *A/AC. 19/SC. 2/PV.6.*

[37] Hearing of Kim Sŏng-su, U.N. Document, *A/AC. 19/SC. 2/PV.11.*

[38] U.N. Document, *A/AC. 18/28.* See also Yi Ki-ha, pp. 193–197; and Pak Kyŏn-sik and Kang Chae-ŏn, *Chōsen no Rekishi* (History of Korea) (Tokyo, 1961), pp. 300–301. This book is written from a Marxist point of view.

Woon-hong were seriously considering convening a joint conference of Northern and Southern leaders to discuss the reunification of Korea by Koreans alone.[39] They felt that there would be no hope to achieve unification, either by a conference of the powers concerned or by the United Nations, as long as the inflexibility arising from the tight bipolarization of power continued. Kimm thought that if a conference of leaders should be suggested by the Communists or by the North Koreans, "the extreme rightists might try to oppose it; but if the suggestion should first come from the United Nations Commission, it might have a greater weight." [40] As a prerequisite for the conference, he thought that it was necessary for the occupation forces in both zones to: (a) restore freedom to political offenders; (b) cancel or suspend warrants for the arrest of political leaders; (c) respect freedom of speech, press, assembly, and association; and (d) agree upon the conditions and time of evacuation of both occupation forces.[41] This proposal was later supported, without reservation, by Kim Koo.

On March 12, 1948, seven prominent leaders, including Kimm Kiu-sic, Kim Koo, Cho So-ang, and Hong Myŏng-hi, issued a joint statement pledging to work for unified Korean independence, and vowing not to participate in a South Korean election that would result in "murder in a family." They then sent a letter to Kim Il-sŏng, Chairman of the North Korean People's Committee, and Kim Tu-bong, Chairman of the North Korean Workers Party, proposing that "measures for the establishment of a unified and democratic

---

[39] Kimm said that the idea of the conference had been brought up in a meeting of 12 parties in December, 1947, when it was sponsored by Mr. Cho So-ang, president of the National Congress and a close associate of Kim Koo's party. Ma Han, *Han'guk Chŏngch'i ŭi Ch'ong Pip'han* (The Whole Criticism of Korean Politics) (Seoul, 1959), pp. 35–40. This analysis is pro-Syngman Rhee's position.

[40] U.N. Document, *A/AC. 19/SC. 2/PV.8.*

[41] *Ibid.*

government should be discussed through a conference of political leaders of North and South." [42]

On March 25, through a broadcast over Pyongyang radio, the Central Committee of the Democratic National Coalition Front (Minjujuŭi Minjok T'ong'il Chŏnsŏn) invited, without announcing the content of Kimm's proposal, all South Korean parties, associations, and organizations opposing separate elections in South Korea to meet in conference on April 14 in Pyongyang with the representatives of the North Korean political parties and social organizations.[43] Kim Il-sŏng sent a formal letter to Kimm officially inviting 15 rightist political leaders from the South to attend the conference, emphasizing the urgency of the joint withdrawal of occupation forces so that Koreans could solve their own problems.[44] The South Korean leaders accepted the invitation, asking only for a guarantee of the personal safety of their representatives.

Prior to his departure, Kimm became hesitant about going to North Korea because: (1) a great many leftists and communists from South were attending the conference, while only 15 prominent rightists (ten from the National Independence Federation and five from the Korean Independence party) would participate; and (2) the problem of what group would take the responsibility for public safety in the event of simultaneous withdrawal of the occupying forces would be extremely difficult to settle. Finally, however, he

---

[42] The text of the letter is in *Interim Activities,* No. 30 (March, 1948), p. 153. See *Seoul Shinmun* or *Dong-A Ilbo,* March 9 and 13, 1948.

[43] U.N. Document, *A/AC. 19/W.43.* See also *Dong-A Ilbo,* March 26, 1948.

[44] The text of the letter is in *Interim Activities,* No. 30 (March, 1948), pp. 153–154. See also *Seoul Shinmun* and *Dong-A Ilbo,* March 28 and 29, 1948. A brief survey of this meeting is in Hong Sŭng-myŏn *et al., Haebang Isip nyŏn* (Twenty Years of Emancipation), Vol. 1 (Kirok P'yŏn) (Seoul, 1965), pp. 294–296. Kim Il-sŏng also invited all leftist groups in South Korea.

and Kim Koo left for Pyongyang on April 19 and 21. Just prior to their departure, Kimm issued a statement containing five principles which were accepted by the North Korean leaders as a basis for discussion. If these principles had been put into effect, there should have been no difficulty over the unification of Korea.

(1) Any form of dictatorship shall be rejected and a truly democratic government should be established.
(2) Monopolistic capitalism shall be rejected and private property ownership should be recognized.
(3) A unified central government shall be established through a general election of the entire nation.
(4) No military bases shall be allowed to any foreign power.
(5) Regarding the early withdrawal of the two occupation forces, the powers concerned should immediately open negotiations for reaching an agreement as to the time and conditions of withdrawal and make a definite pronouncement to the world.[45]

Kimm seemed to be particularly concerned about military withdrawal. He told the subcommittee of the United Nations Commission that the Soviet proposal of simultaneous withdrawal of foreign troops "sounds very sweet, natural, and reasonable to the ears of Koreans as well as to the ears of any third party. However, when Korea is left to herself and when the Allied forces withdraw, we must still remember that there are these 800,000 trained men who are seasoned fighters, part of which number may sweep down at any moment and organize a Soviet Government in South Korea."[46] On these grounds he opposed immediate withdrawal without a guarantee of non-invasion from the North,

---

[45] U.N. Document, *A/AC. 19/W. 43/Add.3.*

[46] He complained that General William P. Dean, the military governor, seemed not quite to agree on the necessity of recruiting and training South Koreans. See the First Part of the Report of the United Nations Temporary Commission on Korea, Vol. III, Appendices IX–XII, Official Records: Third Session Supplement No. 9. U.N. Document, *A/575/Add.2.* p. 81.

and urged the military government to recruit and train at least 200,000 or 300,000 men so that there would be no fear of North Korean military aggression.[47] Being strongly anti-Communist himself, he probably thought that his five principles would help to preserve democracy in case the Koreans succeeded in forming a coalition government in the forthcoming conference.

The first session of the conference opened on April 19 with a speech by Kim Il-sŏng. Attending were 695 representatives from sixteen political parties and forty special organizations of North and South Korea.[48] During the second and third sessions, held on the succeeding days, it became immediately apparent that there would be no discussion. The various parties attending the conference submitted statements to the planning committee, headed by Kim Tu-bong. These statements were read to the sessions, and voting was by a show of hands, with no debate on any question. No one was allowed to talk; everything was passed, although there probably was some opposition. It was a well controlled meeting of the sort common in Communist countries. As one Southern delegate complained, everything seemed to be "well cooked up." Kimm's speech at a dinner party was later distorted and an entirely different version was broadcast over the Northern radio.[49]

---

[47] *Ibid.*

[48] Twenty-four South Korean parties and organizations signed the resolution passed by the conference. U.N. Document, *A/AC. 19/W.43/Add.4,* pp. 3–6. According to McCune, the conference was attended by 545 delegates from North and South Korea including 240 from the South. George M. McCune, "The Korean Situation," *Far Eastern Survey,* September 8, 1948, p. 201. See also Kim Chong-myŏng, *Chōsen Shin Minshushugi Kakumei Shi* (History of Korea's New-Democratic Revolution) (Tokyo, 1953), pp. 205–213; and *Tōitsu Chōsen Nenkan: 1965–66* (One Korea Year Book: 1965–66) (Tokyo, 1966), p. 219.

[49] U.N. Document, *A/AC. 19/W. 43/Add.4.* See also Kim Ch'ang-sun, *Pukhan Sibo nyŏn Sa* (Fifteen Years of History in North Korea) (Seoul, 1961), pp. 209–214; and *Haebang Isip nyŏn, loc. cit.*

In this way, the conference passed three resolutions: (1) the decision of the conference on the Korean political situation; (2) a message to the Korean people; and (3) a message to the governments of the United States of America and the Union of Soviet Socialist Republics. (Neither Kimm nor Kim Koo signed the resolutions; they had the secretaries of their parties sign in their stead.) Each of these three resolutions protested the separate election in South Korea, condemned the United States and UNTCOK, and demanded the immedite withdrawal of foreign troops from the two zones.[50] At the end of the conference on April 30, a joint communiqué was issued, signed by the representatives of 33 North and South Korean political parties and social organizations. The political program proposed in this communiqué can be summarized as follows:

(1) The only solution for the Korean problem under the present condition is the immediate and simultaneous withdrawal of foreign troops from Korea.
(2) Leaders of both North and South declare that they will never permit an outbreak of civil war or any disturbance which might militate against Korean desire for unity after withdrawal of foreign troops.
(3) Following such withdrawal, a political conference of all of Korea will be called for the purpose of forming a "democratic provisional government." The provisional government will then "elect" on the principles of universal, direct and equal elections and on the basis of a secret ballot, a United Korean Legislative Organ, which in turn shall adopt a constitution which shall be the permanent constitution according to which the unified national government shall be formulated.
(4) The political parties and social groups signing this statement will never acknowledge the result of a separate election in South Korea nor support the separate government so established.[51]

---

[50] The three resolutions are in *The Soviet Union and the Korean Question* (London, 1950), pp. 53–54.

[51] The text is in U.N. Document, *A/AC. 19/SC. 4/SR.8*, p. 9; and

Immediately after returning to Seoul, Kimm and Kim Koo issued a statement that North Korean authorities had promised never to establish a separate government, had readily agreed to continue to supply electricity to South Korea, and had guaranteed the release of Cho Man-sik, a famous Christian leader and chairman of the Chosŏn Democratic Party, at the earliest possible date. They expressed their hope that the other problems could also be successfully solved by frequent negotiations between the leaders of both zones. Kimm told a member of the U.N. Commission that "Kim Il-sŏng had proposed the clause about no civil war and he had no reason to distrust it."[52] With these reports, the prestige of Kimm and Kim Koo reached its highest peak. They were accepted as saviors, and their program was supported with enthusiasm.

Subsequent events proved that the South Korean leaders were too naive: less than two weeks after their joint statement, the supply of electricity from North to South was suddenly cut off—apparently as a result of Soviet opposition to the South Korean election.[53] But this action boomeranged against the Communists since it generated intense resentment among South Koreans and caused the virtual elimination of Kimm and Kim Koo from Korean politics. The power shutoff became a political football and rightist groups now charged that the promise of leaders in the North-South conference had proven false and their promise was nothing but a trick to deceive the people.[54] Unfortunately, once the South Koreans felt betrayed in their high expectations, they

---

in Royal Institute of International Affairs, *Documents on International Affairs, 1947–1948* (London, 1952), p. 701.

[52] *Interim Activities,* No. 32 (May, 1948), p. 147.

[53] For the problems of electricity, see George M. McCune and Arthur L. Grey, Jr., *Korea Today* (Cambridge, 1950), pp. 146–152. See also Yi Ki-ha, pp. 193–194.

[54] USAFIK, *Interim Activities,* No. 32 (May, 1948), p. 148. See also Yi Ki-ha, pp. 193–194.

mercilessly tramped down those who they believed had misled them.

A new constitution purporting to apply to all Korea was adopted by the North Korean People's Committee on May 1, 1948, less than two weeks before the South Korean election. In June, Kim Il-sŏng and Kim Tu-bong invited Kimm and Kim Koo to attend a further conference at Haeju, just north of the 38th parallel, to plan for the election. It was reported that in their reply of June 23, the two Southern leaders proposed that the Northerners arrange for the election of 100 representatives to join the National Assembly established in Seoul under the supervision of the United Nations Commission.[55] Sorely disappointed with the moves of the Northern regime, the two leaders had by this time acquiesced in the separate Southern election.

The second joint conference, held on June 29, was not attended by the two South Korean leaders because the Northern leaders had failed to live up to their earlier promises. This conference, dominated by North Koreans, resolved on July 5 that it would not recognize the South Korean National Assembly and Government; instead it would establish a "Korea's Supreme People's Assembly" on the basis of a nationwide general election (to be held on August 25), and a "Korean Central Government" composed of representatives from the North and South. Kimm and Kim Koo, along with 25 political organizations in the South, declared their unqualified disapproval of this unilateral move. The long-cherished desire for unification through the negotiation of Koreans among themselves thus ended in great disillusionment. The efforts of these beloved leaders were abruptly ended by the assassination of Kim Koo by a South Korean army officer on June 26, 1949.[56] Kimm Kiu-sic was taken

---

[55] U.N. Document, *A/575/Add.3,* p. 12.

[56] Kim was assassinated by First Lieutenant Ahn Tu-hi of the Korean army. Ahn was a member of Kim Koo's Han'guk Independence Party. In the special military court, he revealed that his motive for

into custody by North Korean authorities in June, 1950, when the North Korean army briefly occupied Seoul, and it was later reported that he died in North Korea.

Thus, the hectic efforts for the unification of Korea by Korean leaders alone failed dismally. One of the reasons for the failure was the insincerity of the North Korean leaders. In retrospect, however, it is clear that from the beginning the project was bound to fail. First of all, there was no concrete plan to maintain order among the many hostile political groups in the anarchy that would follow the simultaneous withdrawal of occupation troops. Second, with no well-trained forces to cope with the North Korean army, the Southern leaders had to rely completely upon the dubious goodwill of the North. Third, the program for unification was more idealistic than realistic. Finally, the presence of foreign troops destroyed the program before it even had a chance for development: the United States viewed it as a purely Communist device to secure hegemony over all of Korea, and the Soviet Union and North Koreans viewed the United Nations Temporary Commission as "an instrument of American imperialism." The Russian Commander's negative policy toward the Commission demonstrated clearly that his country had no intention of holding elections under its supervision. Without the close cooperation of the military governments in both zones the program was bound to be abortive.

The Korean problem was fundamentally an international one which could be solved only by negotiations among the powers concerned. There was little room for action by Koreans themselves, even though their own well-being was at stake. The efforts of the Korean leaders can be epitomized by the traditional Korean proverb: "When whales fight, the shrimp in the middle get crushed."

---

the assassination was to protect the Republic of Korea and Syngman Rhee because he believed that Kim Koo and his party were doing disservice to the Republic. See *Haebang Isip nyŏn*, pp. 334–340.

9

The Birth of Two Republics and Permanent Division of Korea

The resolution of the General Assembly of the United Nations for the unification of Korea in November, 1947, was but a prelude to the permanent division of this tiny peninsula under the supervision of the international organization. The formal inauguration of the Republic of Korea on August 15, 1948, was the disappointing culmination of American efforts in the United Nations to establish an independent democratic, and unified Korean government. Although it can be argued that the establishment of a separate South Korean government was an inevitable outcome of the struggle between the United States and the Soviet Union during this period, it is also true that both America and the United Nations can, to some extent, be charged with failure.

Korean reaction toward the establishment of a separate South Korean Republic under the supervision of the United Nations varied considerably. Some welcomed the news; they were realistic, and had abandoned hope for national unification under this unprecedented system of hostile, bipolarized power politics. Others viewed the policy as a diplomatic blunder which would bring about a permanent division of the Korean people.

From the viewpoint of the State Department, the establishment of a separate South Korea was the logical way to implement the General Assembly resolution. Policy makers of the Department seemed to feel somewhat relieved now that this increasingly tiresome and unwelcome responsibility was shifted to the United Nations. They also considered themselves successful—because the new republic would be a buffer state, friendly to America. As long as the South Korean government remained hostile to the Soviet Union, Japan—a major American fortress in the Far East—would be safe from Communist aggression.

At the same time, Washington planners were alarmed to see the Red Star rising over the plains of Manchuria. By the spring of 1949 most of Northern China was overrun by the Communists, and Chinese Red soldiers were about to cross the Yangtze River. There was no doubt that Korea would be influenced by the rise of Communist power in her northern neighbor. In order to avoid an unnecessary commitment on the Asian mainland, the United States clearly felt that it was time to withdraw from all Asian involvements. The establishment of the South Korean Republic was thus strangely motivated by seemingly contradictory American desires to withdraw from Asia and to contain Communist power.

ELECTIONS IN SOUTH KOREA

The resolution adopted by the Interim Committee on February 26, 1948, and the subsequent decision of the United Nations Temporary Commission in Seoul to observe the election in South Korea, were undoubtedly welcomed by the American military authorities in that nation. If the Commission had confessed its failure, the field might have been clear for the adoption of the Russian proposal for simultaneous military withdrawal, which would have led to the emergence of another satellite country in Asia. This was something which neither the American commander in Korea, the Supreme Commander for the Allied Powers in Tokyo, nor leaders in Washington desired.

The primary responsibility for preparing and conducting the elections fell to the American military government, simply because UNTCOK had insufficient manpower for such operations. At no time did the Commission have at its disposal more than 30 non-Korean personnel. It was virtually impossible with this small group to observe elections in an area of about 40,000 square miles with a population of about 20 million. UNTCOK's activities were therefore limited to checking legislation and administrative attitudes with sporadic on-the-spot observations of the electoral process.[1]

Prior to the elections, General Hodge issued a "Korean Bill of Rights," an ordinance which provided that there would be no arrests without warrants. He released 3,140 political prisoners, as recommended by the Commission, and allowed them to register as voters and to stand as candidates if they so desired.[2] Every effort was made by the Commission and the military government to assure a free atmosphere for the elections.[3]

On April 28, the United Nations Temporary Commission on Korea adopted a resolution, with five votes in favor and three abstentions, confirming that it would observe the elections on May 10, 1948. The resolution also stated that extensive field observation in various key districts showed there was "a reasonable degree of free atmosphere wherein the democratic rights of freedom of speech, press, and assembly are recognized and respected."[4] The Commission also reported later that their observation groups were not able to collect any evidence of threats or violence against non-

---

[1] See the recommendation of the U.N. Commission on the election law. U.N. Document, *A/AC. 19/53.* It is interesting to know that in the past, 1,000 neutral observers had been employed in the Saar Plebiscite of 1935 which involved a population of only 500,000 voters, and 775 U.S. observers had been used for an election in Nicaragua in 1933 which had a population of approximately one million.

[2] U.N. Document, *A/AC. 19/W.40;* see also Ordinance 176 in AMGIK (American Military Government in Korea), *Gazette.*

[3] U.N. Document, *A/576,* p. 42.

[4] U.N. Document, *A/AC. 19/68.*

registrants, though there were some complaints about malpractice in the conduct of registration.

A ten-day period of registration, during which time 7,837,504 voters actually registered, ended on April 9. The number of registrants represented some 79.7 percent of the potential electorate. Just under 51 percent of the registered voters were men, and about 49 percent were women.[5] South Korea was divided into 200 electoral districts with 13,407 voting places, each district electing one member of the new legislative body. There were 942 candidates, including 17 women, ranging from 11 candidates for the three available seats in Cheju Island, to 145 in Kyŏnggi province for 29 available seats. It was not unusual to have four or five candidates in one district, and in some instances there were as many as ten or more.

Most of the candidates pleaded for support of the election as a step toward achieving an independent Korea; discussions of domestic issues and party platforms were conspicuously absent. Organized campaigns were local rather than national, and in most cases contests were waged between competing candidates whose personalities, family ties, and rival clan organizations played major roles. Personal and clan-oriented campaigns figured to such an extent that many qualified statesmen were unable to defeat unknown, clan-supported, incompetent candidates.

Despite the intensive campaign against the election by the leftists, the military government fully maintained law and order through the help of a civilian "Community Protective Corps" organized by the military authorities shortly before the election.[6] Still, there was considerable bloodshed;[7] on

[5] USAFIK, *South Korean Interim Government Activities,* No. 31 (April, 1948), p. 151. Hereafter cited as *Interim Activities.* Of 942 candidates originally registered, 57 did not stand for election.

[6] This organization was dissolved on May 22, 1948. Benjamin Weems, "Behind the Korean Election," *Far Eastern Survey,* June 23, 1948, p. 142; Robert T. Oliver, "The Korean Election," *Far Eastern Survey,* June 2, 1948, p. 42.

[7] *Interim Activities,* No. 32 (May, 1948), p. 182. For the North

election day itself, 44 persons were killed and 62 wounded, and 68 of 13,407 election booths were attacked. In describing the situation, however, the United Nations Commission stated that "the actual mechanics of voting were generally satisfactory and the secrecy of the balloting was, on the whole, ensured."

For their first democratic election, 7,487,649 of the 7,840,871 registrants, or 95.5 percent of the total number, actually took part in the voting. This represented 75 percent of the total potential electorate,[8] showing that Communist obstruction failed completely. The American and the South Korean Interim Governments described the election as a great victory for democracy and a repudiation of communism, whereas the leftists and those moderates who boycotted it claimed it was a farce and "was held without realization of a free atmosphere." [9] Whatever may have happened, the election indicated a degree of political maturity of the Korean people in 1948. Critics should remember that this was the first election in more than twenty centuries of authoritarian tradition in this nation.

It gradually became clear that no party had won a clearcut majority. Rhee's National Society for Acceleration of Korean Independence controlled 54 seats; the Han'guk Democratic Party, 29 seats; the Taeong Youth Group, 12 seats; the National Youth Groups, 6 seats; and Taehan Labor League, 2 seats. Ten were single representatives of minor parties, and the remaining 85 were elected as independents.

Korean point of view, see Kim Hi-il, *Mije ŭi Chosŏn Ch'imyak Sa* (History of the Invasion of American Imperialism in Korea) (Pyongyang, 1962), pp. 78–82.

[8] The figure is based on the South Korean source. See also U.S. Department of State, *Korea: 1945 to 1948* (Washington, 1948), p. 15; and U.N. Document A/AC. 19/80, p. 121.

[9] See a statement by Kim Koo, *Interim Activities*, No. 32 (May, 1948), p. 143. See also *Yŏktae Kukhoe Ŭiwŏn Sŏngŏ Sanghwang* (Election Results of Congressional Elections) (Seoul, 1964), pp. 11–74. In this chapter the factual information was mostly based on *Seoul Shinmun* and *Dong-A Ilbo.*

Almost half of the 198 men elected were avowed rightists, and none of the Assembly members was registered as Communist, although some observers estimated at the time that 50 out of 85 independents had Communist leanings, while the remaining 35 were inclined toward the moderate right.[10] Thus, the National Assembly that emerged as a result of the election was predominantly conservative in character, substantially composed of the followers of Syngman Rhee and Kim Sŏng-su.[11]

Following the elections, the United Nations Temporary Commission retired to Shanghai to study its conclusion and prepare a report to the General Assembly. It finally adopted the following resolution: The results of the elections are "a valid expression of the free will of the electorate in those parts of Korea which were accessible to the Commission and in which the inhabitants constituted approximately two-thirds of the people of all Korea." [12]

THE REPUBLIC OF KOREA

The National Assembly convened for the first time on May 31, 1948. Rhee was elected Chairman and immediately proceeded to make his appointments, including members of the Constitution Drafting Committee for the establishment of an independent Korean government.

In a letter to the new Assembly, the American commander suggested that: (1) an early resolution might be adopted that would, in effect, reserve a hundred seats for duly chosen

---

[10] For detailed information see *Yŏktae Kukhoe Ŭiwŏn Sŏngŏ Sanghwang* and *Interim Activities,* No. 32 (May, 1948), pp. 137–142; Han Ch'ŏl-yŏng and Kim Chin-hak, *Chehŏn Kukhoe Sa* (History of Constituent Assembly) (Seoul, 1956), pp. 95–97. For the voting behavior of Korean people, see Yun Ch'ŏn-ju, *Han'guk Chŏngch'i Ch'ege Sŏsŏl* (Introductory Theory of Korean Political System) (Seoul, 1961), pp. 295–301.

[11] The parties of these two leaders did not amalgamate, chiefly because of personality factors and leadership problems. See U.N. Document, *A/AC. 19/30/Add.1,* p. 8.

[12] *Korea: 1945 to 1948,* pp. 72–73.

North Korean representatives and keep open the possibility of Korean unification; (2) the Assembly might, early in its deliberations, appoint a liaison committee to have contact with the United Nations Temporary Commission; and (3) the Assembly should avoid precipitate action in the adoption of a constitution.[13]

Accordingly, in a letter dated June 3, Rhee informed the Commission of the establishment of a temporary liaison committee and expressed the hope that it would contact the members whenever it wished to consult the Assembly. A constitution was adopted on July 12, and Rhee was elected the first president of the new government on July 20. By early August he was already proceeding to form a cabinet, since the military government scheduled the transfer of its authority to the new government on August 15. President Rhee also notified Hodge that the Government of the Republic of Korea recognized that it would be necessary for Americans to retain control of vital areas and facilities, such as ports, military camps, railways, lines of communication, and airfields, in order to ease the transfer of authority and the withdrawal of occupation forces.

On August 12, the American government issued a statement which explicitly declared that "it is the view of the United States government that the Korean government so established is entitled to be regarded as the Government of Korea envisaged by the General Assembly resolution of November 14, 1947." It then sent Mr. John J. Muccio as ambassador to Korea.[14] On the same day, the Republic of China extended its "provisional recognition," pending discussion of the U.N. Commission's report by the General Assembly, and appointed Dr. Liu Yu-wan as China's ambassador.[15] The Philippine Republic followed suit, declaring that the new Korean government should be recognized

---

[13] U.N. Document, *A/AC. 19/W.51.*

[14] *Department of State Bulletin,* August 22, 1948, p. 242.

[15] U.N. Document, *A/AC. 19/W.58/Add.1.*

as the government of Korea in accordance with the provisions of the General Assembly's resolution.[16]

On August 15, the new Republic was formally inaugurated in Seoul. General Hodge officially proclaimed that the United States military government in Korea would be terminated at midnight on that date, marking the end of three years of hard service.

THE DEMOCRATIC PEOPLE'S REPUBLIC OF KOREA

The course of events in South Korea brought a prompt response from the Soviet Union and the North Korean regime. As we have observed earlier, a major governmental transformation took place in North Korea in early 1947 with the establishment of the Supreme People's Assembly and the Central People's Committee. Meanwhile, the North Korean Workers Party consolidated its power by successive waves of a rectification campaign. The purge of 1947 alone eliminated an estimated 40,000 to 60,000 "undesirable elements." Kim Il-sŏng further weakened the domestic factions by attacking their leaders, O Ki-sŏp, Ch'oe Yong-dal, Chŏng Tal-hyŏn for "sectarianism and heroism" at the second plenary meeting of the party in 1948.[17] The Soviet-oriented authorities were now firmly established. They pressed the socialization of the North Korean economy, reducing further the private sector and putting greater emphasis upon heavy industry. Major

---

[16] *Korea: 1945–1948*, pp. 102–103.

[17] For detailed information see *Chosŏn Rodongtang Yŏksa Kyojae* (Textbook for the History of the Korean Workers Party) (Pyŏngyang, 1964), pp. 153–248; Pak Sang-hyŏk, *Chosŏn Minjok ŭi Witaehan Yŏngdoja* (The Great Leader of the Korean Nation) (Tokyo, 1964), pp. 148–299; and Yu Ho-il, *Gendai Chōsen no Rekishi* (History of Modern Korea) (Tokyo, 1953), pp. 58–72. Gaimusho (Japanese Ministry of Foreign Affairs), *Sengoni okeru Chōsen no Seiji Josei* (Korean Politics in the Postwar Era) (Tokyo, 1948), pp. 84–95, contains a more objective analysis. See also U.S. Department of State, *North Korea: A Case Study in the Techniques of Takeover* (Washington, 1961), pp. 12–18, and Shannon McCune, *Korea: Land of Broken Calm* (Princeton, 1966), pp. 124–127.

attention was directed toward military and industrial expansion.

Then on November 18, 1947, the North Korean Assembly established a committee to draft a provisional Korean constitution. It is probable that this radical action was taken as a countermove to the unilateral action of the United States in presenting the Korean question to the United Nations. The Soviet intention apparently was to establish a separate government in North Korea unless America changed her declared policy; however, Soviet spokesmen repeatedly denied that preparation of the provisional constitution would mean the inauguration of a separate government. In fact, the constitution adopted in April of 1948 was not ratified officially until September, following the establishment of the Republic of Korea in the South.[18] Meanwhile, the North Korean Assembly officially announced the establishment of the People's Army in February, 1948.[19]

After the failure of another North-South political leaders' conference in May and the successful conclusion of the South Korean election, the North Korean radio announced that a concurrent election had been held secretly in the South to choose 360 South Korean representatives for the 572 members of the Supreme People's Assembly, despite "the barbarous suppression and persecution by South Korean police." They claimed that 77.52 percent of the 8,681,745 eligible voters in South Korea participated in this secret election, while 99.97 percent of the total electors in North Korea actually voted. As McCune has pointed out, these figures are obviously false since they exceed by 650,000 the

[18] U.N. Document, *A/AC. 19/W.25.* An excellent analysis of the North Korean constitution is Pak Tong-un, *Pukhan T'ongch'i Kigu Ron* (Theory of North Korean Government) (Seoul, 1964), pp. 23–35.

[19] Interception of Radio Pyongyang, *Interim Activities* No. 30 (February, 1948), p. 184. Kim Sam-gyu, *Chōsen Gendai Shi* (Modern History of Korea) (Tokyo, 1963), p. 54. The strength of North Korean Forces soon reached 200,000 regular soldiers.

number of votes polled in South Korea in the May 10 election which was held under conditions of official encouragement.[20]

The Supreme People's Assembly for Korea held its first meeting in Pyongyang and ratified the Constitution of the Democratic People's Republic of Korea on September 3, three weeks after the establishment of the Republic of Korea in the South. Kim Il-sŏng was appointed Premier of the Democratic People's Republic of Korea. Next day, the Assembly duly approved Kim's choice of three vice-premiers and a cabinet of twelve ministers which mainly consisted of members of the former People's Committee. Pak Hŏn-yŏng, leader of the South Korean Workers Party, was appointed Vice-Premier and Minister of Foreign Affairs.[21] On October 12, the Soviet Union recognized the North Korean government and, a few days later, Colonel General Shtykov was appointed as the first Soviet ambassador. Shortly thereafter, the Eastern European satellite nations and Outer Mongolia also extended official recognition to this new Communist republic. On September 14, 1948, the Supreme People's Assembly issued an appeal to the governments of the Soviet Union and the United States for the withdrawal of all foreign troops.[22] Russia, of course, accepted the appeal with-

---

[20] See the Democratic People's Republic of Korea, *Outline of Korean Geography* (Pyongyang, 1957), pp. 6–9; and George M. McCune and Arthur L. Grey, Jr., *Korea Today* (Cambridge, 1951), pp. 246–247. According to *Izvestia,* September 23, 1948, 85.2 percent of all persons eligible to vote participated in these elections. *Soviet Press Translation* (Seattle: Far Eastern Institute, University of Washington), November 1, 1948, p. 583. For a detailed analysis of the election, see Pak Tong-un, pp. 19–22.

[21] For the North Korean point of view see Kim Chong-myŏng, *Chōsen Shin Minshushugi Kakumei Shi* (History of Korea's New Democratic Revolution) (Tokyo, 1953), pp. 244–255. For the emulation pattern of the North Korean government, see Glenn D. Paige, "North Korea and Emulation of Russian and Chinese Behavior" in *Communist Strategies in Asia,* ed. A. Doak Barnett (New York, 1963), pp. 228–237.

[22] *Pravda,* September 14, 1948.

out reservation and shortly afterward announced that its troops would be withdrawn by the end of December. With the completion of this operation, the North Koreans attained their full "independence" on December 24, 1948. It was, however, a poorly disguised fact that the Soviets still exercised control over the North through its embassy, advisory personnel, and the Soviet Koreans who held key positions in the government and the ruling Communist Party.[23]

The North Korean regime now greatly increased the tempo of its military and industrial development. It intensified the latter by initiating a two-year economic plan for 1949–1950, and enlarged its armed forces with considerable numbers of heavy weapons left behind by the Soviet troops.[24] A regular military training program with an efficient conscription system was introduced in the summer of 1949.

At the same time, the North Korean Workers Party absorbed its counterpart, the South Korean Workers Party, taking the new name of Korean Workers Party (Chosŏn Rodong Tang). With this "merger," Kim Il-sŏng became the Chairman of this united Communist party while Kim Tu-bong, the leader of the old Yenan faction and the former Chairman of the North Korean Workers Party, was elected to chair the Presidium of the Supreme People's Assembly. Although retaining membership in the powerful Central Committee, Kim Tu-bong definitely lost influence within the party. Pak Hŏn-yŏng, the new Vice-Premier, shared the vice-chairmanship of the new party with Hŏ Ka-i, a Soviet Korean party organizer.[25] With this reorganization of Korean Communist parties, Kim Il-sŏng made himself the undisputed leader of the entire Korean Communist move-

---

[23] *North Korea: A Case Study in the Techniques of Takeover,* pp. 100–103.

[24] *Ibid.*, p. 17.

[25] *North Korea Today,* ed. Robert A. Scalapino (New York, 1963), pp. 14–16. Kim Ch'ang-sun, *Pukhan Sibo nyŏn Sa* (Fifteen Years of History in North Korea) (Seoul, 1961), pp. 115–120.

ment. He was thus able to establish a unified channel of command and to ensure more effective control of South Korean Communist activities. Gradually, the subversive movement in the South was encouraged by material support for sabotage, riots, and guerrilla warfare. The North also intensified border skirmishes along the 38th parallel and stepped up its propaganda campaign.

The Northern regime apparently abandoned hope for the peaceful unification of Korea and instead, prepared for a military conquest of the South. On October 14, 1949, the North Korean government clearly stated in its letter to U.N. Secretary-General Trygve Lie that it reserved the right to unify the whole country "by its own force." [26] The tone and style of this assertion was very similar to that of South Korean leaders, and the prophetic statement of Kimm Kiu-sic to UNTCOK had now become a reality:

> Any Korean who talks about a South Korean unilateral government will go down [in] history as a "bad egg," because once that term is used, the communists in the north under the direction of Soviet Union will establish what is called the "People's Republic," or the "People's Committee." Then you will have two unilateral governments in this little space of something over 85,000 square miles. Not only that, but once such a thing occurs in history, it will go down forever, and it will be perpetuated.[27]

With the establishment of the two rival governments, the prospect for unification became dimmer and dimmer: as the relationship between the two occupation powers worsened, so did the relationship between their offspring.

THE INTERNATIONAL STATUS OF THE TWO REPUBLICS

It was natural for the South Korean government to call itself the only lawful government in Korea, even though it

---

[26] *New York Times,* October 18, 1949.
[27] U.N. Document, *A/575/Add.2,* p. 80.

could physically control only the southern half of the country. It felt that the North Korean government should be condemned not only as an illegal body, but as an immediate threat to international peace. Thus, in a communiqué of July 11, 1948 to the Chairman of UNTCOK, Rhee explicitly stated that the newly elected Korean National Assembly regarded itself as formed in accordance with Part II of the General Assembly resolution of November 14, and as a national—not merely a South Korean—government.[28]

Before the inauguration of the government, a proposed motion urging the establishment of a North-South special unification committee was rejected on the grounds that the establishment of such committee might reflect unfavorably on the claims of the present government as the government of all Korea.[29] The National Assembly later called upon its fellow countrymen in the North to "hold a general election soon in a free atmosphere in accordance with the United Nations resolution; elect the true representatives of the people; and send them to the National Assembly" to fill the seats duly allocated to them.[30] This offer still remains open and the Republic of Korea continues to this day to claim its legal right as a national government of the whole peninsula. The Republic of Korea has held that if the North Koreans refuse voluntarily to accept its authority, the Republic should consider itself fully justified in using any means, including force, of asserting its governmental authority. Article 4 of the Republic's Constitution, for instance, unequivocally defines its national territory as the whole Korean peninsula and its accessory islands.[31] It also believed that any negotiations required to unify the country by peaceful means could be conducted only with the Soviet Union and not with the

[28] U.N. Document, *A/AC. 19/78.*
[29] U.N. Document, *A/575/add.3,* pp. 12–13.
[30] U.N. Document, *A/AC. 19/W.53.*
[31] In Article 103 North Korean constitution also designated the city of Seoul as its capital. Yu Chin-o, *Hŏnbŏp Haeŭi* (Interpretation of Constitution) (Seoul, 1949), pp. 22–23.

North Korean regime.[32] It strongly opposed negotiation conferences between leaders of the North and South, holding that unification should be achieved only through elections in North Korea, held under the observation of the United Nations. Consequently, the establishment of the Republic of Korea closed many avenues that might have led to unification.

The United States had quickly accorded *de facto* recognition to the Government of the Republic of Korea pending consideration by the General Assembly at its forthcoming third session. When the General Assembly considered the Korean question toward the end of its Paris meeting, the American delegation exerted strong influence upon the member states to recognize the Republic as "the only lawful government in Korea." [33] As for the Russians, the Republic of Korea had become anathema to her prestige and security. The delegations of the Soviet bloc in the General Assembly continuously charged that the establishment of the U.N. Commission itself was a direct violation of international agreements, that the Republic of Korea had no legal or constitutional basis, and that it did not reflect the wishes of the Korean people. Instead, Russia insisted, the Democratic People's Republic in North Korea should be recognized, as it was organized by "democratic" elections throughout the country.

The members of the Temporary Commission themselves were initially divided between the American and Soviet positions. On the one hand, the representatives of China and the Philippines held that the National Assembly could be regarded as the government envisaged in Part II of the General Assembly resolution of November 14, 1947, because the

---

[32] U.N. Document, *A/936*, p. 14.

[33] See the statement by John Foster Dulles in the Political Committee in the General Assembly. U.N. *Official Record, the First Committee of the General Assembly, Third Session,* 1948, Part 1, pp. 961–962.

elections were declared "a valid expression of the free will of the electorate" by the Commission. They strongly stated that the government was entitled to be accorded *de jure* recognition as a national government of Korea. But the representative of Australia contested this view on the ground that, since the people in North Korea did not participate in the election of May 10, the government was not in a position to extend its jurisdiction over the whole nation.[34] As a compromise, at its 69th meeting (June 25, 1948) UNTCOK unanimously adopted the following statement of its official attitude: "The results of the ballot of May 10, 1948, are a valid expression of the free will of the electorate in those parts of Korea which were accessible to the Commission and in which the inhabitants constituted approximately two-thirds of the people of Korea."[35]

This resolution was officially announced to the Korean National Assembly on June 30 by Mr. Miguel A. P. Valle, then Chairman of the Commission.[36] Although this speech carefully refrained from recognizing the national character of the Assembly, it was wrongly interpreted in some press comments. To rectify the misunderstandings, he reemphasized to the liaison committee of the National Assembly that while the Commission had not questioned the right of the elected representatives to constitute the National Assembly and to establish a government, it had carefully avoided any responsibility of "recognizing the title of the Assembly as National."[37] He apparently felt bound to explain this in order to avoid future misunderstandings, and to eliminate the possibility of the South Korean government using the Commission to justify its claim of jurisdiction over the whole country.

In its final report to the General Assembly, however, the

---

[34] U.N. Document, *A/AC. 19/82; A/AC. 19/77;* and *A/AC. 19/W.59.*

[35] U.N. Document, *A/AC. 19/84* or see *A/575/Add.3,* p. 3.

[36] *Ibid.*

[37] U.N. Document, *A/AC. 19/SC. 4/SR.15,* pp. 2–7.

United Nations Temporary Commission on Korea seemed to suggest unification under the government which was established by the May 10 elections, since "this government does provide a basis from which it may be possible to proceed to unification by peaceful methods of negotiation."[38] The Commission stressed that for the social, political, and economic well-being of the Korean people, immediate unification was absolutely essential. The need for setting up some procedure for peaceful negotiations was urgent and must take place before withdrawal of the occupation forces, so that the peninsula would not be abandoned to the arbitrary rule of rival political regimes whose military forces might find themselves driven into internecine warfare. UNTCOK did not, however, present a positive recommendation for unification because it felt that "the task of defining methods for peaceful relations between the governments of North and South Korea would be futile so long as the opposing ideologies and politics 'continue in opposing each other.'"

When the report of the Commission finally came to the forum of the General Assembly of the United Nations, the Soviet Union again did its best to delete the Korean question from the agenda, asserting that the Commission was an illegal body. After many heated discussions in the First Committee, the United States introduced a draft resolution urging that: (1) the United Nations ought to put "the seal of legitimacy" on what has been done in Korea under its auspices in order to maintain the Republic of Korea's prestige and authority at home and abroad; (2) the United Nations should continue a commission in Korea in order to help the new government end the wartime military occupation by observing the withdrawal of forces as soon as practical; and (3) the United Nations Commission should help the Korean people to reunite and to end the economic disorder and fears of a civil war.[39]

---

[38] U.N. Document, *A/575/Add.3* (October 15, 1948).

[39] U.N. Document, *A/C.1/426.* This was submitted jointly by Australia, China, and the United States.

The Soviet Union challenged this proposal by submitting its own draft resolution which asked for: (1) the termination of the Temporary Commission on Korea; (2) a new means of reestablishing Korea as an independent democratic state; and (3) condemnation of the South Korean election.[40] At the 236th meeting of the First Committee, the American draft resolution was adopted by 41 to 6, with 2 abstentions. After careful consideration of the report of the First Committee, the final resolution was finally adopted on December 12, 1948 in the General Assembly by roll call vote of 48 to 6 with 1 abstention.[41] The General Assembly by this action officially recognized the legal standing of the Republic of Korea.

The resolution declared that "there has been established a lawful government having effective control and jurisdiction over that part of Korea where the Temporary Commission was able to observe and consult and in which the great majority of the people of all Korea reside," and that this government was based on an election which was "a valid expression of the free will of the electorate of that part of Korea." The resolution then emphasized that this is "the only such government in Korea." It recommended that the occupation powers withdraw their forces as early as practicable. It also established a commission to continue the work of the Temporary Commission, and called upon members of the United Nations to afford "every assistance and facility" to the new commission in its tasks of promoting unification, removing the economic and social barriers caused by division, and observing and verifying the actual withdrawal of forces. The resolution authorized the Commission to travel, consult, and observe throughout Korea and instructed it to report at the next session of the General Assembly. The new Commission was to consist of representatives from the nations that were

---

40 U.N. Document, *A/C.1/427/Corr.1.*

41 Sweden abstained in the voting, while the six Soviet bloc nations opposed the resolution. U.N. Document, *A/806.*

affiliated with its predecessor, with the exception of Canada and the Ukrainian S.S.R., and was to establish itself in Seoul within 30 days.

The new resolution, it will be noted, carefully avoided declaring the Republic of Korea the national government of Korea, though it did not declare specifically that it was not. Actually the wording of paragraph two of the resolution was vague enough to be interpreted either way. In fact, Mr. Chang Myŏn, chief representative of the Republic of Korea in the United Nations, had expressed in the First Committee the desire that the wording be changed to confirm "the claim of the Republic of Korea that it was, in effect, the government envisaged in the Assembly Resolution of the 14th of November, 1947, that it was prevented from exercising its jurisdiction over all of Korea only by force and that the sovereignty of the entire Korean nation resided in it." [42] Mr. Setalvad of India disagreed, while cautioning that, as it stood, paragraph two might be interpreted to imply "the recognition of the southern government as the national government envisaged in the November 14th resolution." [43] The representatives of Burma, Syria, and New Zealand agreed that no government created as a result of the election held only in the southern zone could possibly be regarded as a "national government" of all Korea. They also believed that if Russia would ask the United Nations to send a commission to North Korea to find out who really represented the people in that area, the two governments could be merged, elections could be held under the new authority, and an entirely new government could be established.[44] This was an entirely different interpretation from that made by China, the Philippines, and the Republic of Korea.

---

[42] U.N. *Official Record, the First Committee of the General Assembly, Third Session,* 1948, pp. 966–967.

[43] *Ibid.,* pp. 973–974.

[44] *Ibid.,* p. 1015. See the statement of Mr. Fraser of New Zealand.

In order to clarify the First Committee's stand on this point, Dulles stated that "paragraph two of this joint resolution (A/C.1/426) had been carefully worded to state only what was indisputably true and did not assert that the present government was, in fact, the government of all Korea, nor deny that another regime existed in another part of Korea. It was a carefully drawn statement which had been considered very thoroughly by the sponsors of the draft resolution."[45] Dulles' statement was also so carefully worded that its meaning remained evasive. It could be interpreted to mean either that the United States did not recognize the Republic of Korea as a national government, or that although the present government was not *ipso facto* the government of all Korea, it was *ipso jure* the national government having jurisdiction over all the country. He explicitly denied the existence of another lawful government in other parts of Korea.

Whatever Dulles' meaning and intent may have been, the Republic of Korea is still using the resolution to support its own claim that the Republic is the only legal national government in Korea. But to others of the United Nations, the status of Korea has not been clearly defined, and they treat her as a government which has effective authority only in South Korea. This state of affairs is in reality unimportant, however, because it is clear that Korea's future will not be determined on the basis of superior legal claim alone, but rather by the Republic's ability—cultural, economic, and political—to resist the aggression of its rival regime in the North.

The new United Nations Commission on Korea, like its predecessor, tried without success to contact the Soviet commander and the North Korean leaders.[46] The Commission

---

[45] *Ibid.*, p. 1023.

[46] U.N. *Official Record,* Report of the United Nations Commission on Korea, General Assembly, Fourth Session, Supplement No. 9 (*A/936*), pp. 5–6.

even declared its readiness to assist in discussions between representatives of the North and South to consider possibilities for unification. It offered assistance in the resumption of legitimate trade between the two zones on a trial basis, and proposed the cessation of inflammatory propaganda to lessen the tensions.[47]

All offers were completely frustrated, not only by the uncooperative attitude of the North Korean regime, but also by the South Korean government because these programs radically differed from its own unification plan. The South Korean government urged that the Commission take the following steps: (1) persuade the Soviet Union to dissolve the North Korean regime as well as all political parties and social organizations thereof, so that the Southern government could conduct a general election in the North under the observation of the United Nations Commission; (2) supervise the immediate and complete withdrawal of foreign troops from North Korea and lend its good offices for "the immediate dissolution" of the People's Army; and (3) declare any international agreements or treaties concluded by the Northern regime as "null and void." [48] Rhee emphatically opposed any attempts to make direct contact with the authorities in the North because he felt that it would imply recognition of the regime. The Commission's activities were, as a result of these attitudes, strictly limited to South Korea, a fact noted in the North Korean charge that it was a "running dog of American imperialism."

As the danger of civil war grew and the insecurity of the Republic of Korea mounted due to the anticipated early withdrawal of American occupation forces, the United States, Australia, China, and the Philippines introduced into the fourth General Assembly session a draft resolution which, in effect, authorized the Commission to observe and

---

[47] *Ibid.*, p. 9.

[48] U.N. Document, *A/AC. 26/9,* statement of Col. B. C. Lim. See also U.N. Document, *A/AC. 26/SC. 1/1 and 6 and 23.*

report any development that might lead to, or otherwise involve, military conflict in Korea. The resolution, finally passed, also authorized the Commission to appoint observers to accomplish these aims.[49]

Apparently sensing the danger ahead, the Foreign Minister of the Republic of Korea officially requested in June, 1949, that the United Nations Commission "continue its work in Korea and stated that the continuation of the work of the Commission on Korea for at least another year would be greatly appreciated by his government." [50] The Republic earnestly requested that a unit of United Nations military observers of high rank be stationed in Korea to stop unlawful attacks by the North Korean regime.[51] Though the establishment of the U.N. military observers and the continued presence of the Commission had little power to deter military attack from the North, it undoubtedly lent some feeling of security to the people of South Korea. Because of the presence of the Commission, the United Nations was able to react quickly when the North Korean army attacked the South in June, 1950.

The fundamental dilemma of the Korean problem lies primarily in the strategies and national goals of the two superpowers, although the historic interests of China and Japan are also not negligible. It is apparent that the problem cannot be solved until the United States and the Soviet Union take some positive steps together to lift the barrier at the 38th parallel, and to restore the independence and unity that were promised at the Moscow Conference of Foreign Ministers in December, 1945. Until this happens, the efforts of the United Nations will be futile within the present scope of power provided by the Charter. Without having a more effective enforcement agency for its resolution, the United Nations has practically no means for the unification of Korea.

---

[49] The draft resolution was adopted by 48 to 6, with 3 abstentions.
[50] U.N. Document, *A/AC. 26/36.*
[51] U.N. Document, *A/AC. 26/40.*

10

Withdrawal of American Occupation Forces and the Allocation of Economic Aid

By late 1948 there had been serious developments in the Far East which compelled American concern over its position in Korea. The Chinese situation became the heart of the Far Eastern problem and ultimately affected the American approach to other questions. The hopelessness of the earlier American efforts to sustain the Nationalist regime was made clear by the complete failure of General Marshall's mission. The Nationalist Government was rapidly losing the support of Chinese public opinion and the confidence of its own armies. On military fronts, the Chinese Communists began in early 1948 to advance swiftly. By autumn they were occupying cities in north China and Manchuria almost at will. Tientsin and Peking surrendered in January, 1949. In May the Reds entered Shanghai and began the conquest of China's most industrially developed area.[1] The Nationalist forces by autumn of 1949 had been driven into southwestern

[1] *New York Times,* April 22 and 24, 1949. See also O. Edmund Clubb, *Twentieth Century China* (New York, 1964), pp. 289–297; and Tang Tsou, *America's Failure in China: 1941–50* (Chicago, 1963), pp. 500–503.

China and Formosa, and on October 1 the People's Republic of China was finally inaugurated in Peking.

KOREA IN AMERICAN MILITARY STRATEGY

The Communist victory in China now made the defense of South Korea appear to America as strategically impracticable. Given the limits of American economic and military resources at this time, it could well be argued that all available resources should be channelled to Europe. The Communist coup in Czechoslovakia, the Berlin blockade, and the rapid absorption of the Eastern European nations into the Soviet camp during this period repeatedly called attention to the urgency of maintaining Europe against the Soviet threat. The Americans were reluctant to disperse their limited military resources to the continent of Asia, despite the fact that the Soviet threat to Western Europe was largely economic, political, and psychological in character, while in Asia its aims were outright military and political annexation. There had been indications since its initiation that the United States was finding it nearly impossible to fit the Korean situation neatly into its containment policy. It had apparently concluded that Korea was not a sufficiently important strategic asset to warrant the commitment of scarce American manpower and military supplies.[2]

The Truman administration was also faced with serious reductions of military manpower and appropriations during this period. On February 18, 1948, General Gruenther made a statement at the White House in the presence of Marshall, Forrestal, and the Joint Chiefs of Staff concerning America's available military strength and the strength considered necessary for effective containment. The General pointed out that the United States had only 140,000 men in Asia, including 20,000 in Korea, instead of the required 180,000, and predicted that the total army shortage would reach 165,000

[2] William Reitzel *et al.*, *United States Foreign Policy, 1945–1955* (Washington, 1956), p. 179.

by the end of 1948. The navy also faced an acute shortage of manpower which might require the laying-up of more than 100 ships. Only the personnel situation in the Air Force was found to be satisfactory.[3]

Gruenther showed that in Korea the Joint Chiefs of Staff now faced a major problem in securing 10,000 additional troops urgently needed by General Hodge. According to *The Forrestal Diaries* Gruenther at this time indicated Greece, Italy, Korea, and Palestine as possible explosion points in the world, warning that a commitment in any one of these areas would probably reduce the reserve of the United States to a dangerous degree. The army had at this time a total strength of only 630,000 men, distributed in four under-strength divisions in Japan, with five divisions in Europe and another five under-strength divisions in the United States.[4] This acute shortage of manpower made it clear that America could not afford a military commitment on any part of the Asian continent.

As we have seen earlier, the Joint Chiefs of Staff had already made a careful study of the military aspects of troop withdrawal from Korea in the latter part of 1947. Their views were further reinforced by the recommendation of General Wedemeyer after his fact-finding mission to China and Korea. All agreed that the United States had little strategic interest in maintaining its under-manned occupation units on the peninsula.[5] When the Soviet delegation in the Joint Commission in Seoul proposed the simultaneous withdrawal of occupation troops from both zones, it was not, therefore, an unwelcome surprise. For the United States, the

---

[3] *The Forrestal Diaries*, ed. Walter Millis (New York, 1951), p. 375.

[4] U.S. Congress, *Military Situation in the Far East*, Hearings before the Senate Committee on Armed Services and the Committee on Foreign Relations, 82nd Congress, 1st Session (Washington, 1951), pt. 3, p. 2327.

[5] Harry S. Truman, *Years of Trial and Hope* (New York, 1956), pp. 325–326. When the Joint Chiefs of Staff made their report to the President, they had available to them the Wedemeyer report.

Soviet offer seemed to be the best opportunity to implement the recommendations of General Wedemeyer and the Joint Chiefs of Staff. Indeed, many people in the State Department were inclined to believe that it seemed to "be a good opportunity." Under this pressure Secretary Marshall said in a Cabinet luncheon on September 29, 1947, that "he was giving close study to the question of getting out of Korea." Harriman, the former Ambassador to Russia, raised the question of whether America could get out without losing face. The Secretary of State replied "that was the aspect of the question to which he was giving most serious thought." [6]

Although policy planners agreed that the United States should withdraw its occupation troops from Korea as soon as possible, they were not ready to accept the Soviet proposal for withdrawal, made at the Joint Commission in September, 1947, without consideration of its political and military consequences. Foreseeing the Soviet intention, Wedemeyer predicted that "there is strong possibility that the Soviet Union will withdraw their occupation forces and thus induce our withdrawal. This probably will take place as soon as they can be sure that the North Korean puppet government and its armed forces which they have created, are strong enough, and sufficiently well indoctrinated to be relied upon to carry out the Soviet objectives without the actual presence of the Soviet troops." [7] The General was of the opinion in September, 1947 that the North Korean People's Army of approximately 125,000 troops, equipped and trained by the Soviet Union, was vastly superior to the American-trained constabulary of 16,000 South Koreans equipped with Japanese small arms.

THE STRATEGY OF WITHDRAWAL

America's Korean policy became much more complicated after the case was presented to the United Nations, since it

[6] *The Forrestal Diaries,* pp. 321–322.

[7] Albert C. Wedemeyer, *Wedemeyer Reports* (New York, 1958), p. 475.

became more difficult to withdraw American forces unilaterally without instruction from the United Nations. Furthermore, internal politics in Korea had deteriorated so greatly that if the occupation forces withdrew without leaving a reliable Korean security force, there was a strong possibility of a Communist-dominated South Korea. The decision for withdrawal was thus delayed through 1948 while diplomatic maneuvering led to the U.N. action that created the Republic of Korea in the South.[8] Americans took the official stand that in the opinion of the United States government the question of withdrawal of occupation forces from Korea must be considered an integral part of the solution of the problem of unification.[9]

In the United Nations, the majority opinion was that the withdrawal ought not to take place until the government of South Korea had established its own armed forces. Mr. Castro of El Salvador especially warned the members of the General Assembly that there was an army of about 170,000 in North Korea and if the United States forces would withdraw prematurely "it was clear that this army would come down from the north." [10] The U.S. draft resolution, which was later adopted by the General Assembly by a vote of 48 to 6 with 1 abstention, therefore vaguely "recommended that the occupation powers should withdraw their occupation forces from Korea as early as practicable." [11]

Despite its victory on this issue in the United Nations, America was actually in a hurry to prepare for withdrawal in order to relieve itself of the financial and military burden. In fact, as a result of a high-level study carried out some

---

[8] Harold M. Vinacke, *The United States and the Far East: 1945–1951* (Stanford, 1952), pp. 62–65.

[9] Letter of Lovett to Molotov, delivered on October 18, 1947. U.S. Department of State, *Korea: 1945 to 1948* (Washington, 1948), p. 50.

[10] U.N. *Official Record, the First Committee of the General Assembly, Third Session,* 1948, p. 1021.

[11] U.N. Resolution 195 (III), in *Year Book of the United Nations 1948–49,* p. 290. Sweden abstained from voting.

time early in 1948, a definite decision to withdraw U.S. forces had been reached long before the Soviet announcement. In April, the National Security Council had reported to the President that the United States could do one of three things: (1) abandon Korea; (2) continue political and military responsibility for it; or (3) extend to the Korean government aid and assistance for the training and equipping of their own security forces and offer extensive economic help to prevent a breakdown. The Council recommended that the President choose the last course, which he promptly did.[12]

Subsequently, the Department of the Army directed the Commanding General of USAFIK to create conditions for American withdrawal at the end of 1948. Hodge thus was instructed to train and equip Korean security forces for the protection of South Korea from any but an outright act of aggression from beyond its border.[13] A month after the establishment of the new Republic, the United States military forces began a phased withdrawal on September 15th according to a plan called CRABAPPLE (or later, TWIN BORN) which was scheduled to remove all American troops from Korean soil by the end of 1948.[14]

ARMED INSURRECTIONS IN THE SOUTH

The move soon proved to be a hasty one. The South Korean government was not ready or able to control the situation. Its own small security forces were grossly under-equipped, largely untrained, and in some cases politically unreliable. There were serious shortages of spare parts and of all types of technical equipment. The ill-equipped and ill-trained small numbers of the South Korean army seemed to

---

[12] *Years of Trial and Hope*, p. 328.

[13] U.S. Department of the Army, "History of United States Military Advisory Groups to the Republic of Korea," MS., pt. 1, p. 47. Based on the Department of the Army Radio Communication, OUT 99374 to CG, Korea, April, 1948. Hereafter cited as *KMAG History*.

[14] *Ibid.*, p. 55. Based on Historical Report, GHQ. SCAP & FECOM P & O File 091 Korea.

be inadequate to cope even with internal security problems, such as suppression of riots and armed revolts.

Soon after the initial withdrawal of American troops, South Korea was plagued by sabotage, demonstrations, and armed insurrections in various localities. Infiltration of subversive elements from the North rapidly mounted and domestic unrest intensified to an almost uncontrollable degree. Communists penetrated into various levels of governmental organizations including the colleges, high schools, and the constabulary forces. On October 2, 1948, less than two months after the inauguration of the Republic of Korea, a constabulary unit on Cheju Island rebelled against the central government. The government immediately ordered the 14th Constabulary Regiment, stationed in the seaport of Yŏsu, to suppress the insurrection, but the regiment, under the leadership of Lt. Kim Chi-hoe and other Communist-indoctrinated junior officers, suddenly revolted and occupied the city of Yŏsu and its sister city, the education center of Sunch'ŏn. The 4th Regiment, dispatched from the provincial capital of Kwangju to control the situation, also joined the rebellion, with local Communists and large numbers of students. This became the first major revolt against the new Republic.[15] Led by 2,000 rebellious troops, it quickly spread to the towns of Posŏng, Kwanyang, and Pŏlkyo in southern Chŏlla province. Although all these towns were recaptured by loyal troops within about a week, several hundred rebel troops escaped to the almost impenetrable Chili mountain area nearby and became guerrilla forces to harass the new government. Before escaping, they established people's committees and tribunals and executed about 500 government officials and so-called "reactionary elements." According to a

[15] *Seoul Shinmun* and *Dong-A Ilbo*, October 19–30, 1948. The factual statements in this chapter are based on *Seoul Shinmun* and *Dong-A Ilbo*. See also Kim Sam-gyu, *Konnichi no Chōsen* (Today's Korea) (Tokyo, 1956), pp. 28–32; and Hong Sŭng-myŏn *et al.*, *Haebang Isip nyŏn* (Twenty Years of Emancipation) (Seoul, 1965), Vol. 1, pp. 322–325.

report of the U.N. Commission in Korea, 9,536 rebels were killed or captured between October, 1948 and August, 1949.

On November 2, 1948, a second revolt broke out at Taegu among other constabulary troops. Though it also was quickly suppressed, maintenance of law and order became extremely difficult as many civilian Communists joined the guerrilla forces. In many rural areas, the central government may have ruled during the day, but Communist guerrillas ruled at night. On November 13, President Rhee declared martial law in one-fourth of South Korea.[16]

After the Taegu revolt, Rhee requested an additional security force of 50,000 to check subversive elements. In order to form and train such a force, he asked that a permanent United States military and naval mission be established at once.[17] In addition, the National Assembly appealed to the United States to maintain troops in Korea until its own security forces were capable of maintaining order.[18]

In this emergency situation, the complete withdrawal of American troops would almost certainly have meant the downfall of the new republic. Under these threatening circumstances, the State Department seems to have become confused and its policy lines unclear. The Far East seemed to be on the verge of collapse in the surge of the Communist tide; it was urgent to build a dike somewhere. The Department had expressly requested the temporary halt of troop withdrawal and had asked that a regimental combat team of 7,500 men be allowed to remain for some time.[19] Yet Am-

---

[16] *Seoul Shinmun,* November 2–8, 1948; for the Communist point of view, see Kim Hi-il, *Mije ŭi Chosŏn Ch'imyak Sa* (History of the Invasion of American Imperialism in Korea) (Pyongyang, 1962), pp. 99–111 and Kim Chong-myŏng, *Chōsen Shin Minshushugi Kakumei Shi* (History of Korea's New Democratic Revolution) (Tokyo, 1953), pp. 261–271.

[17] Letter of Rhee to Ambassador Muccio. "KMAG History," MS, pt. 1, p. 61.

[18] U.S. Department of State, *The Conflict of Korea,* Far Eastern series 45 (Washington, 1951), p. 17.

[19] *Military Situation in the Far East,* pt. 3, p. 2008.

bassador Muccio and General John B. Coulter, who succeeded Hodge in August, 1948, repeatedly assured the Koreans that there had been no change in United States policy concerning the withdrawal of American troops.

In December, the Soviet withdrawal left the Americans as the only foreign troops on the peninsula, a most embarrassing situation. The Russians were spreading propaganda that the United States intended to stay longer for the purpose of using Korea as an important military base in Asia.

WITHDRAWAL OF AMERICAN OCCUPATION FORCES

Although such an action could only aid Moscow's military and political strategy, it was, nevertheless, announced on December 28, 1948, that the United States would evacuate one full American Army division. The U.S. XXIV Corps left Korea in January for deactivation in Japan, leaving only the 5th Regimental Combat Team.[20] In February, Secretary of the Army Kenneth C. Royall and General Wedemeyer spent some time in Seoul and reviewed with Rhee the question of troop withdrawal and the training of the Korean army.[21] The departments of State and Defense and the National Security Council completed in March a thorough review of the United States Korean policy. The National Security Council concluded that further support and assistance to Korea should not include the presence of American occupation forces and that a complete evacuation of U.S. troops was politically and militarily desirable; preparation should be made to permit complete withdrawal by June 30, 1949. The Council also concluded that legislative authority should be sought for military assistance for the fiscal year of 1950, and that thereafter aid should depend on the development of Korea's own military strength. It further recommended that

[20] "KMAG History," MS, pt. 1, p. 61.

[21] Excerpts from the hearing of Ambassador Muccio at the United Nations Commission, U.N. Document, *A/AC. 26/SR.33.*

there be established a U.S. Military Advisory Group to train ROK (Republic of Korea) armed forces. President Truman approved the Council's recommendations.[22]

Subsequently, USAFIK was instructed to complete its withdrawal not later than June 30, and to establish a military advisory group with 500 officers and enlisted men.[23] With the first public announcement about the withdrawal of American troops, Rhee issued a statement proclaiming that the South Korean army was rapidly reaching the point at which our security can be assured, provided the Republic of Korea is not called upon to face attack from a foreign source.[24] He added that discussions were now underway between the representatives of the Republic and the United States concerning the establishment of a date in the course of several months for the withdrawal from Korea of U.S. troops.

A radio message from the Supreme Commander in Japan on May 15 ordered General William L. Roberts, who had assumed Command of USAFIK in January, 1949, to proceed with the final evacuation of his troops from Korea. On May 28, the first of four groups of the 5th Regimental Combat Team moved from Inchon en route to Hawaii, followed by a second, third, and fourth on the 18th, 21st, and 29th of June respectively. In accordance with paragraph II of the resolution of the U. N. Commission of June 20, Sub-Commission III engaged in the observation and verification of the withdrawal. By June 29, the evacuation of American troops was completed;[25] USAFIK headquarters was deactivated at midnight the next day. At the same time, the interim mili-

---

[22] "KMAG History," MS, p. 62, based on NSC file 8/2, Sect. 1-A BK 1, Case 5/8.

[23] *Ibid.*, based on Department of the Army, RAD WX 86933, April 9, 1949.

[24] *New York Times,* April 19, 1949.

[25] U.S. Department of State, *Chronology of Events concerning Korea, 1943–October 1, 1950.* DRF Information Paper No. 362. Unclassified mimeographed paper, p. 7.

tary agreement entered into by Hodge and Rhee in August, 1948, automatically lapsed and Rhee assumed complete control of the South Korean forces.[26]

Knowing America's determination to withdraw its troops regardless of the internal situation of the country, Rhee realized that retention of a small task force would not "mean much." He was now more interested in a statement from American authorities that the United States would solidly stand by Korea in case of outside aggression. He thought that a strong statement or an agreement to that effect would be more salutary than the retention of a task force.[27] As a hesitant response to Rhee's request, Truman recommended to Congress that there be a continuation of economic assistance to South Korea.[28] The next day, the State Department issued a press release on U.S. policy, which read in part:

> In pursuance of the recommendation contained in the General Assembly's resolution of December 12, 1948, to the effect that the occupying powers should "withdraw their occupation forces from Korea as early as practicable," the United States Government will soon have completed the withdrawal of its occupation forces from the country. As is clear from the broad program of assistance outlined above, this withdrawal in no way indicates a lessening of the United States support in the Republic of Korea, but constitutes rather another step toward the normalization of relations with that Republic. . . .[29]

Neither in this nor in subsequent statements was there a guarantee of the territorial integrity and sovereignty of the Republic against the possibility of future aggression from

---

[26] U.N. *Official Record, General Assembly, Fourth session*, Supplement No. 9 (*A/936*), p. 31.

[27] U.N. Document, *A/AC. 26/SR.33.*

[28] *Chronology of Events Concerning Korea, 1943–October 1, 1950*, p. 7. Truman asked the Congress for 100 million dollars for the ECA program for Korea for the fiscal year 1950.

[29] U.S. Congress, Senate Committee on Foreign Relations, *The United States and the Korean Problem, Documents, 1943–1953* (Washington, 1953), pp. 26–27.

the North. Nor was there any promise of a mutual defense program in the event of large-scale Communist aggression in the Far East, or even of adequate military assistance to the Korean armed forces in the near future—except for a plan to establish a small American military training program and to transfer existing military equipment to the South Korean army. Moreover, there was no guarantee of any further effort toward unification; it seemed that the United States had completely transferred this responsibility to the United Nations.

American policy toward Korea in this critical period was apparently directed toward one immediate and primary objective: to end its unwanted political and military commitments in the country as soon as possible. Though the development of South Korean strength was desirable as a bulwark against Communist aggression, it seems that troop withdrawal was of more concern than the build-up of security forces. Military authorities in Washington recognized the inability of South Korea's armed forces to deter outside aggression, but the situation was not corrected by the subsequent American program of economic and military aid. In fact, the inadequacy and resulting failure of the aid program further demonstrated American reluctance to commit herself to this area.

ECONOMIC AID

When the National Security Council recommended the evacuation of American forces, the conclusion was reached that the prospect for Korea's survival may be considered favorable as long as it can continue to receive large-scale aid from the United States.[30] Actually, in view of the fact that the new Republic was created through the efforts of American diplomacy and America's previous commitment, the

---

[30] *Years of Trial and Hope,* p. 328. Department of State, *The Conflict of Korea,* p. 7. Ko Sŭngje, *Han'guk Kyŏngje Ron* (Theory of Korean Economy) (Seoul, 1957), pp. 7–33.

United States had a special relationship to the Republic. In addition, for its own security and prestige in Asia, America could not afford a complete abdication of responsibility. The President recognized that without positive economic assistance, there could be no real hope of "achieving a unified, free, and democratic Korea."

Since 1945, three factors had greatly aggravated the ills of the South Korean economy. First, the refusal of the Soviet Union to permit the free exchange of goods had effectively cut off South Korea from normal industrial activities. Second, the sudden exodus of Japanese left Korea bereft of trained management and technical personnel. The Korean people had long been denied the opportunity to develop technical skills to match the industrial development of their economy.[31] Third, the legacy of a colonial economy, with a heavy influx of refugees from the North, effected a further dislocation of the economy. During the 35 years of Japanese domination, the national economy of Korea had been integrated into the overall economy of the Japanese empire so that it lacked self-sufficiency, and its production was seriously unbalanced.

In the summer of 1947, manufacturing industries were operating at 20 percent of their prewar level and were continuing to reduce or to close down production. Meanwhile, Korea turned from a food-exporting nation into a food-deficit nation because of sharp increases in population and low production resulting from fertilizer shortages.[32]

In an effort to meet serious basic needs, the occupation authorities under the Department of the Army used funds

---

[31] John P. Lewis, *Reconstruction and Development in South Korea* (Washington, 1955), p. 9. For an excellent analysis of the colonial economy, see Cho Ki-jun, *Han'guk Kyŏngje Sa* (Economic History of Korea) (Seoul, 1962), pp. 257–422.

[32] Half a million tons of fertilizer valued at nearly 60 million dollars were imported to South Korea in the three years of military occupation. USAFIK, *South Korean Interim Government Activities*, No. 34 (July, 1948), p. 2.

from Government and Relief in Occupied Areas Appropriations (GARIOA) almost exclusively for such items as food, clothing, fertilizer, and petroleum.[33] Assistance to the major industrial facilities themselves was virtually ignored. Supplementing the military government, the United Nations Relief and Rehabilitation Administration (UNRRA) provided considerable amounts of economic assistance for relief purposes before completion of its mission to Korea in June, 1947. Because of the uncooperative attitude of the Soviet Union in its occupation zone, the assistance from UNRRA was limited to less than one million dollars.[34]

Toward the end of the occupation, there was a gradual shift from relief to economic assistance in terms of capital investment, despite General Wedemeyer's advice against a program of rehabilitation or industrialization in the absence of unification. Along with this shift, the army obtained authority to purchase raw materials with its GARIOA funds. William M. McGovern, who spent two months as a consultant for Congressional committees observing the situation in the Far East, was less concerned about the perils of geographical division than about the absence of clear-cut policy and the lack of competent American technicians to assist Korean reconstruction and development.[35] After withdrawal, however, long-range economic planning became more urgent because the strength and internal stability of the Republic of Korea were of direct importance to the national security of the United States in Asia.[36] Under Secre-

---

[33] Department of the Army's total allocations under the GARIOA program to Korea were as follows: 1946—$6,000,000; 1947—$93,000,-000; 1948—$113,000,000; 1949—$144,000,000; total—$356,000,000.

[34] George Woodbridge, *History of the UNRRA Administration,* Vol. 11 (New York, 1950), p. 463.

[35] William A. Brown, Jr. and Redvers Opie, *American Foreign Assistance* (Washington, 1953), p. 373.

[36] U.S. Congress, House, *Economic Assistance to the Republic of Korea,* 81st Congress, 1st Session, House Document 212 (Washington, 1950). This is the message from the President to Congress.

tary of State Webb emphasized before the House Committee on Foreign Affairs in June, 1949, that a modest capital equipment program was indispensable for building a viable Korean economy. He further stated that "without a continuation, for the present, of outside assistance not only for essential relief, but also to help the Korean people to bring themselves closer to a level of economic self-support, the Korean economy will suffer a rapid, inevitable collapse. Under such circumstances, only the Communists would win."[37] Therefore, the concern of the United States for the new Republic had two goals: (1) capital investment, and (2) strengthening Korean security forces.

ACTIVITY OF THE ECA

Under an economic agreement with the Republic of Korea,[38] effective January 1, 1949, the United States now undertook to provide economic assistance in accordance with their previous agreement of December, 1948.[39] The President of the United States by executive order transferred the authority for the continuance of an economic program from the Department of the Army to the Economic Cooperation Administration, which had originally been established to carry out the Marshall Plan in Europe and to administer aid to China. Responsibility was given to this agency on the understanding that the program presented to Congress would be a real economic recovery program with emphasis on long-range capital development. At this time the U.S. also extended *de jure* recognition to the government of the Republic of Korea, on the basis of the resolution of the General Assembly on December 12, 1948.

The ECA proceeded to launch a large-scale program of

---

[37] *Department of State Bulletin,* June 19, 1949, p. 785.

[38] The text of the agreement is in U.S. Congress, *Background Information on Korea* (Washington, 1950), pp. 22–27.

[39] The text of the agreement on financial and property settlement is in *Korea: 1945 to 1948,* pp. 104–112.

assistance, designed to fill the economic vacuum and to promote economic stability in an effort to contribute to the political stability of the new Republic. To insure that the aid would go to Western-oriented Korea alone, the Congress passed an amendment to the bill (H.R. 5330) which read: "Notwithstanding the provisions of any other law, the Administration shall immediately terminate aid under this [Act] in the event of the formation in the Republic of Korea of a coalition government which includes one or more members of the Communist Party or the party now in control of the government of northern Korea." [40] While this amendment clearly shows that the United States would not tolerate any future government which included a Communist in its cabinet, no definite policy was indicated with regard to defending Korea in case of possible attack from the Communists.

The ECA was the sole agency operating the aid program during the period between the establishment of the Republic and the outbreak of the Korean War.[41] For the fiscal years 1948, 1949, and 1950, the agency had plans for a three-year effort emphasizing these lines of development: (a) coal and electric power production; (b) agricultural production; (c) fisheries; (d) mineral resources; (e) transportation and communications; (f) the textile industry; (g) the training of Korean technicians and specialists; and (h) the conversion of Japanese-built war factories to peacetime purposes. The principal products financed by ECA were coal, bread, grains, cotton, machinery and vehicles, and petroleum.[42]

---

[40] Public Law 447, 81st Congress, 2nd Session, the Far East Economic Assistance Act of 1950, House Report No. 2495, *Background Information on Korea,* p. 31.

[41] Brookings Institution, *The Administration of Foreign Affairs and Overseas Operations* (Washington, 1951), p. 29.

[42] ECA, *Fifth Report to Congress for Period April 3–June 30, 1949* (Washington, 1949), pp. 83–88. See also *Economic Aid to The Republic of Korea* submitted by ECA in June, 1949.

In the fiscal year 1949–50, Truman had available only 60 million dollars to be spent in economic aid before February 15, 1950.[43] Therefore, on June 7, 1949, he sent a message to Congress asking for the sum of 150 million dollars for the Korean program for the 1949–50 fiscal year.[44] But despite the warning from Secretary of State Acheson that the Republic would fall "within three months" if economic assistance were not provided, the Korean issue received scant attention in the first session of the 81st Congress. The Senate passed the requested Korean aid bill, but in January, 1950, a parallel bill was rejected by the House, 193 to 191, with most of the negative votes coming from the Republican members.[45]

This defeat was partly caused by a maneuver of the opposition in the House to force the Administration to increase aid to the Chinese Nationalists, but it was also an expression of a feeling that further help for Korea would be useless.[46] The Republican opposition was extremely critical of continued aid, charging that the Administration had no overall policy for saving Asia. It was generally thought that with the fall of China (and with Formosa expected to go the same way), there was no chance for the survival of Korea in case of aggression from the North.[47] It was argued that Washington was not merely backing another loser, but also that "there is every reason to believe that the lending of economic assis-

---

[43] U.S. Congress, House Report No. 962, *Aid to Korea,* 81st Congress, 1st Session (Washington, 1949), pp. 21–26. *Background Information of Korea,* p. 27.

[44] *Department of State Bulletin,* June 19, 1949, pp. 781–783.

[45] *Ibid.,* February 6, 1950, p. 212. See also *Aid to Korea,* 81st Congress, First Session, HR 962.

[46] One hundred and seventy Democrats and twenty-one Republicans voted for the Korean Aid Bill. The opposition consisted of sixty-one Democrats, one hundred and thirty Republicans, and Mr. Marcantonio. *Ibid.*

[47] See an article written by Mr. Hanson Baldwin in *New York Times,* June 11, 1949.

tance at this time will only enhance the prize to be taken by force of arms and internal intrigue." [48]

The President and his Secretary of State, however, did not accept this reasoning. The day following the defeat of the aid bill, Acheson warned Truman that "this action, if not quickly repaired, will have the most far-reaching adverse effects upon our foreign policy, not only in Korea but in many other areas of the world." [49] The Administration believed that if limited assistance were continued, the Republic would have a good chance of survival as a free nation; should such aid be denied, that chance might well be lost and all previous American efforts wasted. The State Department argued that a strong Republic supported by economic aid would alone serve as a nucleus for the eventual peaceful unification of the entire country on a democratic basis,[50] and stressed the possible impact of the downfall of Korea upon the people of South and Southeastern Asia and the Pacific islands.

The unfavorable reaction from the Administration and general public to the defeat of the Korean aid bill brought about a reconsideration of the measure. On January 22, Mr. Acheson asked the House Foreign Affairs Committee to reverse the earlier vote: the Administration was ready to pay the price of seeing the Chinese Nationalists brought into the bill. On the following day, the Committee approved a new bill, the Far Eastern Economic Assistance Act, and the House itself passed it, 240 to 134, on February 9. It was approved by the Senate on the next day and signed by the President about a week later.[51] The Act allocated 103 mil-

[48] See the opinion of the minority views in *Aid to Korea,* 81st Congress, First Session, House Report 962: pt. 2, Minority Views to accompany H. R. 5330, p. 2.

[49] Letter from Acheson to Truman, January 20, 1950. *Department of State Bulletin,* February 6, 1950, p. 212.

[50] *Ibid.,* March 20, 1950, p. 455.

[51] *The United States in World Affairs, 1950,* ed. Richard P. Stebbins (New York, 1951), pp. 91–93.

lion dollars to Nationalist China, providing at the same time 60 million for South Korea—that is, 40 million less than the amount requested by the Administration. Under this and other legislation, a total of $110,000,000 was made available for the fiscal year ending June 30, 1950.[52]

It can hardly be said, in comparison with the amounts devoted to China and the European countries, that this aid was overly generous. Furthermore, the long delay by Congress came at a critical time; economic development in Korea was temporarily impeded and inflation was becoming serious. Nonetheless, it did enable Korea to make significant progress toward achieving a viable economy in the brief period before it was engulfed by the Korean War. One of the quickly conspicuous achievements was an increase in rice production: a large quantity of fertilizer imported from the United States allowed the Republic once again to become not only self-sufficient in basic foodstuffs, but actually to export some rice.[53] Progress in industrial production was also remarkable. Electric power, for instance, reached an average of 57.7 million kilowatts a month in the second quarter of 1949, a 19 percent gain over the previous three months and 50 percent higher than a year earlier.[54] The sharply increasing coal supplies enabled industrial plants to increase production, with results that the output in March, 1949, was the highest since the end of the war. Per capita gross national product in that year reached an estimated post-World War II high of $86. In addition, the living standard of the people reached the highest point since 1945, though it was still lower than during the prewar period.

If there had been no delay in economic aid, and if the Republic had enjoyed immunity from military attack, there

---

[52] *Conflict of Korea,* p. 8. For detailed information see U.S. Congress, House Report 2495, *Background Information on Korea,* pp. 27–33.

[53] Brown and Opie, *American Foreign Assistance,* p. 372.

[54] *The Fifth Report to Congress,* p. 84.

were strong indications that Korea would have reached self-sufficiency by the beginning of 1953. Because of the delay in Congressional action, the country had received at the time of the North Korean attack goods representing less than half the total allocated amount. Moreover, if the United States had started its long-range development plan three years earlier despite the opposition of the Soviet Union, Korea might have been sound enough economically to have prevented the Northern invasion.

It was unfair, as well as unrealistic in terms of American interest, to create an anti-communist government and then fail to provide it with American moral and material support. While it maintained that "strength is not simply a matter of arms and forces, it is a matter of economic growth, social health and vigorous institutions, public and private,"[55] the United States actually showed little interest in the Republic. American attitudes of resignation, hesitation, and withdrawal had a role in encouraging the aggression from the North, and thus in producing the tragic Korean War.

[55] A part of President Truman's State of the Union message, *New York Times,* January 13, 1950.

11

United States Policy on the Eve of the Korean War

Bewildered by the fall of the Chinese mainland, the United States seemed to be in a state of shock; it was several months before she began to search for a more effective Far Eastern policy. The issuance of the White Paper on China and the subsequent collapse of the Nationalist regime on the mainland were disturbing signs to the Asian people. It seemed that the United States no longer intended to resist Communist aggression on the Asian continent. In fact, General MacArthur later wrote that there was a directive from Washington that "all available material should be used 'to counter false impressions' that the retention of Formosa would save the Chinese government, and that its loss would damage seriously the interests of either the United States or of other countries opposing Communism." [1]

In Korea, the United States seemed to withdraw completely its political and military commitments. According to the General, the Joint Chiefs of Staff had drawn up a defense strategy in Asia which was based "on the assumption that under no circumstances would the United States engage in the military defense of the Korean peninsula." The occupa-

[1] Douglas MacArthur, *Reminiscences* (New York, 1964), pp. 321 and 324.

tion forces were evacuated in spite of a strong protest by the Korean National Assembly; the Korean aid bill received cold treatment by Congress; increasingly urgent requests for military assistance were given little attention. This series of events gave the impression that America no longer wished to support the Republic, even if there were outright aggression from the North. The meager economic and military aid that had been promised seemed to be a farewell gift to an abandoned country, and the possibility of civil war became more real than ever before.

The Asian peoples felt that the position of the United States in Korea differed from her position in China because of her wartime pledge and the military occupation. After all, the Republic was a creation of American Asian policy, and the United States had been the first country to extend *de facto* and *de jure* recognition to the government.[2] America was also a strong advocate in the General Assembly and in the Security Council of the admission of the Republic to the United Nations.[3] It was the American delegation which vehemently opposed the membership application of the Democratic People's Republic. It seemed, therefore, that abandonment of Korea to communism could forecast abandonment of the whole of Asia, and could be viewed as a sign of the unreliability of the United States policy.

ORIGIN OF THE SOUTH KOREA ARMY

Almost from the beginning, occupational authorities recognized that further development of the South Korean police force alone would be inadequate to meet national defense needs. As early as November 13, 1945, the military government created an "Office of the Director of National

---

[2] The United States accorded *de jure* recognition on January 1, 1949. *Department of State Bulletin,* January 9, 1949, p. 59.

[3] The Republic of Korea applied for membership in January, 1949 (U.N. Document, *S/1238*), but was vetoed in the Security Council by the Soviet Union on February 15, 1949.

Defense" with jurisdiction over the Bureau of Police and a newly established "Bureau of Armed Forces," to be comprised of Army and Navy departments. In December, however, the State-War-Navy Coordinating Committee concluded that the matter of establishing armed forces was too closely related with the unsettled problems of American commitment and recommended that action to establish a Korean army and navy be deferred.[4] Although it was apparent that the occupational authority believed in the need for Korean forces, Washington became increasingly hesitant. In this connection General Hodge wrote:

> I was very interested in establishing a Korean army from the beginning of the occupation, not only to relieve American troops of many details in handling Korean security but to get a start for the future when we accomplish our mission of setting up a Korean government. I was met with much opposition at higher levels apparently in the belief that at that stage of our relations such a move might be misunderstood by the Russians and be a source of difficulty when it came to the coordinating of the American and Russian zones of Korea into a single nation.[5]

Washington's hesitation seemed to be reasonable as, at this time, the Joint U.S.-Soviet Commission was soon to meet in

---

[4] Except where otherwise indicated, the information in this chapter is based on: (1) U.S. Department of the Army, "History of American Military Advisory Groups in Korea," MS, n. d., hereafter cited as *KMAG History*. The manuscript was published in 1962 as *Military Advisors in Korea: KMAG in Peace and War,* prepared by Major Robert K. Sawyer and edited by Walter G. Hermes. The original manuscript contains information not available in the published volume. *KMAG History,* pt. 1, p. 9. This is based on USAFIK, Files, AGO Record Center, Kansas City, Mo. (2) U.S. Department of State, *The Conflict of Korea,* released October, 1951; (3) U.S. Congress, *Background Information on Korea,* House Report No. 2495, 1950; (4) U.S. Congress, *Military Situation in the Far East,* 5 pts., 1951; (5) Department of State, *Mutual Defense Assistance Program, A Fact Sheet,* 1950; and (6) *First Semi-annual Report on the Mutual Defense Assistance Program,* House Document No. 613, 1950.

[5] Letter of Hodge to Maj. General Orlando Ward, March 18, 1952, as quoted in "KMAG History," MS, pt. 1, p. 29.

Seoul. The establishment of armed forces in South Korea would certainly reduce hopes for unification.

Knowing that it was impractical for the time being to establish armed forces, the military government set up a plan called BAMBOO. This was to organize a police constabulary reserve consisting of 25,000 men to be trained along infantry lines. Recruitment was begun in January, 1946. By the end of the month nearly three companies had been formed and trained in the Seoul area alone, using a limited amount of clothing and equipment from abandoned Japanese stocks under the direction of the United States army.[6] Using a stock pile of 60,000 Japanese rifles and 15 rounds of ammunition for each weapon set aside by the occupation forces, eight regiments were organized by April, 1946, having a total strength of slightly over two thousand men.[7]

Concern over Soviet reaction during this period led Washington to order the military authority to change the title of the Korean "Department of National Defense" to "Department of Internal Security." Later it substituted the "Bureau of Constabulary and Coast Guard" for the "Bureau of Army and Navy." [8] This action greatly lowered the morale of the constabulary, and many officers resigned in protest. Morale deteriorated further through the increasing competition between the regular police force and the constabulary for prestige and jurisdiction. The subsequent revolts of the constabulary, stimulated by Communist elements, were partly the result of this deterioration. The prestige of the constabulary

---

[6] SCAP, *Summation of Non-military Activities in Japan and Korea,* No. 4 (January, 1946), p. 285, and No. 5 (February, 1946), p. 287.

[7] Locations of the regiments were Seoul, Pusan, Kwangju, Taegu, Iri, Taejŏn, Ch'ungju, and Ch'un Ch'ŏn, USAFIK, *Summation of U.S. Army Military Government Activities in Korea,* No. 7 (April, 1946), p. 12.

[8] USAMGIK Ordinances No. 63 (March 29, 1946); No. 64 (April, 1946); and No. 86 (June 15, 1946) in the *Official Gazette,* USAMGIK (United States Military Government in Korea).

fell so low that there were difficulties in recruiting members.

With the change of overall United States policy to containment, emphasis switched to consolidation of the power in the South against the North Korean buildup. It was in this atmosphere that Wedemeyer recommended, and the National Security Council concurred, that the United States actively train and equip the Korean Security forces.[9] However, as noted earlier, MacArthur preferred to wait until the General Assembly expressed its wishes. Yet even after the U.N. resolution had passed, and Washington planners felt the urgency for effective security forces, MacArthur in Tokyo advised against establishing a South Korean army. The reasons given this time were limited training facilities, the lack of competent Korean officers, and the diminishing ability of the XXIV Corps to foster such an army. Instead, he recommended that "the strength of the constabulary be increased to 50,000." [10] Because MacArthur thought that "the United States would have to give up active military support of the ROK forces" in case a serious military threat developed in Korea, he recommended that the remaining American forces be completely withdrawn by May of 1949.[11] Therefore, the South Korean constabulary in the winter and spring of 1947–48 remained limited to only 18,000–20,000 men. In a closed session of the House Appropriations Committee on March 26, 1947, General Hodge had estimated the strength of the North Korean army at 120,000 to 150,000 soldiers.[12] When the Department of the Army instructed Hodge to create conditions for American withdrawal, Hodge directed

---

[9] Albert C. Wedemeyer, *Wedemeyer Reports* (New York, 1958), p. 475.

[10] "KMAG History," MS, pt. 1, p. 44 based on Rad. Msg. CX 5847 and JCS Dc. 1483/51, Appendix "B," March 10, 1948.

[11] *Military Advisors in Korea*, pp. 37–38.

[12] James Steward, Chief of Civilian Information of Military Government in South Korea, was quoted in an Associated Press dispatch, July 26, 1948, as setting the total of the North Korean Forces at 125,000.

the XXIV Corps units to set up a school to train the Koreans in the use of American equipment. American provisional military advisory groups were organized under the command of General Roberts after the establishment of the Republic; this was the first practical step to train Korean forces. A law for the organization of the armed forces was passed by the Korean National Assembly in November, 1948, and at the same time departing units of American troops turned over much-needed supplies to the Koreans. Now, while still lacking mortars and heavy machine guns, the Korean army was "perhaps 70 percent equipped with American small arms and automatic weapons." [13]

By March, 1949, security forces of the Republic had grown to about 114,000 of which 65,000 were army, 4,000 coast guard, and 45,000 police. The army had equipment for only 50,000 men, while approximately one-half of the police and coast guard were equipped with American side arms and carbines; the remainder had Japanese equipment of a similar type.[14] In the opinion of one American military advisor, the Republic of Korea army in June, 1949, "could have been the American Army in 1775." [15] He observed that unless one took into consideration intense national pride, there was little to recommend it as a military force. In the face of an extreme arms shortage, the Koreans produced 20,000 Japanese rifles which they had hidden when U.S. forces were destroying Japanese arms in 1945 and 1946. However, most of these weapons were unserviceable, as well as without ammunition. Nonetheless, the summer of 1949 marked the first time since the Sino-Japanese War of 1894 that the Koreans had been left alone in their country, free of foreign troops. They were at last able to assume control of their own forces.

---

[13] See Report of the United Nations Commission on Korea, U.N. *Official Record, Fourth Session of General Assembly,* Supplement No. 9, pp. 22–23.

[14] *The Conflict of Korea,* p. 9.

[15] *Military Advisors in Korea,* p. 69.

SOUTH KOREAN ARMED STRENGTH

The Provisional Military Advisory Group (PMAG) that had officially ended on July 1, 1949, was reborn as the United States Military Advisory Group to the Republic of Korea (KMAG). KMAG was under jurisdiction of Ambassador Muccio as a part of the American Mission in Korea, and directly under the Department of the Army for operational control. Muccio himself had no control over the advisory group as a military organization. His relationship with General Roberts, KMAG Commander, revolved primarily around American military assistance to Korea. On other matters, such as military command or administration, Roberts reported directly to the Pentagon.[16] General MacArthur's responsibility for KMAG was reduced to logistic support as far as the Korean waterline, and to protection for Americans in Korea. In compliance with the Department of the Army's instructions, however, the Far East Commander was kept informed of political and military events occurring on the peninsula.

In May, 1949, the Russians were believed to have entered into an agreement with the North Koreans to equip six infantry and three motorized divisions and to provide 20 destroyers and 220 aircraft.[17] Yet by June, 1950 when the war began, the ROK army had grown to only 98,000 and their equipment from the United States was sufficient for only 65,000. There were, besides a conventional army headquarters, eight infantry divisions—the 1st, 2nd, 3rd, 5th, 6th, 7th, 8th, and Capitol—all in various stages of organization.[18] But probably only one, the Capitol Division, was near full

---

[16] *Ibid.*, pp. 46–49.

[17] *Survey of International Affairs, 1949–1950,* ed. Peter Calvocoressi (London, 1953), p. 466.

[18] Kukpangbu (the Ministry of National Defense), *Han'guk Chŏllan Inyŏn Chi* (the Record of the First Two Years of the Korean War) (Seoul, 1953). For the chart of the strength of ROK Combat divisions, see Roy E. Appleman, *U.S. Army in the Korean War: South to the Nakton, North to the Yalu* (Washington, 1961), p. 15.

strength; the others were handicapped because equipment for six divisions had to be spread through eight.

KMAG never was able to assign advisors down to the level of every Korean battalion. Furthermore, because of the acute internal disorder caused by guerrilla forces, the Koreans did not have enough time to complete training before they were deployed in anti-guerrilla operations. In the six-month period from July to December, 1949 alone, Korean army units were compelled to mount 542 counter-guerrilla actions, or nearly three a day. By the time of the Northern attack, only 30 of the Republic's 67 army battalions had completed training at even the company level, while the North Koreans had completed training on the level of battalion operations.[19]

As for a navy, the South Korean coast guard had 6,145 men with an assortment of approximately 90 vessels, ranging from Japanese minesweepers to picket boats, of which less than one-half were operational. The Republic had practically no air force, because America was in no way committed to support one with advisors or materials.[20] Air power, then, consisted of 1,865 men, with 14 planes that had been received in 1948 for liaison purposes only. Therefore, the Korean government purchased out of its meager budget 10 AT-6 training aircraft from a private American firm.

MILITARY AID PROGRAM

The equipment delivered to Korea originally cost the United States about $56,000,000 with a 1949 replacement value of approximately $110,000,000. In addition, the United States turned over to Korea $85,000,000 worth of equipment and supplies of military origin that still had considerable

---

19 *Military Advisors in Korea*, pp. 73–75.

20 There is more detailed information on the strength of the Korean armed forces on the eve of the Korean War in *The Conflict in Korea*, p. 10.

value for defense purposes. These included trucks, tractors, trailers, and medical supplies.[21]

On July 25, 1949, the day the United States signed the North Atlantic Treaty, President Truman asked Congress to authorize "military aid to free nations" as an essential phase of American policy to resist Communist aggression. In his message to Congress, the President, in the interests of administrative efficiency and flexibility, proposed to consolidate with the Western European program the existing programs of military aid to Greece and Turkey, Iran, Korea, the Philippines, and countries of the Western Hemisphere.[22] The Mutual Defense Assistance Act became law on October 6, and the appropriations for carrying it out were made available three weeks later. Under this act, Truman provided for a total expenditure of $1,314,010,000 of which one billion was for North Atlantic Treaty signatories; $211,370,-000 for Greece and Turkey; $27,640,000 for Iran, Korea, and the Philippines; and $75,000,000 for use at the President's direction in the "general area" of China. Only $10,200,000 —less than eight-tenths of one percent of the total expenditure—was allocated to Korea. Additionally, before any assistance could be granted to a recipient country under the terms of the Act, a bilateral agreement had to be concluded; Korea signed on January 26, 1950.[23] The aid under this agreement, however, was to be mostly in the form of maintenance material and spare parts for the substantial quantity of military equipment already given. About 90 percent of it was devoted to ordnance supplies and equipment.

General Roberts, as the chief of the military advisors, of course had first hand information on the potential strength of Korean armed forces. Apparently worrying about inade-

---

[21] *Military Advisors in Korea,* pp. 96–97.

[22] Public Law 329, 81st Congress. The necessary appropriations were included in Public Law 430 (H.R. 6427), approved October 28, 1949.

[23] For the text of the treaty see, U.S. Department of the Army, *United States Agreement with Republic of Korea* (Washington, 1954), pp. 9, 11.

quate supplies of military aid, he had recommended, through Ambassador Muccio, that Korean MDAP aid be supplemented by part of the $75,000,000 allotted to the general area of China. Muccio strongly endorsed this recommendation on the grounds that a strong defense force in Korea would contribute to the accomplishment of the policies and purposes set forth in the Act.[24] According to their estimate, sufficient funds should be allocated to bring Korean total military assistance in the fiscal year 1950 to a minimum of $20,000,000. In KMAG's semiannual report dated December 31, 1949, Roberts outlined a specific recommendation for additional aid, falling within an approximate dollar limitation of $9,800,000.[25]

After a few months of surveys and reviews, Congress finally approved only $10,970,000 for Korea's military aid on March 15, 1950.[26] But that did not mean that supplies and equipment began to flow immediately into Korea. Owing to the necessary six to nine month period for rehabilitating available equipment, and one to two years necessary for manufacturing new equipment promised by this program, by June 25, 1950, only about $52,000 worth of signal equipment, and spare parts valued at $298,000 were en route; at the time of the North Korean attacks, material valued at less than $1,000 had been received.[27] Therefore, practically no equipment through Mutual Defense Aid was available to the South Korea armed forces at the time of the Northern aggression.

The reason for the delay in shipment, Secretary Acheson stated in testimony, was that "in view of the status of equipment of the armed forces in 1950, the military equipment for Korea had to come either from new procurement or out of

---

[24] For a detailed information on MDAP, see U.S. Congress, *Background Information on Korea,* pp. 33–40.

[25] *Military Advisors in Korea,* p. 102, based on SA Rpt., KMAG, December 31, 1949.

[26] *Military Situation in the Far East,* pt. 3, p. 1993.

[27] *Ibid.,* pp. 1992–1994; and *The Conflict in Korea,* p. 11.

stocks on hand, which needed extensive rehabilitation and repair; and this could not be done in the 90 days between the time the program was established and the invasion." [28]

By June, 1950, spare parts in all categories were exhausted by the South Korean security forces. American military advisors in Korea estimated that 15 percent of the army's weapons and 35 percent of its vehicles were unserviceable. With the equipment on hand, it was estimated that full-scale defensive operations could not be supported for a period longer than 15 days. KMAG repeatedly warned that "Korea is threatened with the same disaster that befell China."

STRENGTH OF NORTH KOREAN FORCES

The Soviet Union had a more active assistance policy for the aiding of the North Korean forces. Early in 1946, the Soviet occupational authority had established a force of 20,000 men as a border constabulary (Boan Tae) and army (In Min Gun), supplied with Japanese rifles. In 1948 its strength was increased to 60,000 men with a few tanks and aircraft. About 16,000 of these were seasoned veterans who had fought with the Chinese Communist or Soviet armies in World War II. They gave the North Korean People's army a quality and efficiency that it would not otherwise have had.[29] Moreover, when the Soviet occupation troops withdrew in December, 1948, North Korean security forces received a large quantity of military supplies. The Soviets left as many as 150 advisors for each North Korean army division for the purposes of training and organization.[30]

Under the terms of a reciprocal aid agreement concluded

[28] Testimony of Acheson in U.S. Congress, *Military Situation in the Far East,* pt. 3, p. 1992.

[29] Unless otherwise specified, data on the development of North Korean Forces may be found in (1) Roy E. Appleman, *United States Army in the Korean War,* Chapter II, and (2) Robert K. Sawyer, *Military Advisors in Korea,* pp. 104–109.

[30] For Russian equipment and training in North Korea, see two articles by Hanson Baldwin in the *New York Times,* July 5 and 9, 1950.

on March 17, 1949, the Russians agreed to furnish North Korea with arms and equipment for six infantry divisions and three mechanized "units" and for eight battalions of "mobile" border constabulary.[31] In 1949–50, the Soviet Union supplied 10 reconnaissance aircraft, 100 Yak fighter planes, 70 attack bombers, and 100 Russian T-34 and T-70 tanks and heavy artillery. It is reported that by June, 1950, ground forces exceeded 135,000 men, including approximately 77,838 in seven assault infantry divisions, 6,000 in the tank brigade, and 18,600 in the highly indoctrinated border constabulary. In early 1950 Communist China repatriated about 12,000 Koreans from the Chinese Communist forces. Veterans hence made up one-third of the North Korean People's army by June, 1950.[32]

Thus the North Korean armed forces were far superior to the Southern forces in training, firepower, and equipment when they clashed on June 25, 1950.[33] Even though the South Korean army was only slightly smaller than the aggressor from the North, the fighting capacity of the two forces was incomparable. And the weakness of the Southern army was in a large part due to the inadequate American military assistance policy. The South Koreans lacked tanks, medium range artillery, heavy mortars, recoilless rifles, and fighter planes. The half-heartedness of American support of ROK forces later revealed itself in the failure of those forces to defend themselves successfully against Northern aggression.

Unfortunately, while American occupational authorities were thinking in terms of the "Bureau of National Defense"

---

[31] For the text of the treaty, see *Source Materials on Korean Politics and Ideology*, comp. Donald G. Tewksbury (New York, 1950), pp. 127–128; and Indian Council of World Affairs, *Selected Documents: East Asia 1947–50*, ed. Vidya Prakash Dutt (London, 1958), pp. 449–451.

[32] Appleman, *loc. cit.*

[33] U.N. Document, *A/1350*, pp. 27–28. Allen S. Whiting, *China Crosses the Yalu* (New York, 1960), p. 38.

in 1946, the Soviets were already sending thousands of Koreans to Russia for specialized training. While less than a hundred American advisors were nursing the South Korean constabulary with unserviceable rifles through the 1946–1949 period, the Soviet occupational authority was engaging in an active training program, including artillery and tank-maneuvering tactics. While the United States wasted time in endless discussion between the Administration and Congress on the Korean aid program, the Soviet Union supplied fighter planes, bombers, medium tanks, and heavy artillery.

However, the fundamental difference between the two national policies was that the United States, unlike Russia, was hesitant to commit itself on Korean problems. United States military assistance to the Republic was firmly based upon the policy that the military establishment there was basically an internal security force. Washington aimed to provide equipment only to enable Koreans (1) to preserve internal security, (2) to prevent border raids and incursions from north of the 38th parallel, and (3) as a by-product to deter armed attack and other aggression by the forces of North Korea.[34] American strategy was based upon the thesis that a Korean war would not be limited to Korea alone; and in the eventuality of an all-Asian war, Korea would only be a liability to the free world. Policy planners did not seem to take seriously the opinions of local advisors or leaders, including General Roberts and Syngman Rhee, that war was very possible. (In April, 1950, two months before the Northern invasion, the Department of the Army directed Roberts to prepare a plan for a scaled reduction of KMAG personnel.)

It was certainly true that the United States had to determine the extent of its assistance to Korea not only in terms of the demands of the Korean situation itself, but in the light of worldwide commitments. Korea was seen as only one of the

---

[34] *Background Information on Korea*, p. 34.

many free countries endangered by Communist aggression. In addition, America had to furnish military aid to the North Atlantic Treaty nations and also to Greece, Turkey, Iran, the Philippines, and other endangered countries. It was also true, as we have already observed, that the small Republic, with serious economic and internal security problems from marauding guerrillas and revolts, appeared incapable of supporting a large security force immediately or of maintaining more complex weapons of war. Furthermore, Rhee and his government were too bellicose in their attitude toward the North Korean regime; American officials feared Southern attack on the North if offensive weapons were provided. Yet, after all this has been considered, the fact remains that with more extensive economic and military aid, the Republic could have fostered more effective defense forces to deter the Korean War.

KOREA AND THE AMERICAN DEFENSE PERIMETER

From the summer of 1948, military action had flared intermittently along the 38th parallel. These border incidents had been isolated and local in nature while the nominal task force of the United States remained in Korea. After its withdrawal, however, large-scale attacks became more common. On May 3, 1949, North Korean troops launched a large-scale attack in the Kaesŏng area,[35] and during the following six months, hundreds of separate engagements took place along the border. In fact, daily contact between the two opposing troops was no longer unusual.

While most of these skirmishes were only patrol actions, some engagements resulted in heavy casualties on both sides. Provocation reached a peak in the latter part of 1949: in the month of August alone, 527 cases of military clashes were reported. The situation deteriorated to such an extent that in September the United Nations Commission warned

---

[35] *Seoul Shinmun*, May 14, 1949; Kim Sam-gyu, *Konnichi no Chōsen* (Today's Korea) (Tokyo, 1956), pp. 32–44.

the General Assembly of the growing possibility of full-scale war. It also reported that "embittered propaganda and hostile actions which now make up the relations between the two parts of Korea rendered the prospect of the unification more and more remote." [36]

The position of the Republic of Korea grew more and more precarious because of the official and unofficial indications (discussed earlier) from the United States that she would virtually abandon the Republic in the event of an Asian military conflict. In search of an effective Asian policy, and also in answer to the American public, Secretary of State Acheson made his much-criticized remarks before the National Press Club on January 12, 1950. With regard to American security in the Pacific he said:

> This defensive perimeter runs along the Aleutians to Japan and then goes to the Ryukyus. We hold important defense positions in the Ryukyu Islands. We will at an appropriate time offer to hold these islands under trusteeship of the United Nations. But they are essential parts of the defensive perimeter of the Pacific, and they must and will be held. The defensive perimeter runs from the Ryukyus to the Philippine Islands . . .[37]

The Republic of Korea and Formosa were conspicuously absent from the line of his "defensive perimeter." Furthermore,

[36] The United Nations Commission on Korea said that border raids from the North were frequently reported, and that they were supposed to be increasing in intensity. U.N. Document, *A/936*, Vol. 1, p. 33. On the other hand, the guerrilla operations in the South were also intensified by partisans armed and partly supplied by North Korea. A North Korean source claimed that in April of 1950 the guerrillas, numbering somewhere between 50,000 to 65,000, attacked various government installations more than 1,400 times, inflicting 2,500 casualties. It claimed that 666 "reactionary" elements were purged during the same period by peasant rebellions. See Kim Chong-myŏng, *Chōsen Shin Minshushugi Kakumei Shi* (History of Korea's New Democratic Revolution) (Tokyo, 1953), pp. 300–301; and *Military Advisors in Korea*, pp. 74–75.

[37] For the full text of Acheson's statement, see *Department of State Bulletin*, January 23, 1950, pp. 111–116.

he made it clear that "no person can guarantee these areas against military attack"—that is, those areas outside the "defensive perimeter." He remarked that such a guarantee would hardly be sensible or necessary within the realm of practical relationship. If such an attack occurred, "the initial reliance must be on the people attacked to resist it and then upon the commitments of the entire civilized world under the Charter of the United Nations which so far has not proved a weak reed to lean on by any peoples who are determined to protect their independence against outside aggression."

This was the first clear-cut statement on a United States defense perimeter in Asia. It seemed a most surprising statement, though, as we have seen earlier, the National Security Council had decided as early as September, 1947, that Korea had no strategic value for American defense. The same conclusion had been reached in the Council when it reviewed the overall policy on Korea in 1949. MacArthur had also already (in March, 1949) told G. Ward Price, a British journalist, that America's line of defense ran through a chain of islands from the Philippines to the Aleutians through the Ryukyu Archipelago.[38] Later that year he confirmed the same story to William R. Mathews of the *Arizona Daily Star*. At this time, the General mentioned that "anyone who commits the American army on the mainland of Asia ought to have his head examined."[39]

Thus, Acheson's statement was really nothing but a confirmation of long-standing American military strategy; but it was certainly an unwise and unskilled diplomatic maneuver to broadcast it openly to the world. And only seven weeks before the North Korean attack, Senator Tom Connally, the

---

[38] Richard H. Rovere and Arthur M. Schlesinger, Jr., *The General and the President* (New York, 1951), pp. 100–102.

[39] *Ibid.*, p. 100. See also *Reminiscences*, p. 322; and John W. Spanier, *The Truman-MacArthur Controversy and the Korean War* (New York, 1965), pp. 16–17.

Democratic chairman of the Senate Foreign Relations Committee, went further than Acheson to state publicly that South Korea would have to be abandoned. He hinted that the United States would probably not intervene in the event of large-scale military conflict, since Korea was not "very important." [40] Virtually tantamount to an invitation for Communist aggression on Korea and Formosa, Acheson's and Connally's statements meant to ordinary people that Korea was considered outside the defense perimeter of the United States and that, if the North attacked, the Republic would have to depend upon its own strength until the United Nations took measures to stop the invasion.

Since the United Nations could not take any such measures without the consent of the Security Council in which the Soviet Union held a veto power, it must have appeared to the Kremlin and the North Korean government that the South was not only hopelessly weak defensively, but also had been abandoned by its former friend. Acheson's statement and the unofficial indications from MacArthur and Connally seem to have had great influence when the North Korean and Kremlin strategists planned for the invasion.[41] They may well have concluded that they now had an opportunity to achieve the unification of Korea through military force without serious risk of American involvement.

Although the United States remained unconcerned about a possible invasion from the North, she did become increasingly worried over South Korea's critical economic situation and its political development. On April 3, Acheson warned of a cut in the new economic assistance program unless adequate action was taken by the Republic to curb its mounting inflation, and expressed concern about a current rumor that

---

[40] This was remarked in an interview for *U.S. News and World Report*. See Trumbull Higgins, *Korea and the Fall of MacArthur* (New York, 1960), p. 14.

[41] Phillip E. Mosely, "Soviet Policy and the Korean War," *Journal of International Affairs*, Spring, 1952, pp. 107–114.

the election due in May, 1950, would be postponed.[42] Ambassador-at-large Philip C. Jessup also reminded the members of the Korean National Assembly of Truman's State of the Union message which declared: "Strength is not simply a matter of arms and force. It is a matter of economic growth and social health and vigorous institutions, public and private. We can achieve peace only if we maintain our productive energy, our democratic institutions, and our firm belief in individual freedom."[43]

Elections were held on May 30. There were 210 seats to be filled and 2,209 candidates ran. Between 86 and 90 percent of the electorate went to the polls, though the Communists again tried to cause a boycott. This election resulted in a much more representative legislative body, which convened June 19 in a hopeful atmosphere conducive to continued progress.[44] Economic and social conditions were also improving, despite continued unrest and disorder instigated by Communist guerrillas.

When Dulles, then consultant to the Secretary of State, came that month to Korea, he belatedly gave the Republic this assurance:

> The American people give you their support, both moral and material, consistent with your own self-respect and your primary dependence on your own efforts.
>
> We look on you as, spiritually, a part of the United Nations which has acted with near unanimity to advance your political freedom, which seeks your unity with the north and which, even though you are technically deprived of formal membership, nevertheless requires all nations to refrain from any threat or use of force against your territorial integrity or political independence. . . .

---

[42] *Department of State Bulletin,* April 17, 1950, p. 602.

[43] *New York Times,* January 13, 1950.

[44] Cablegram from the U.N. Commission on Korea, June 26, 1950. U.N. Document, *S/1505,* June 26, 1950; see also U.N. *Yearbook of the United Nations,* 1950, pp. 253–256. See also Taehan Min'guk Kukhoe (National Assembly), *Yŏktae Kukhoe Sŏngŏ Sanghwang* (Election Results of Congressional Elections) (Seoul, 1964), p. 173.

> The free world has no written charter, but it is no less real for that. Membership depends on the conduct of a nation itself; there is no veto. Its compulsion to common actions are powerful, because they flow from a profound sense of common destiny.
>
> You are not alone. You will never be alone so long as you continue to play worthily your part in the great design of human freedom.[45]

Although this greatly encouraged the Koreans, it left many questions unanswered. There was no clear-cut, definite commitment of American military assistance in the event of outright aggression from the Northern regime. Nothing was said about plans for American intervention to protect the South, nor was there any indication of intent to conclude a mutual defense treaty. It carefully avoided even mentioning a promise for more active economic and military aid. The speech was emotionally well phrased, but it contained nothing that was substantially new. As we now know from captured documents dated prior to Dulles' talk, North Korea was already prepared to attack.[46]

Military preparation in the North had increased rapidly during the early months of 1950. Large shipments of arms and equipment were flown in from the Soviet Union. American as well as Korean intelligence agencies had become aware of the growingly aggressive posture of North Korea. As early as October 10, 1949, the Chinese Ambassador to South Korea, Shao Yu-lin, had warned that North Korea might invade South Korea with the help of Moscow and Peking.[47] On March 10, 1950, General MacArthur's headquarters reported to the Joint Chiefs of Staff in Washington that there were indications that North Korea planned a large-

---

[45] *Department of State Bulletin,* July 3, 1950, pp. 12–13.

[46] See the captured document, reconnaissance Order No. 1, dated June 18, 1950. *The Conflict in Korea,* pp. 25–36.

[47] Robert T. Oliver, *Why War Came in Korea* (New York, 1950), p. 17.

scale invasion around June, 1950.[48] Yet on March 25, MacArthur reported that there would be no civil war that spring or summer and that instead, continued guerrilla warfare was likely.[49] On May 10, there were public warnings from the Republic's Ministry of Defense that its intelligence reports indicated that the North Korean army, estimated to have a total strength of 183,000 men equipped with planes and tanks, was moving toward the 38th parallel.[50]

The signs were clear. The responsible authorities in Seoul, Tokyo, and Washington already knew that there were growing indications of attacks from the North during the spring of 1950. Yet Pentagon authorities and KMAG advisors agreed with MacArthur's estimation and decided that no attack was imminent. And even if there were one, they thought that the ROK army would be "able to meet any test the North Korean army might impose on it." Indeed, in June, 1950, General Roberts and KMAG's senior G-1, G-2, and G-3 advisors and several other key personnel were being transferred, further indicating American complacence. The South Korean army itself was not on guard: on the day of the invasion, Seoul was surprised by repeated broadcasts cancelling leaves and calling for soldiers who were on leave in the city.[51]

Three weeks before its attack, the North Korean regime had once more proposed that a general election be held on August 15, the fifth anniversary of the Korean liberation, in order to form a united all-Korean parliament. They also pro-

---

48 *Military Situation in the Far East,* pt. 3, p. 1990. See also Charles A. Willoughby and John Chamberlain, *MacArthur 1941–1951* (New York, 1954), pp. 351–352; and Izidore F. Stone, *The Hidden Story of the Korean War* (New York, 1952), pp. 19–20.

49 *Military Situation in the Far East,* pt. 3, p. 1990.

50 *New York Times,* May 10, 1950 and U. N. Documents, *S/1506,* p. 28–29.

51 "KMAG History," MS p. 119. For the South Korean story, see Kukbangbu (Ministry of Defense) *6.25 Sabyŏn Sa* (History of the Korean War) (Seoul, 1959).

posed to exchange the South Korean-held Communist leaders, Kim Sam-yong and Yi Chu-ha, for the North Korean-held nationalist leader Cho Man-sik. Although the proposal of the election was immediately rejected, and the proposal for the personal exchange conditionally accepted by the Southern government, the two proposals seemed to create a mood favorable to peaceful unification and considerably lessened the tensions between the two regimes. The sudden overture of the Northern regime was to prove to be nothing after all but a tactical gesture to camouflage its impending aggression.

At 4 a.m. Korean time on June 25, 1950, an artillery barrage was directed across the 38th parallel from the north. Two hours later approximately 80,000 North Korean forces supported by 150 T-34 tanks crossed the parallel near Ongjin, Kaesŏng, and Ch'un Ch'ŏn, and carried out landing operations from the sea north and south of Kang-nŭng.[52] At 1100 hours the North Korean wireless station at Pyongyang broadcast a declaration of war. The next day, Kim Il-sŏng, the Premier of North Korea, called upon his forces to "liberate" the South, asserting that the North was forced to wage a just war for the unification and independence of the motherland, and for freedom and democracy.[53]

In the early morning of June 25, 1950 the first official word of the attack was dispatched by an American military attaché in Tokyo to the Assistant Chief of Staff, Department

---

[52] Report of the American Ambassador in Korea to the Secretary of State, Department of State, *United States Policy in the Korean Crisis* (Washington, 1950), p. 11. See also T. R. Fehrenbach, *This Kind of War* (New York, 1963), p. 21. Appleman, pp. 19–30.

[53] The North Korean government still maintains that the war was initiated by the Southern regime. For documentation of this claim, see M. N. Pak, *Wie die amerikanische agression in Korea vorbereitet wurde* (Berlin, 1953); and Kim Hi-il, *Mije ŭi Chosŏn Ch'imyak Sa* (History of the Invasion of American Imperialism in Korea) (Pyongyang, 1962), pp. 136–153. A scholarly work that is sympathetic to the North Korean point of view is D. Frank Fleming, *The Cold War and Its Origins: 1917–1960,* Vol. II (New York, 1961), pp. 592–601.

of the Army in Washington.[54] Muccio later reported, in his first radio message to the Department of State, that "it would appear from the nature of the attack and manner in which it was launched that it constitutes an all-out offensive against the Republic of Korea." [55]

When Muccio's report was received at 9:26 p.m. June 24 (Washington time), neither Truman nor his Secretary of State was in the capital. The President was at Independence, Missouri, for a weekend visit and Acheson was resting at his farm in Maryland. They were informed of the aggression by phone.[56] Truman at first wanted to fly back to Washington but Acheson dissuaded him because the scale and nature of the attack were still uncertain. However, they decided that the aggression should be brought to the attention of the United Nations immediately. Assistant Secretary of State John Hickerson thus notified the U.N. Secretary General Trygve Lie; shocked, Lie exclaimed, "This is war against the United Nations." [57]

Upon the request of the United States, an emergency session of the Security Council was convened on Sunday afternoon to consider the Korean crisis. The Council adopted a resolution by a vote of 9 to 0, with one abstention (Yugoslavia), calling the North Korean military action "a breach of the peace." The resolution asked for: (1) the immediate cessation of hostilities; (2) the North Koreans to withdraw their armed forces to the 38th parallel; and (3) all members to render every assistance to the United Nations in the execution of this resolution and to refrain from giving assistance to the North Korean authorities.[58] The Soviet delegation was absent—it had boycotted the Security Council since January, 1950, as a protest against the seating of Nationalist

---

[54] Appleman, p. 37.

[55] *United States Policy in the Korean Crisis,* p. 11.

[56] David Rees, *Korea: The Limited War* (New York, 1964), p. 21. See also Eric F. Goldman, *The Crucial Decade: America, 1945–1955* (New York, 1956), pp. 146–155.

[57] *Ibid.,* p. 148.

[58] U.N. Document, S/1501.

China in the organization instead of the newly born Communist regime.

After Truman's return to Washington, he and his advisors in the State and Defense departments discussed the situation at Blair House on the evening of June 25. The resolute President then authorized MacArthur to employ his air and naval powers to assure the delivery of the needed military supplies to the South Korean army and to protect the evacuation of American dependents.[59] Truman later wrote that there was "the complete, almost unspoken acceptance on the part of everyone that whatever had to be done to meet this aggression had to be done." He further recorded "there was no suggestion from anyone that either the United Nations or the United States could back away from it." [60]

The next evening, after a second meeting, Truman authorized MacArthur to use American naval and air forces in support of the Republic against all targets south of the 38th parallel. Truman also ordered the Seventh Fleet dispatched to the Formosa Strait to prevent attacks by the Chinese Communists against Taiwan.[61]

Meanwhile, the United Nations Commission in Korea was closely watching the military developments. On June 27 the Commission reported to U.N. headquarters that the North Korean action was a "well-planned, concerted, and full-scale invasion of South Korea." That night, the U.N. Security Council resolved to call upon members to "furnish such assistance to the Republic of Korea as may be necessary to repel the armed attack and to restore international peace and security in the area." [62] American air and naval support

---

[59] *Years of Trial and Hope,* pp. 334–337.

[60] *Ibid.*

[61] *Ibid.*, p. 337. See also, Appleman, p. 38. *United States Policy in the Korean Crisis,* p. 18.

[62] In the voting, India and Egypt abstained while Yugoslavia cast the negative vote. The Soviet delegate was still absent. An excellent analysis of this resolution is in Leland M. Goodrich, *Korea: A Study of United States Policy in the United Nations* (New York, 1956), pp. 112–114.

alone was unable to stop the advance of the well-armed North Korean forces. Nor could the under-armed South Korean troops stop the Russian-made tanks. During the first three days of hopeless battles all defense lines were completely broken. Disorganized retreat of the Southern forces further worsened the situation. Seoul fell early on June 28 and the total collapse of South Korea seemed imminent. In these circumstances, MacArthur was instructed from Washington, on June 30 (Tokyo time) to: (1) use naval and air forces against military targets in North Korea but to stay well clear of the Manchurian and the Soviet borders; (2) employ army combat units to ensure the retention of a port and air base in the general area of Pusan-Chinhae; (3) defend Formosa against invasion by the Chinese Communists and, conversely, prevent Chinese Nationalists from using Formosa as a base of operations against the mainland of China. The directive specifically noted that this instruction "did not constitute a decision to engage in war with the Soviet Union." [63]

After making a personal field trip to Korea, MacArthur realized the need for immediate use of American land forces and requested permission to move a U.S. regimental combat team into Korea. He reported to Army Chief of Staff, General J. Lawton Collins, "time is of the essence and clear-cut decision without delay is essential." [64] Therefore, on the morning of June 30 Truman approved, without hesitation, the immediate dispatch of one American regiment to the combat zone. After meeting with State and Defense department officials a few hours later, he further ordered the transfer of two American divisions from Japan to Korea and a naval blockade of the North Korean coast.[65] In the afternoon the President announced his decision to the world; and Warren Austin, American delegate in the United Nations,

[63] See the summary of the instructions in Appleman, p. 46.
[64] *Ibid.*, p. 47.
[65] *Military Situation in the Far East*, pt. 2, p. 1012.

told the Security Council of American large-scale military intervention in accordance with the Council's resolutions of June 25 and 27. Thus, the United States had now clearly committed its land, air, and naval forces in Korea—the peninsula which American military leaders had so long considered of little strategic value.

What were the major reasons for the sudden and complete reversal of American Far Eastern policy? Truman's message to MacArthur partially explained them. He stated that "we were fighting in Korea . . . to carry out our commitment of honor to the South Koreans and to demonstrate to the world that the friendship of the United States is of inestimable value in time of adversity." [66] Beside this idealism, however, North Korean aggression suddenly was seen as "a challenge to the whole system of collective security, not only in the Far East, but everywhere in the world." [67] Officials thought that if South Korea was allowed to be overrun by an unprovoked armed attack, a chain of similar events would be set up. They considered this a test that would decide whether other nations would be intimidated by the show of military force. It was thus a direct challenge to the free world. Truman remarked that "the Russians were trying to get Korea by default, gambling that we would be afraid of starting a third world war and would offer no resistance." [68]

Furthermore, Korea was vitally important to the security of Japan. If the peninsula was lost, the Pacific Ocean would no longer be the private lake of the American navy. Once the policy of containment failed in Asia, the American alliance system in Europe could be affected by a psychological

[66] *The General and the President,* p. 104. An excellent study of the American decision-making process during this time is Richard C. Snyder and Glenn D. Paige, "The United States Decision to Resist in Korea; The Application of an Analytical Scheme," *Administrative Science Quarterly,* Vol. III, no. 3 (December, 1958), pp. 341–378.

[67] Acheson's testimony, *Military Situation in the Far East,* pt. 3, pp. 1715–1716.

[68] *Years of Trial and Hope,* p. 335.

chain reaction. Inaction in Korea might have been interpreted by allies as an indication of American fear of direct confrontation with the Soviet Union, and as an attitude of appeasement. Thus, it would be feared that the United States might not abide by its pledges to any of its friends. Additionally, the United Nations would be greatly weakened because it, along with the United States, had played godfather at the birth of the South Korean government; a military attack not only struck at the fundamental purposes of the United Nations Charter, but also defied the competence and authority of the world body. Lastly, if the Truman Administration had not taken positive action, the rising forces of McCarthyism would have accused it of being hopelessly "soft" on communism and of having "sold out" not only in China but also in Korea.

RESPONSIBILITY FOR WAR

Who was mainly responsible for the outbreak of the Korean War? Was it the Soviet Union, the United States, Communist China, North or South Korean leaders? This question is difficult to answer mainly because of the lack of reliable documentary evidence. The answer so far found is more or less based on circumstantial evidence or conjecture.

From such reliable sources as South Korean and American documents, we can safely conclude that neither the American nor the South Korean government initiated the Korean War on June 25, 1950. An immediate on-the-spot investigation made by the United Nations Commission on Korea confirmed this fact.[69] But the North Korean government, as well as its Communist allies, claims that the war was carefully planned by American and South Korean authorities as early as 1949. According to allegedly captured documents

[69] See "The Report of the United Nations Commission on Korea to the Secretary General" in *United States Policy in the Korean Crisis,* p. 21, and Appleman, pp. 19–35. See also *The Conflict in Korea,* pp. 12–69. U.N. Document, S/1496.

from Syngman Rhee's personal files and South Korean government archives, the United States ordered the South Korean army to provoke the war against the North, and finally it was Dulles who set the date for the major attack after his trip to Korea on June 18, 1950.[70] The North also claims that the trips of Secretary of Defense Louis A. Johnson and Chief of Staff Omar N. Bradley to Japan in the earlier part of June were for the purpose of charting the final strategy of the war.

However, the Western world generally interprets the war as the result of Soviet efforts to divert Western pressures from Europe to the Far East. The West also claims that it was a by-product of the grand strategy of the Soviet Union to expand its sphere of influence and ideology whenever and wherever it could. It is also popularly interpreted as a Soviet test of American determination to resist open, armed attack by the Communists. The truth appears to be that Russia initiated the conflict mainly because the United States had shown little interest in Korea, and accordingly Russia thought she could seize control of the South without risking total confrontation.

It is possible that the Kremlin may have planned and directed the Korean War as a means of counteracting the Americans' unilateral move to conclude a separate peace treaty with Japan.[71] Washington's decision in 1949, as the fall of mainland China became an imminent and nightmarish reality, to proceed with a treaty with Japan, bypass-

---

[70] See Kim Hi-il, pp. 119–135. This book explains the North Korean views in much more detail than the official history *Chŏson T'ong Sa* (Outline History of Korea) (Tokyo, 1959), Vol. 3, pp. 165–166. For views sympathetic to the North Korean interpretation, in English, see Stone, *The Hidden Story of the Korean War,* pp. 1–107; and Fleming, *The Cold War and Its Origins,* Vol. II, pp. 592–601. A collection of documents is in *Wie die amerikanische agression in Korea vorbereitet wurde.*

[71] Whiting, *China Crosses the Yalu,* pp. 37–40. See also Spanier, *The Truman-MacArthur Controversy and the Korean War,* Chapter II (pp. 15–40).

ing the Soviet Union, might have been interpreted as an attempt to prepare another defense organization like NATO in Asia by creating a strongly anti-Communist nation in Japan. Russia's fear of the rise of a rearmed Japan was strongly indicated in the Sino-Soviet Treaty of Alliance concluded between Stalin and Mao Tse-tung on February 14, 1950. The treaty was specifically aimed against "the revival of Japanese imperialism and the resumption of aggression on the part of Japan or any other state that may collaborate in any way with Japan in acts of aggression." [72]

Under this imaginary threat of "American imperialism," and with a seemingly bright prospect of easy victory in Korea, the Soviet leaders apparently ordered the war to ensure the safety of Asian Communism and at the same time to weaken the American position in Japan. Because of geographical proximity, and because of the resultant psychological effect, the American position would become untenable if the whole Korean peninsula were controlled by the Communists. As George Kennan has pointed out, the question of Japan may not have been the only factor, but "it would be surprising if [it] had no effect at all." [73]

Another interesting interpretation of the Soviet origin of the Korean War has been presented by Edgar Snow. He implies that the war was "Stalin's design to bring the United States into irreconcilable conflict with China," because American authorities suggested their interest in the recognition of Communist China in the spring of 1950.[74] With the benefit of hindsight, he points out that as a result of this war China has been barred from membership in the United Na-

---

[72] The text of the treaty is in Alvin Z. Rubinstein, *The Foreign Policy of the Soviet Union* (New York, 1960), pp. 269–275. For an interpretation of the treaty, see Robert C. North, *Moscow and Chinese Communists* (Stanford, 1953), pp. 266–267.

[73] George Kennan, "Japanese Security and American Policy," *Foreign Affairs*, October, 1964, p. 15.

[74] Edgar Snow, *The Other Side of the River: Red China Today* (New York, 1962), pp. 654–655.

tions, China's dependence on Russia greatly increased, and most of all, the pending rapprochement between China and the United States was postponed for an indefinite period of time. True or not, this argument is difficult to document. It assumes that Stalin coldly calculated immediate American intervention, and the defeat of North Korea which made Chinese intervention inevitable.

Mao Tse-tung was most likely informed of the impending North Korean attack by Stalin when Mao was in Moscow in February of 1950. In fact, the timely relocation of the seasoned Chinese Fourth Field Army from Southern China to Manchuria just prior to the Korean War, and the transfer of approximately 12,000 Korean troops from the Chinese Red Army to North Korea during 1949–1950, seem to suggest that Communist China was well aware of the forthcoming attack by the North Korean army.[75] It is, however, unlikely that China played a major role in the preparation of the war as it was not then closely allied with the North Korean leadership. Nor was the Sino-Korean relationship during the period 1949–50 particularly friendly, owing to the increasing conflict over the allocation of electric power along the Yalu River. The status of the Korean minority in Manchuria and the settlement of border problems between the two nations also had some cooling effects. In other words, at present there is still little evidence to show that Communist China closely participated in the planning stage of the Korean War.[76] To China, her own internal problems and the liberation of Taiwan and Tibet were more urgent.

Some share of responsibility for the war must also be borne by the Koreans themselves. It has been speculated that the North Korean leaders initiated the war without Russia's knowledge in order to trap her into a position where she had no choice but to support their policy of "unification

---

[75] Whiting, pp. 43–46.
[76] *Ibid.*

by force."[77] However, in the light of North Korean political development during the prewar period, the North could not have waged such a well-planned and costly war without previous approval by Stalin. It is equally true that it was difficult for the leaders in the North to resist orders from the Soviet Union, or later from Communist China, because of their heavy reliance upon these nations for the maintenance of their power. But perhaps these Northern leaders genuinely believed that the cause of international communism was more important than the welfare of their own people.

The South Korean leaders also can be blamed. As we have seen earlier, their failure to develop a stable, democratic government and their extremely bellicose attitudes toward the North Korean regime caused the half-hearted and unduly hesitant American economic and military aid policy in Korea. Their diplomatic failure or apathy in recruiting more effective American public support for their cause also weakened them. However, if all Korean leaders had only worked with patience and tolerance for the peaceful unification of their country, refusing to become puppets of the big powers, they would have been able to settle their differences without the recourse to war that destroyed more than a million of their own countrymen and caused inestimable material loss. Although many of the difficult Korean problems were not their fault and the solutions often beyond their control, there still were neglected opportunities for the Korean people to play a greater role in the development of their own destiny. After all, many of these problems were the results of interaction between the Koreans and the big powers. As Kim Pyŏng-no, the late Chief Justice of the South Korean Supreme Court, often said to me, "Korean problems are basically problems of Korea's own creation; if they failed to reconcile their own differences they must blame their own lack of ability, foresight, and love." Ultimately, history will judge Ko-

---

[77] Spanier, pp. 23–24.

rean leaders in the light of how successfully and selflessly they served their own people.

In final retrospect, if the United States had had—and had made clear—a firm and unqualified determination to defend the free world, the Korean War would probably never have taken place. If the United States had not turned from a policy which gave hope and support to those new nations whose independence was endangered by communism, to what seemed—in Korea at least—to be a "policy of drift," it is likely that she would not have had to return to fight the "most disheartening and frustrating, the coldest and dreariest, the least inspiring and the least popular war in American history." [78]

---

[78] Rutherford M. Poats, *Decision in Korea* (New York, 1954), p. XI. Hugh Gaitskell once wrote that it was not the departure of the American troops in itself which led to the Korean War, but the accompanying statements of Mr. Acheson and General MacArthur that the Americans had no strategic interest in Korea. Hugh Gaitskell, "Disengagement: Why? How?" in *Foreign Affairs* (April, 1958), p. 554.

12

Summary and Conclusion

This study has contended that, in addition to the already widely discussed effects of the uncooperative Soviet attitude and the Korean internal political situation following World War II, the formulation and administration of American foreign policy played an important part in frustrating the original plan for the independence and unification of Korea.

The foreign policy of a nation involves a process of challenge and response to defend national interest. Thus, the policy of the United States should ideally be studied with an eye to America's own interests, the pattern of the Soviet challenge, and the internal Korean political situation. These and many other minor factors interacted in such a complex fashion that no one factor can assume full responsibility. However, because it would be impossible in the space available to deal in detail with all phases of such a complex problem as Korean unification, this study has reluctantly been limited to only the critical factor of American foreign policy toward Korea.

My first hypothesis has been that the "personal diplomacy" of President Roosevelt, with his and President Truman's heavy reliance on the advice of the military during the wartime conferences, was one of the major causes of the division of Korea. Decisions on the Far East during this period were basically and essentially military and thus founded on predominantly military considerations. Because of this, policy toward the Soviet Union became, in almost all respects, one of unreserved cooperation. Furthermore, because of Korea's remoteness from military strategy at the time, Roosevelt gave little attention to the future political implications of the problem. At this juncture Korea was simply not important to the United States. Thus, independence was promised almost as an afterthought: the actual aim was the punishment and weakening of Japan. However, as Dulles later pointed out, while military victory may be indispensable in time of war, if the moral and material power marshalled to win victory is not used to attain political objectives, the sacrifice becomes a cruel waste.

No aspect of the wartime conferences reflected the dominance of personal diplomacy so clearly as did the Far Eastern political discussions. On Korea, Roosevelt decided almost everything himself with little or no reference to the State Department. At Cairo, the phrase "in due course" was added in this way. Even in the most crucial conference at Yalta, the State Department delegation did not participate, and the Conference consisted essentially of personal talks among Churchill, Roosevelt, and Stalin.

Roosevelt's personal thought was that it would be necessary to educate the Koreans for enlightened self-government on the model of the Philippines. He thus planted the seed of great confusion: at Cairo, the President proposed forty years of political tutelage; then, at Yalta, he shortened this time limit to "thirty to twenty years." Had he been attentive to the State Department's recommendations prior to the Yalta Conference, and had he reached some agreement on a unified Korean administration in accordance with those recommendations, there would not have been the original problem of the 38th parallel. Likewise, if Truman had given more serious consideration to the recommendations of his civilian ambassadors, such as Harriman and Pauley, there might not have been the problem of a divided

Korea. Even without the cooperation of the Soviet Union, it is still possible that the United States could have settled many unnecessary problems, such as the 38th parallel and unified military administration, had adequate political consideration been given to the process of policy formulation. A clearly defined agreement either by Roosevelt at Yalta, or Truman at Potsdam would have served this purpose.

Contrary to a widely held view that the division of Korea was a secret agreement made either at Yalta or Potsdam, it has been shown that the division appears to have originated in War Department recommendations in Washington. The 38th parallel, as a dividing line in Korea, had never been the subject of discussion among the wartime leaders. The division was neither debated nor bargained for by either side. It was intended to be a purely military demarcation of a temporary nature for accepting the surrender of Japanese forces in Korea. It was proposed by the United States to limit the Soviet occupation of the whole peninsula since America could not then send sufficient forces to receive the Japanese surrender any further north. Proposing this boundary was a grave mistake: experience in Eastern Europe should have shown that the military occupation would have great political implications for the future. It could possibly have been averted if the Americans had previously reached some agreement with the Soviets on the nature of the military occupation, and if the two had set up a concrete plan for trusteeship under a unified administration as recommended by the State Department.

My second hypothesis is that the widespread lack of coordination between the local occupation authorities in Seoul and the policy planners in Washington became a constant source of confusion and inconsistency, thus hindering further the unification of Korea. American policy itself was characterized by a lack of internal coordination between the agencies of policy formulation on the one hand, and policy administration on the other. Although the Japanese surrender came sooner than expected, it came almost twenty months after the Cairo pledge on Korean independence. During this period no preparation was made for occupation. Yet if American policy had been thoughtfully planned, and had competent administrative personnel been obtained and carefully trained, frequent changes and deviations would not have been necessary.

The near-vacuum in the initial period of the military occupation was filled by General Hodge, Commander of United States Armed Forces in Korea; since the State Department failed to provide needed instructions, he had to make many decisions on his own. American policy should naturally have been shaped or modified in close coordination with the local military commander. Instead, when Washington finally did adopt a plan, it conflicted with actions Hodge had already taken. Thus, after he had already begun to strengthen the forces of the rightists, he was officially instructed to shift his support to the moderate groups, creating an almost uncontrollable situation in the South. The General was finally placed in such a difficult position that he offered his resignation to save face for his country. Yet many of Hodge's dilemmas could have been effectively solved by close coordination between the two levels of the government.

This and much other confusion between policy makers and policy administrators brought about many contradictions; consequently, the Korean leaders and people began to distrust the Americans. The Soviet command took advantage of the situation, using it for propaganda purposes as in the case of Shtykov's unilateral press release on the decision of the Moscow Conference. The American proposals at the Conference itself provide a good illustration of the lack of understanding of Korean feelings and aspirations. Even though it was apparent at this time that Koreans would unanimously oppose any trusteeship, no matter how temporary, the United States nevertheless suggested a government through a high commissioner and an executive council of representatives of the Four Powers. This American tendency to ignore the role of the people in determining their own destiny was in part the result of irresponsible political activities and the lack of unity in the South. But the policy of non-consultation aroused strong anti-American sentiments among the Korean leaders, who felt they were being dictated to by the United States. This was exemplified by the frequent conflicts between Hodge and Syngman Rhee and Kim Koo, as well as by the vehement anti-trusteeship movement.

Further difficulty was caused by the American tradition of conducting foreign policy in moral and ethical terms, greatly reducing the scope and methods of negotiations at the conference table. In a bipolarized world, it is extremely difficult to manage foreign policy merely in terms of law, moral principles, or ideal systems unless the other party takes the same approach. Nonetheless, because of her previous agreement with Stalin, the United States continuously supported the idea of trusteeship. Furthermore, as we have seen in the proceedings of the Joint Commission and in the General Assembly's debate on Korean independence, while the United States preached international law, Western concepts of freedom of speech, and the moral obligation against the enslavement of peoples, her opponent was indulging in constant territorial expansion and duplicity whenever it was to her advantage. Thus, the negotiations in the Joint Commission and General Assembly of the United Nations became time-consuming and futile. Had the United States sought a more realistic solution than trusteeship, and had she renounced the Moscow Agreement rather than antagonize Korea, her policy would have been far more effective.

The sudden shift in American strategy that appeared with the enunciation of the Truman Doctrine in the spring of 1947 caused new kinds of problems. For one thing, as America began to develop defense treaties and alliances, the Soviet reaction in Korea was immediate: their delegation to the Joint Commission unilaterally renounced its previous agreement with the United States to consult the Anti-Trusteeship Committee, thus creating a total impasse. Further, it had been the judgment of responsible military authorities in 1947 that from the point of view of its own security, the United States had little strategic interest in maintaining troops in Korea, which in any case were much needed elsewhere. The internal South Korean situation, with the impossible conditions created by 354 political and social organizations and almost hopeless economic circumstances, was also prompting American withdrawal. Unconditional withdrawal would, however, violate the avowed principles of Truman's containment policy. It would leave South Korea to be overrun by the Communists and would be a severe blow to American prestige in Asia. In the summer of 1947 the United States was thus faced with the problem of how to avoid responsibility for an embarrassing situation in Korea without losing face with the Korean people and the rest of the world.

After the failure of the Joint Commission, the United Nations was almost the only remaining means through which the free world could negotiate with the Soviet Union. The United States, therefore, planned to establish a united Korean government in the name of the United Nations, transferring most of its responsibility to the international organization. It was apparent at this time, however, that once the case was brought before the General Assembly, two separate governments, rather than unification through the international body, would be the result. Still, the United States made her heavy and unrealistic demands on the world body, knowing that the organization was too weak to bear such a burden. Indeed, when the General Assembly adopted its resolution on November 14, 1947, calling for elections throughout Korea under the observation of UNTCOK, the Soviet Command predictably denied the Commission permission to enter its zone. As a result, while in the South the Republic of

Korea was organized on August 15, 1948, under the supervision of the Commission, the Soviets established the Democratic People's Republic of Korea in the North. Thus, it was as a result of power politics that two separate governments within one nation came into being, and the will of the Korean people was largely ignored.

Even after the establishment of the Republic of Korea in accordance with the overall containment policy toward the Soviet Union, the Americans failed to reconcile successfully the objectives of two different departments of the government. The military leaders continued to view the immediate withdrawal of occupation forces as almost imperative because of manpower shortages and the perceived strategic insignificance of Korea in the event of a large-scale war on the Asian continent. The State Department, on the other hand, was primarily concerned with forthcoming political repercussions among the peoples of South and Southeastern Asia, then living under the threat of Communist domination. This threat would become even greater should the Republic of Korea be overrun. Therefore, the State Department argued that troop withdrawal would be premature, and that only through a large-scale positive economic aid program would the Republic survive.

No aspect of American foreign policy toward Korea more dramatically reveals its inadequacy and ineffectiveness than its economic and military aid strategy. When the United States forces entered Korea in September, 1945, they found that the economy of the country had been seriously impaired, making difficult the task of restoring independence on a stable economic basis. Even though the State Department felt that a continuation of limited assistance would give South Korea a good chance to survive as a free nation, the United States showed little interest in economic development. During the military occupation, the $356,000,000 appropriated to the Department of the Army under the GARIOA program for government and relief was spent in a preventive program dealing with disease and unrest, instead of in needed capital investment. With the establishment of the Republic of Korea, the ECA launched a supposedly large-scale program of economic assistance. Yet despite the repeated warnings from Secretary of State Acheson that the Republic would fall if assistance were not provided, the initial Korean Aid bill was rejected in Congress. And as finally approved, the ECA legislation provided only $110,000,000 for 1950 to develop industrial and agricultural production. The action came too late to help the Korean economy; the North Koreans attacked before the money was available.

As for military aid, although it had long been discussed, it was not until March, 1949, that basic American policy decisions were made by the National Security Council. The cause of the delay again was chiefly the lack of a definite Korean policy on the part of high-ranking policy planners in Washington. Since America was extremely reluctant to commit herself, military assistance to the Republic was based upon the concept that the military establishment existed only to quell internal disorders. Thus, when the well-equipped North Korean army attacked on June 25, 1950, the South Korean security forces were totally unprepared.

My third and final hypothesis is that the ineffectiveness of American policy was largely due to Korea's assumed remoteness from American national interests. Indeed, there was little concern about the situation until June, 1950. Lack of information, the disinterestedness of current congressional leadership, the changing climate of American public opinion, the necessity of shifting world strategy to meet Soviet challenges, and the political and economic situation in Korea itself all contributed to the inadequacy. But the fundamental determining factor seems to lie in the problem of recognizing the national interests of the United States.

America, in a sense, was primarily a Europe-oriented power; its national interest and security lay more in Europe than in Asia. Since the nineteenth century, her interest in the Far East had been more economic and commercial than military and political. Russian interests in Asia, on the other hand, were traditionally political in nature, as witnessed by her constant efforts to gain convenient access to a warm seaport and to the Pacific.

Because of the fundamentally different nature of the national interests of these two powers, there appeared two different attitudes toward Korean independence and unification. In the name of national interest, the Russians persistently demanded a division of Korea either at the 39th or 38th parallel and clearly stated in the Joint Commission that they could not tolerate Korean hostility to the Soviet Union. On the other hand, the leaders of the United States constantly viewed the Korean problem as an "unhappy burden" and "a needless liability to the free world." Political, military, and geographical factors made it difficult for America to evolve a policy consistent with both her moral commitment to Korean unification and her own self-interest.

Yet, an effective, consistent, and firm United States policy can still contribute in the future to the establishment of a democratic, unified Korean government when the opportune time presents. The people, who are one in language, culture, and race, still aspire to unity. Without preparation or an effective Korean policy, however, the chances of unification will slip away, while the danger of permanent Communist domination will remain.

Hopefully, the Koreans have learned some lessons from their tragic past. Unless, or until, the present system of international relations changes, the pressures and influences of foreign powers will continue to beset, trouble and even dominate Korea's future. The repetition of history is not inevitable, but considering Korea's strategic geographical location, it is possible that events similar to those of the past may haunt Korea's future.

The best hopes for Korea's future, under the existing circumstances, must be found in the people themselves. A strong, happy, healthy and well-educated people, coupled with a stable, growing economy, can provide the basis for a politically strong and secure democracy on Korean soil. However, the task of nation-building is not a matter of political, economic, and institutional stability alone; unless this new nation is built on a firm moral foundation, the edifice is bound to collapse when adverse winds buffet it.

If the only feasible means for Korea's peaceful unification lie in the arts of persuasion and conciliation, those arts should be taught, learned and practiced by the people and especially by their leaders. If another fratricidal, internecine war is to be avoided, if Korea is to face its present problems in order to eventually rectify them, and if Korea is to put away the past misunderstandings and build for the brighter future of a unified nation, then a new, more courageous and less selfish outlook, blended with an infinite amount of patience is demanded of every Korean, in the North and in the South. Almost a new religion, a new morality, and a new nationalism are necessary to rebuild our ancient and, at the same time, young nation. As an old Korean proverb says, "Even if you are caught by a tiger, you will survive as long as your mind is alert."

Selected Bibliography

This bibliography is not meant to be exhaustive, and includes only those government publications, books, pamphlets, and periodicals which the author found useful.

DOCUMENTS AND OFFICIAL AND SEMI-OFFICIAL PUBLICATIONS

a. Canada

Department of External Affairs. *Canada and the Korean Crisis.* Ottawa, 1950.

———. *Documents on the Korean Crisis.* Ottawa, 1950.

b. China

Chang, Chi-yün. *Record of the Cairo Conference.* Taipei: China Culture Publishing Foundation, 1953. (In Chinese and English.)

c. Japan

Gaimusho (Ministry of Foreign Affairs). *Chōsen Jihen no Kei-i* (Details of the Korean Conflict). Tokyo, 1951.

———. *Komura Gaikō Shi* (History of Komura's Diplomacy). 2 vols. Tokyo: Shinbun Getskan Sha, 1955.

———. *Nihon Gaikō Bunsho* (Japanese Foreign Affairs Documents). Tokyo: Nihon Kokusai-Rengō Kyokai, 1935–1956.

33 vols. This series is the Japanese equivalent of *Papers Relating to the Foreign Relations of the United States.*

———. *Nihon Gaiko Hyakunen Shōshi* (A Short Hundred Years History of Japanese Diplomacy). Tokyo: Yamata Shoin, 1963.

———. *Our Position in the Korean Conflict.* Tokyo, 1950.

———. *Sengoni okeru Chōsen no Seiji Josei* (Korean Politics in the Postwar Era). Tokyo, 1948.

d. Korea (North)

Ch'oego Inmin Hoeŭi. *Choguk T'ong'il ŭi Sŏgwang* (The Dawn of the Country's Unification). Edited by Pae, Il-san. Pyongyang: Pyonghwa Ch'ulp'an Sa, 1960.

———. *Chōsen Minshushugi Jinmin Kyowakoku Saiko Jinmin Kaigi, dai niki dai hachikai kaigi* (Proceedings of the Eighth Session of the Second Supreme People's Assembly of the Democratic People's Republic of Korea). Pyongyang: Gaigoku Shuppansha, 1960.

Democratic People's Republic of Korea. *Documents and Materials of the Third Congress of the Workers Party of Korea.* April 23–29, 1956. Pyongyang: Foreign Language Publishing House, 1956.

———. *Documents of the Fourth Congress of the Workers Party of Korea: Document and Materials.* Pyongyang: Foreign Language Publishing House, 1961.

———. *For the Peaceful Unification of the Country—Documents on the Sixth Session of the Second Supreme People's Assembly of the Democratic People's Republic of Korea.* Pyongyang: Foreign Language Publishing House, 1959.

———. *Outline of Korean Geography.* Pyongyang: Foreign Language Publishing House, 1957.

Kim Il-sŏng. *All for the Country's Unification and Independence and for Socialist Construction in the Northern Part of the Republic.* Pyongyang: Foreign Language Publishing House, 1961.

———. *Chosŏn Inmin ŭi Minjok chŏk Myŏngjŏl 8.15 Haebang 15 Chunyŏn Kyŏngch'uk Taehoe esŏ han Pogo* (Korean People's National Fete Day: A Report of the 15th Anniversary of National Independence Day). Pyongyang: Chosŏn Nodongdang Ch'ulp'an Sa, 1960.

———. *Chosŏn Nodongdang Che 4 ch'a Taehoe esŏ han Chung-ang Wiwŏnhoe Saŏp Ch'onghwa Pogo* (Report of the Central Committee's Achievement at the 4th Congress of the Workers Party). September 11, 1961. Pyongyang: Chosŏn Nodongdang Ch'ulp'an Sa, 1961.

———. *Kim Il-sŏng Sŏngjip* (Selected Works of Kim Il-sŏng). 6 vols. Pyongyang: Choson Nodongdang Ch'ulp'an Sa, 1960.

———. *Modŭn Him ŭl Choguk ŭi T'ongil Tongnip Kwa Kong-whaguk Pukbanbu esŏŭi Sahoejuŭi Kŏnsŏl ŭl Wihayŏ Uri Hyŏngmyŏng ŭi Sŏngkyŏk kwa Kwaŏp e Kwanhan T'eje (1955, 4 wol)* (All for the Nation's Unification and the Establishment of Socialism in North Korea: Thesis on Our Revolutionary Characteristics and Works, April, 1955). Pyongyang: Chosŏn Nodongdang Ch'ulp'an Sa, 1960.

———. *Nodongdang ŭi Chojik jŏk Sasang jŏk Kanghwa nŭn Uri Sŭngni ŭi Kich'o* (The Strength of Organization and Ideology of Workers Party Is the Fundamental of Our Victory). A Report at the 5th Central Committee of the Workers Party of Korea, December 15, 1952. Pyongyang: Chosŏn Nodongdang, Ch'ulp'an Sa, 1956.

———. *P'al-iro Haebang Ijunyŏn Kinyŏm Pogo* (A report of the 2nd Year's Anniversary of National Independence Day). Pyongyang: Chosŏn Yosŏng Sa, 1947.

Kukka Kyehoek Wiwŏnhoe, Chung'ang T'onggyeguk. *Chosŏn Minjujui Inmin Konghwaguk Inmin Kyŏngje Palchŏn Tanggye* (Statistical Survey of the Economic Development in the Democratic People's Republic of Korea). Pyongyang: Kungnip Ch'ulp'an Sa, 1961.

Ministry of Foreign Affairs. *Documents and Materials Exposing the Instigators of the Civil War in Korea: Documents from the Archives of the Rhee Syngman Government.* Pyongyang, 1950.

e. Korea (South)

Executive White Paper Publication Committee. *Haengjŏng Paeksŏ, 1962* (Korean Executive White Paper, 1962). Seoul, December, 1962.

Kongbosil (Office of Public Information). *A Handbook of Korea* (written by Jai Hyon Lee). Seoul, 1955.

———. *Korean Report: Report from the Cabinet Ministers of the Republic of Korea.* Vol. I (1948–1952) and Vol. II (1952–1953). Washington: Korean Pacific Press, 1952– .

———. *Kwanbo* (Official Gazette). Seoul, 1949– . Published weekly as *Chukan Digest,* 1945–1949.

———. *Reference Handbook; Government of the Republic of Korea.* Seoul, 1949.

———. *Republic of Korea Army.* Seoul, 1954.

———. *Republic of Korea Economic Summation.* Seoul, monthly since 1948. This is the continuation of *Summation of South Korean Interim Government.*

———. *Statistics of Damage Suffered during the Korean War, June 25, 1950–July 27, 1953.* Seoul, 1954.

Kukpangbu (Ministry of National Defense). *Han'guk Chŏllan Illyŏn Chi* (Record of the First Year of the Korean War). Seoul, 1951.

———. *6.25 Sabyŏn Sa* (History of the Korean War). Seoul, 1959.

Kukhoe (National Assembly). *Kukhoe Simnyŏn Chi* (Ten Years' History of the National Assembly of the Republic of Korea). Seoul, 1958.

———. *Kukhoe Ŭisa Rok* (Record of National Assembly Debate). Seoul, 1948– .

———. *Yŏktae Kukhoe Uiwŏn Sŏngŏ Sanghwang* (Election Results of Congressional Elections). Seoul, 1964.

Kukka Chaegŏn Ch'oego Hoeŭi, Han'guk Kunsa Hyŏngmyŏn Sa P'yŏnjip Wiwŏnhoe. *Han'guk Kunsa Hyŏngmyŏng Sa* (History of Korean Military Revolution). Seoul, 1963.

Kwado Ippŏp Uiwŏn. *Nam Chosŏn Kwado Ippŏp Ŭiwon Sokkirok* (Stenographic Reports of Interim Legislative Assembly of Southern Korea). Seoul, 1946.

Naemubu (Ministry of Home Affairs). *Kani Ch'ong In'gu Chosa Pogosŏ* (Population Census of Korea: Summary Report). Seoul, 1958.

Naeoe Munje Yŏnguso. *Onŭl ŭi Pukhan—Pukkoe Tokchae Kujo ŭi Haebu* (Today's North Korea—Analysis of the Structure of North Korean Dictatorship). Seoul: Naeoe Munje Yŏn'guso, 1962.

Oemubu (Ministry of Foreign Affairs). *Han'guk T'ong'il Munje: Yaksa wa Munhŏn (1943–1960)* (Problems of Korean Unification: Brief History and Documents, 1943–1960). Seoul, 1960.

———. *Oemu Haengjŏng ŭi Simnyŏn* (Ten Years of Foreign Affairs Administration). Seoul, 1959.

———. *Taehan Min'guk Oegyo Yŏnp'yo: 1948–1961* (Diplomatic Chronology of the Republic of Korea: 1948–1961). Seoul, 1961.

———. *The Unification of Korea: Unfinished Task of the United Nations.* Seoul, 1961.

Puhŭngbu (Ministry of Reconstruction). *Development of the Korean Economy.* Seoul, 1958.

———. *Korea's Continuing Development.* Compiled and published by Economic Planning Bureau, Ministry of Reconstruction. Seoul, 1959.

f. Soviet Union

Ministry of Foreign Affairs. *American Armed Intervention in Korea.* London: Soviet News, 1950. (A Soviet News booklet.)

———. *The Soviet Union and the Korean Question.* Moscow, 1948. Reprinted in London, 1950.

———. *Stalin's Correspondence with Churchill, Attlee, Roosevelt and Truman: 1941–1945.* Moscow, 1957. Reprinted in London: Lawrence and Wishart, 1958.

g. United Nations

Official Records of the General Assembly, 1947–1951.

Official Records of the General Assembly from Second Session to Fifth Session constituted one of the principal sources for this study. Records used in this study numbered some twenty to thirty volumes and include the summary records of the First Committee, the Ad Hoc Political Committee, the Interim Committee, and the General Committee; Verbatim Records of Plenary Meetings and General Assembly Resolutions; and proceedings and reports of the United Nations Temporary Commission on Korea and its successor, the United Nations Commission on Korea, which were published as supplements to the Official Records. (When the symbol is followed by "PV," a verbatim record is indicated; "SR" denotes summary records; and "W" denotes working papers.)

Official Records: Security Council. Several numbers of the *Official Records of the Security Council* were used. The symbol is S/.

How the United Nations Met the Challenge of Korea. Lake Success, New York, 1953.

The Korean Question Before the United Nations: September, 1947 to October, 1949. New York, 1950.

United Action in Korea. New York, 1951.

United Nations Review. Monthly. This was preceded by the *United Nations, Weekly Bulletin,* semi-monthly, January, 1948, through June, 1954.

Yearbook of the United Nations. New York. Since 1946.

UNKRA. *An Economic Programme for Korean Reconstruction.* New York, 1954. (Mimeographed. Prepared by Robert R. Nathan Associates.)

h. United States

Commission on Organization of the Executive Branch of the Government. *Administration of Overseas Affairs.* Washington, 1949.

———. *Task Force Report on Foreign Affairs.* Washington, 1949.

House. *Aid to Korea.* 81st Congress, 1st Session. Report of the Committee on Foreign Affairs. House Report No. 962, 2 pts., July 1, 1949, Washington, 1949. Pt. 2 is *Aid to Korea: Minority Views.*

———. *Background Information on Korea.* House Report No. 2495. Report of the Committee on Foreign Affairs Pursuant to House Resolution 206. 81st Congress, 2nd Session, July 11, 1950. Washington, 1950.

———. *Economic Assistance to Certain Areas in Far East,* 81st Congress, 2nd Session. House Report 1571. Washington, 1950.

———. *First Semi-Annual Report on the Mutual Defense Assistance Program.* 81st Congress, 2nd Session. House Document No. 613. Washington, 1950.

———. *Korean Aid.* 81st Congress, 1st Session. Hearing on House

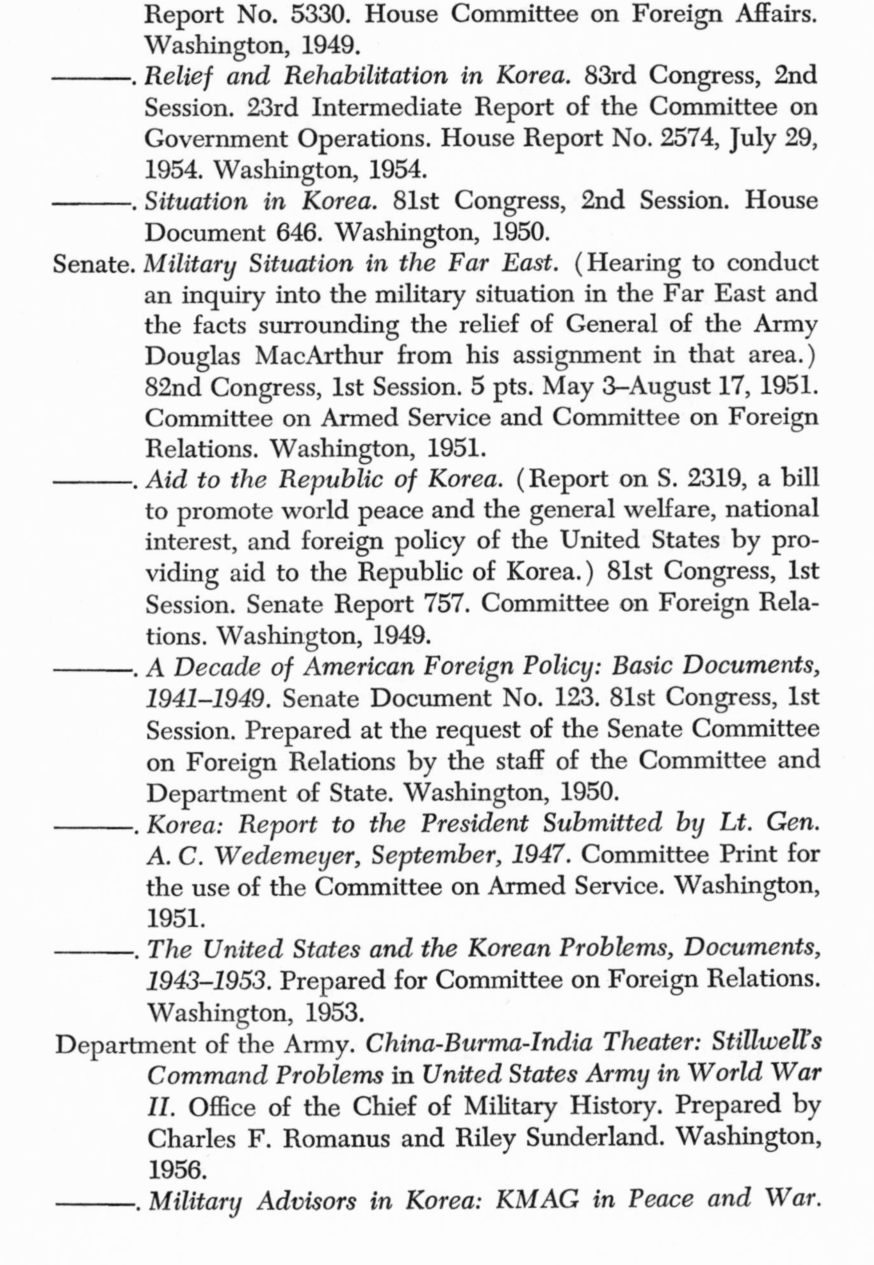

Report No. 5330. House Committee on Foreign Affairs. Washington, 1949.

———. *Relief and Rehabilitation in Korea.* 83rd Congress, 2nd Session. 23rd Intermediate Report of the Committee on Government Operations. House Report No. 2574, July 29, 1954. Washington, 1954.

———. *Situation in Korea.* 81st Congress, 2nd Session. House Document 646. Washington, 1950.

Senate. *Military Situation in the Far East.* (Hearing to conduct an inquiry into the military situation in the Far East and the facts surrounding the relief of General of the Army Douglas MacArthur from his assignment in that area.) 82nd Congress, 1st Session. 5 pts. May 3–August 17, 1951. Committee on Armed Service and Committee on Foreign Relations. Washington, 1951.

———. *Aid to the Republic of Korea.* (Report on S. 2319, a bill to promote world peace and the general welfare, national interest, and foreign policy of the United States by providing aid to the Republic of Korea.) 81st Congress, 1st Session. Senate Report 757. Committee on Foreign Relations. Washington, 1949.

———. *A Decade of American Foreign Policy: Basic Documents, 1941–1949.* Senate Document No. 123. 81st Congress, 1st Session. Prepared at the request of the Senate Committee on Foreign Relations by the staff of the Committee and Department of State. Washington, 1950.

———. *Korea: Report to the President Submitted by Lt. Gen. A. C. Wedemeyer, September, 1947.* Committee Print for the use of the Committee on Armed Service. Washington, 1951.

———. *The United States and the Korean Problems, Documents, 1943–1953.* Prepared for Committee on Foreign Relations. Washington, 1953.

Department of the Army. *China-Burma-India Theater: Stillwell's Command Problems* in *United States Army in World War II.* Office of the Chief of Military History. Prepared by Charles F. Romanus and Riley Sunderland. Washington, 1956.

———. *Military Advisors in Korea: KMAG in Peace and War.*

Office of the Chief of Military History. Prepared by Major Robert K. Sawyer and edited by Walter G. Hermes. Washington, 1962.

———. SCAP. *Summation of Non-Military Activities in Japan and Korea.* These summations are the most exhaustive source of information on United States Military Government in Korea. Following the first five numbers, the reports on Korea, originally appended to those on Japan, appeared separately with the imprint *Summation of U.S. Army Military Government Activities in Korea.* Command-in-Chief U.S. Army Forces, Pacific, No. 6 (March, 1946) to No. 22 (July, 1947). No. 23 of the series appeared with the imprint *South Korea Interim Government Activities,* United States Army Forces in Korea, No. 1, August, 1947. Then followed twelve more volumes, Nos. 24 to 35 (September, 1947, to September–October, 1948), with the added line "Prepared by National Economic Board."

———. *Strategic Planning for Coalition Warfare, 1941–1942* in *United States Army in World War II.* Office of the Chief of Military History. Prepared by Maurice Matloff and Edwin M. Snell. Washington, 1953.

———. *U.S Army Area Handbook for Korea.* Prepared by Foreign Area Studies Division, Special Operations Office. Washington: The American University, 1964.

———. *United States Army in the Korean War: South to the Nakton, North to the Yalu.* Office of the Chief of Military History. Prepared by Roy E. Appleman. Washington, 1961.

———. *Washington Command Post: The Operations Division in United States Army in World War II.* Office of the Chief of Military History. Prepared by Roy S. Cline. Washington, 1951.

Department of Defense. *The Entry of the Soviet Union into the War Against Japan: Military Plan, 1941–1945.* Processed. Washington, 1955.

Department of the Navy. *History of United States Naval Operations: Korea.* Prepared by James A. Field, Jr. Washington, 1962.

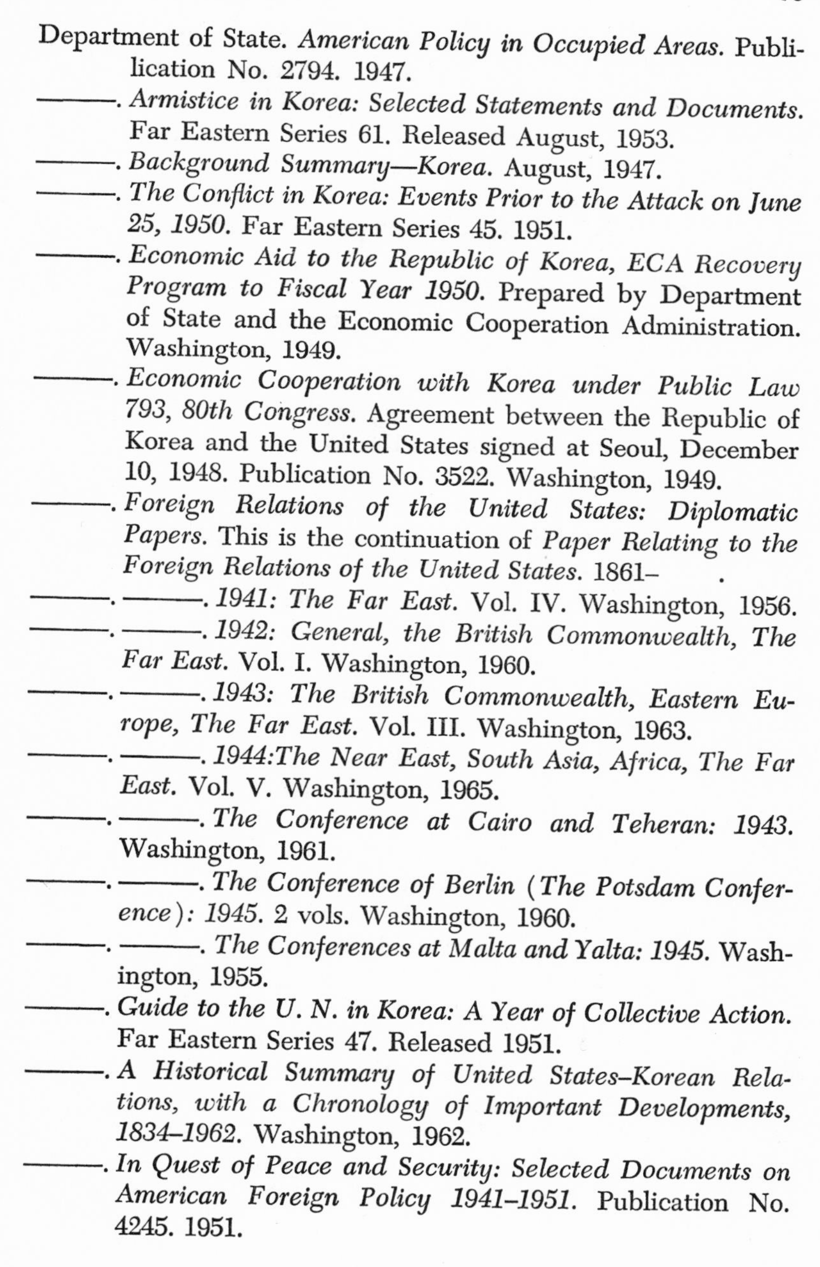

Department of State. *American Policy in Occupied Areas.* Publication No. 2794. 1947.

———. *Armistice in Korea: Selected Statements and Documents.* Far Eastern Series 61. Released August, 1953.

———. *Background Summary—Korea.* August, 1947.

———. *The Conflict in Korea: Events Prior to the Attack on June 25, 1950.* Far Eastern Series 45. 1951.

———. *Economic Aid to the Republic of Korea, ECA Recovery Program to Fiscal Year 1950.* Prepared by Department of State and the Economic Cooperation Administration. Washington, 1949.

———. *Economic Cooperation with Korea under Public Law 793, 80th Congress.* Agreement between the Republic of Korea and the United States signed at Seoul, December 10, 1948. Publication No. 3522. Washington, 1949.

———. *Foreign Relations of the United States: Diplomatic Papers.* This is the continuation of *Paper Relating to the Foreign Relations of the United States.* 1861– .

———. ———. *1941: The Far East.* Vol. IV. Washington, 1956.

———. ———. *1942: General, the British Commonwealth, The Far East.* Vol. I. Washington, 1960.

———. ———. *1943: The British Commonwealth, Eastern Europe, The Far East.* Vol. III. Washington, 1963.

———. ———. *1944:The Near East, South Asia, Africa, The Far East.* Vol. V. Washington, 1965.

———. ———. *The Conference at Cairo and Teheran: 1943.* Washington, 1961.

———. ———. *The Conference of Berlin (The Potsdam Conference): 1945.* 2 vols. Washington, 1960.

———. ———. *The Conferences at Malta and Yalta: 1945.* Washington, 1955.

———. *Guide to the U. N. in Korea: A Year of Collective Action.* Far Eastern Series 47. Released 1951.

———. *A Historical Summary of United States–Korean Relations, with a Chronology of Important Developments, 1834–1962.* Washington, 1962.

———. *In Quest of Peace and Security: Selected Documents on American Foreign Policy 1941–1951.* Publication No. 4245. 1951.

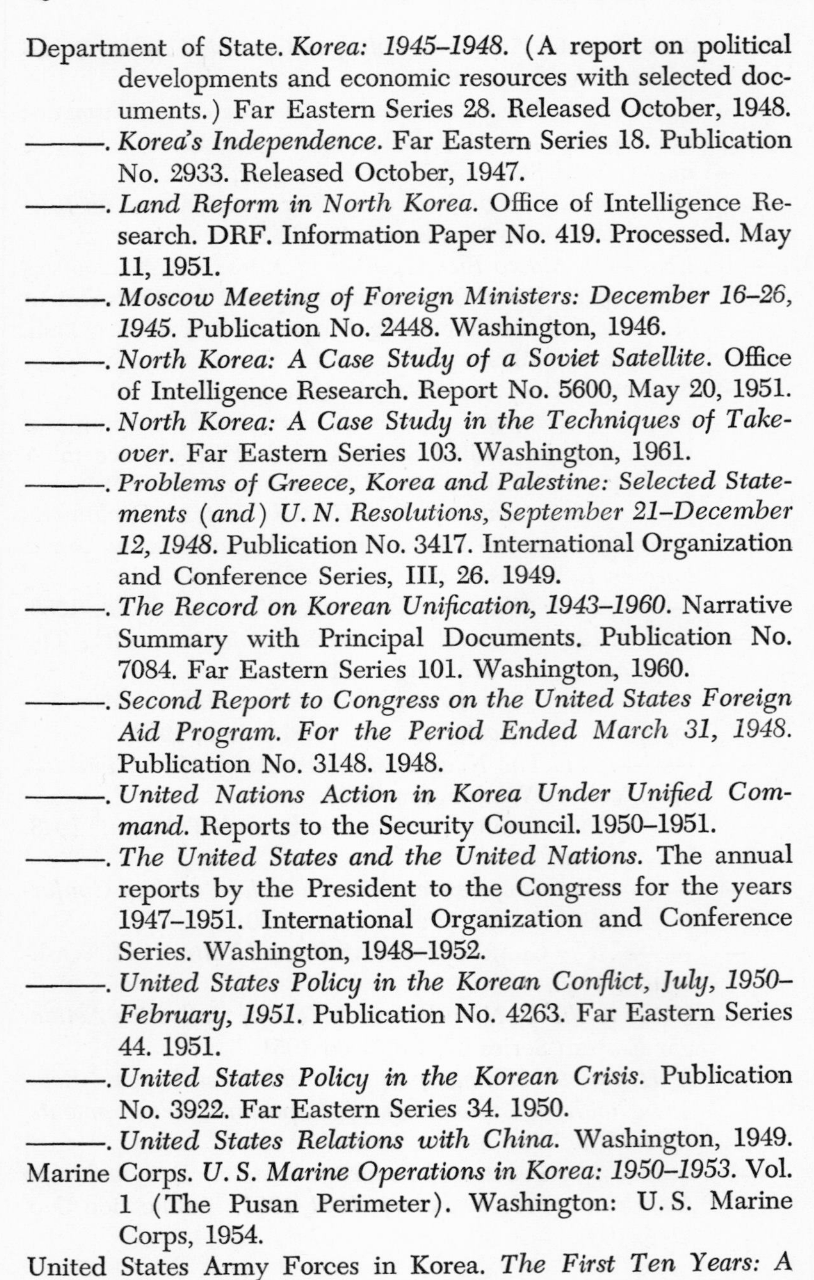

Department of State. *Korea: 1945–1948.* (A report on political developments and economic resources with selected documents.) Far Eastern Series 28. Released October, 1948.

———. *Korea's Independence.* Far Eastern Series 18. Publication No. 2933. Released October, 1947.

———. *Land Reform in North Korea.* Office of Intelligence Research. DRF. Information Paper No. 419. Processed. May 11, 1951.

———. *Moscow Meeting of Foreign Ministers: December 16–26, 1945.* Publication No. 2448. Washington, 1946.

———. *North Korea: A Case Study of a Soviet Satellite.* Office of Intelligence Research. Report No. 5600, May 20, 1951.

———. *North Korea: A Case Study in the Techniques of Takeover.* Far Eastern Series 103. Washington, 1961.

———. *Problems of Greece, Korea and Palestine: Selected Statements (and) U. N. Resolutions, September 21–December 12, 1948.* Publication No. 3417. International Organization and Conference Series, III, 26. 1949.

———. *The Record on Korean Unification, 1943–1960.* Narrative Summary with Principal Documents. Publication No. 7084. Far Eastern Series 101. Washington, 1960.

———. *Second Report to Congress on the United States Foreign Aid Program. For the Period Ended March 31, 1948.* Publication No. 3148. 1948.

———. *United Nations Action in Korea Under Unified Command.* Reports to the Security Council. 1950–1951.

———. *The United States and the United Nations.* The annual reports by the President to the Congress for the years 1947–1951. International Organization and Conference Series. Washington, 1948–1952.

———. *United States Policy in the Korean Conflict, July, 1950–February, 1951.* Publication No. 4263. Far Eastern Series 44. 1951.

———. *United States Policy in the Korean Crisis.* Publication No. 3922. Far Eastern Series 34. 1950.

———. *United States Relations with China.* Washington, 1949.

Marine Corps. *U. S. Marine Operations in Korea: 1950–1953.* Vol. 1 (The Pusan Perimeter). Washington: U. S. Marine Corps, 1954.

United States Army Forces in Korea. *The First Ten Years: A*

Short History of the Eighth United States Army 1944–1954. Washington, 1954.

———. *Summation of South Korean Interim Government.* Monthly from August, 1947, to September–October, 1948. Seoul.

———. *Summation of U. S. Military Government Activities in Korea.* Monthly from March, 1946, to July, 1947. Seoul (?).

———. XXIV Corps. Troop Information and Education Section. *Korea.* Seoul, 1948.

United States Military Government in Korea. *Chukan Digest.* Weekly gazette published in Seoul. In Korean language with English translation. October, 1945– .

———. *Final Report and History of the New Korean Company.* Prepared by C. Clyde Mitchell. Seoul, 1948.

———. *Korea: Present Agricultural Position of South Korea.* Seoul, 1947.

———. *Manual of Military Government Organization and Function.* Seoul, 1948.

———. *Official Gazette.* Both in English and Korean language. Seoul, 1945– .

———. *Political Development in South Korea, 1947.* Processed. Seoul, 1948.

———. *Revised List of All Korean Political Parties and Social Organizations at the National Level under USAMGIK, Ordinance No. 55.* Processed. Seoul, January 22, 1948.

II. UNPUBLISHED MANUSCRIPTS

Han, Pyo-wook. "The Problem of Korean Unification: A Study of the Unification Policy of the ROK, 1948–1960." Ph.D. dissertation at the University of Michigan, 1963.

Sawyer, Robert K. "History of United States Military Advisory Groups to the Republic of Korea." Prepared for the Office of Military History, Department of the Army. Parts I and II, n. d. This was later published under the title, *Military Advisors in Korea: KMAG in Peace and War,* but some material in the original manuscript was omitted.

Soh, Jin-chull. "Some Causes of the Korean War of 1950: A Case Study of Soviet Foreign Policy in Korea (1945–1950) with Emphasis on Sino-Soviet Collaboration."

Ph.D. dissertation at the University of Oklahoma, 1963.
Suh, Dae Sook. "Korean Communism and the Rise of Kim." Ph.D. dissertation at Columbia University, 1964.
Yoon, Yŏn-kyo. "U.N. Participation in Korean Affairs, 1945–1954." Ph.D. dissertation at the American University, 1959.

III. BOOKS IN WESTERN LANGUAGES

Allen, Richard C. *Korea's Syngman Rhee: An Unauthorized Portrait.* Tokyo: Charles E. Tuttle Co., 1960.
The American Assembly. *The United States and the Far East.* New York: Columbia University Press, 1956.
Ball, W. MacMahon. *Nationalism and Communism in East Asia.* Melbourne: Melbourne University Press, 1952.
———. *Japan: Enemy or Ally.* New York: The John Day Co. 1949.
Barnett, A. Doak. *Communist China and Asia.* New York: Harper and Brothers, 1960.
———. (ed.). *Communist Strategies in Asia.* New York: Frederick A. Praeger, Inc., 1963.
Beech, Keyes. *Tokyo and Points East.* New York: Doubleday and Co., 1954.
Beloff, Max. *Soviet Policy in the Far East: 1944–1951.* London: Oxford University Press, 1953.
Berger, Carl. *The Korean Knot: A Military and Political History.* Philadelphia: University of Pennsylvania Press, 1957.
Brookings Institution, International Studies Group. *The Administration of Foreign Affairs and Overseas Operations.* Washington, 1951.
———. *Major Problems in United States Foreign Policy.* Washington, issued annually since 1947.
Brown, William A., Jr. and Redvers Opie. *American Foreign Assistance.* Washington: Brookings Institution, 1953.
Butow, Robert J. C. *Japan's Decision to Surrender.* Stanford: Stanford University Press, 1954.
Byrnes, James F. *Speaking Frankly.* New York and London: Harper and Brothers, 1947.
Cagle, Malcolm W. and Frank A. Manson. *The Sea War in Korea.* Annapolis: United States Naval Institute, 1957.

Caldwell, John C. *Still the Rice Grows Green: Asia in the Aftermath of Geneva and Panmunjom.* Chicago: Henry Regnery Co., 1955.

———. *The Korean Story.* Chicago: Henry Regnery Co., 1952.

Calvocoressi, Peter (ed.). *Survey of International Affairs* (issues of 1947–1948, 1949–1950, and 1951). London: Oxford University Press.

Campbell, John C. (ed.). *The United States in World Affairs* (issues of 1945–1947, 1947–1948, and 1948–1949). New York: Harper and Brothers. Issues of 1950, 1951, and 1952 were edited by Richard P. Stebbins.

Carleton, William G. *The Revolution of American Foreign Policy.* New York: Random House, 1957.

Chang, Tao-li. *Why China Helps Korea.* Bombay: People's Publishing House, 1951.

Chung, Henry. *The Case of Korea.* New York: Fleming H. Revell, 1921.

———. *The Oriental Policy of the United States.* New York: Fleming H. Revell, 1919.

———. *The Russians Came to Korea.* Washington: Korean Pacific Press, 1947.

Chung, Kyung Cho. *Korea Tomorrow: Land of the Morning Calm.* New York: The Macmillan Co., 1956.

———. *New Korea.* New York: The Macmillan Co., 1962.

Churchill, Winston S. *Closing the Ring.* Boston: Houghton Mifflin, 1951.

———. *The Gathering Storm.* Boston: Houghton Mifflin, 1948.

———. *The Grand Alliance.* Boston: Houghton Mifflin, 1950.

———. *Their Finest Hour.* Boston: Houghton Mifflin, 1949.

———. *Triumph and Tragedy.* Boston: Houghton Mifflin, 1953.

Clark, Mark W. *From the Danube to the Yalu.* New York: Harper and Brothers, 1954.

Cohen, Bernard C. *The Political Process and Foreign Policy: The Making of the Japanese Peace Settlement.* Princeton: Princeton University Press, 1957.

Conroy, Hilary. *The Japanese Seizure of Korea: 1868–1910.* Philadelphia: University of Pennsylvania Press, 1960.

Council on Foreign Relations. *Documents on American Foreign Relations.* Various Compilers. Boston and later Princeton,

N.J.: World Peace Foundation. Since 1952, New York: Harper and Brothers for the Council on Foreign Relations. Published annually since 1939.

Dallin, David J. *The Rise of Russia in Asia.* New Haven: Yale University Press, 1949.

———. *Soviet Russia and the Far East.* New Haven: Yale University Press, 1948.

———. *Soviet Foreign Policy After Stalin.* New York: J. B. Lippincott Co., 1961.

Dean, John R. *Strange Alliance.* New York: The Viking Press, 1947.

Dean, William P. *General Dean's Story.* New York: The Viking Press, 1954.

Dennett, Tyler. *Roosevelt and the Russo–Japanese War.* New York: Doubleday and Co., 1925.

Dille, John. *Substitute for Victory.* New York: Doubleday and Co., 1954.

Dulles, Foster Rhea. *America's Rise to World Power: 1896–1954.* New York: Harper and Brothers, 1955.

Dulles, John Foster. *War or Peace.* New York: The Macmillan Co., 1957.

Economic Research Center of Korea. *Industrial Structure of Korea.* Seoul: Korea Traders Association, 1962.

Fairbank, John K., *et al. Next Step in Asia.* Cambridge: Harvard University Press, 1949.

Farley, Miriam S., and Vera M. Dean. *Korea and World Politics.* Toronto: Canadian Institute of International Affairs, 1950.

Fehrenbach, T. R. *This Kind of War.* New York: The Macmillan Co., 1963.

Feis, Herbert. *Between War and Peace: The Potsdam Conference.* Princeton: Princeton University Press, 1960.

———. *The China Tangle: The American Effort in China from Pearl Harbor to the Marshall Mission.* Princeton: Princeton University Press, 1953.

———. *Churchill-Roosevelt-Stalin: The War They Waged and the Peace They Sought.* Princeton: Princeton University Press, 1957.

———. *Japan Subdued.* Princeton: Princeton University Press, 1961.

Fleming, D. Frank. *The Cold War and Its Origins: 1917–1960.* 2 vols. New York: Doubleday and Co., 1961.

Frankel, Ernest. *Korea ein Wendepunkt im Völkerrecht.* Berlin: Gebr. Weise, 1951.

Friedrich, Carl J., and Associates. *American Experience in Military Government in World War II.* New York: Rinehart Co., 1948.

Gayn, Mark J. *Japan Diary.* New York: W. Sloane Associates, 1948.

Geer, Andrew. *The New Breed.* New York: Harper and Brothers, 1952.

Gitovich, A. and B. Bursov. *North of the 38th Parallel.* Translated by George Leonof. Shanghai: Epoch Publishing Co., 1948.

Goldman, Eric F. *The Crucial Decade: America, 1945–1955. New* York: Alfred A. Knopf, 1956.

Goodrich, Leland M. *Korea: Collective Measures against Aggression.* New York: Carnegie Endowment for International Peace, 1953.

———. *Korea: A Study of United States Policy in the United Nations.* New York: Council on Foreign Relations, 1956.

Goodrich, Leland M., and Edvard Hambro. *Charter of the United Nations; Commentary and Documents.* Boston: World Peace Foundation, 1949.

Gordenker, Leon. *The United Nations and the Peaceful Unification of Korea.* The Hague: Martinus Nijhoff, 1959.

Grajdanzev, Andrew J. *Korea Looks Ahead.* New York: Institute of Pacific Relations, 1944.

———. *Modern Korea.* New York: John Day Co., 1944.

Green, A. Wigfall. *The Epic of Korea.* Washington: Public Affairs Press, 1950.

Grew, Joseph C. *Turbulent Era: A Diplomatic Record of Forty Years, 1904–1945.* Edited by Walter Johnson, assisted by Nancy H. Hooker. 2 vols. Boston: Houghton Mifflin Co., 1952.

Griswold, A. Whitney. *The Far Eastern Policy of the United States.* New York: Harcourt, Brace and Co., 1938.

Gugeler, R. A. *Combat Actions in Korea.* Washington: Combat Forces Press, 1954.

Gunther, John. *The Riddle of MacArthur.* New York: Harper and Brothers, 1951.

Ha, Tae-hung. *Korea—Forty-Three Centuries.* Seoul: Yonsei University Press, 1962.

Hakwon Sa. *Korea: Its Land, People and Culture of All Ages.* Seoul: Hakwon Sa, 1960.

Han, Sul-ya. *Hero General Kim Il-song.* Tokyo: Chosŏn Shinbo Sa, 1962.

Harrington, Fred H. *God, Mammon and the Japanese: Dr. Horace N. Allen and Korean-American Relations, 1884–1905.* Madison: University of Wisconsin Press, 1944.

Higgins, Marguerite. *The War in Korea.* New York: Doubleday and Co., 1951.

Higgins, Trumbull. *Korea and the Fall of MacArthur.* New York: Oxford University Press, 1960.

Holborn, Hajo. *American Military Government, Its Organization and Policies.* Washington: Infantry Journal Press, 1947.

Hu, Hung-lick. *Le Problème Coréen.* Paris: A. Pedone, 1953.

Hull, Cordell. *The Memoirs of Cordell Hull.* 2 vols. New York: The Macmillan Co., 1948.

Huntington, Samuel P. *The Soldier and the State: The Theory and Politics of Civil-Military Relations.* Cambridge: Harvard University Press, 1957.

Indian Council of World Affairs. *Selected Documents: East Asia 1947–1950.* Edited by Vidya Prakash Dutt. London: Oxford University Press, 1958.

Isaacs, Harold R. (ed.). *New Cycle in Asia.* New York: The Macmillan Co., 1947.

Jones, F. C., Borton, Hugh, and B. R. Pearn (eds.). *Survey of International Affairs: The Far East, 1942–1946.* London: Oxford University Press, 1955.

Jones, Joseph M. *The Fifteen Weeks, February 21–June 5, 1947.* New York: The Viking Press, 1955.

Joy, Charles T. *How Communists Negotiate.* New York: The Macmillan Co., 1955.

Kahn, Ely Jacques, Jr. *The Peculiar War.* New York: Random House, 1951.

Kase, Toshikazu, *Eclipse of the Rising Sun.* Edited by David Nelson Rowe. London: Jonathan Cape, 1951.

Kelsen, Hans. *The Law of the United Nations: A Critical Analysis of Its Fundamental Problems.* New York: Frederick A. Praeger, Inc., 1950.

Kennan, George F. *American Diplomacy 1900–1950.* Chicago: University of Chicago Press, 1951.

———. *Realities of American Foreign Policy.* Princeton: Princeton University Press, 1954.

Kennedy, Edgar S. *Mission to Korea.* London: Derek Verschoyle, 1952.

Kenney, Malcolm. *A History of Communism in East Asia.* New York: Frederick A. Praeger, Inc., 1957.

Kim, Chang Soon (ed.). *The Culture of Korea.* Honolulu: Korean–American Cultural Association, 1946.

King, Ernest J. *Fleet Admiral King: A Naval Record.* New York: W. W. Norton, 1952.

Korean Provisional Government. *Memorandum: Korea's Role in the Anti-Axis War.* Chungking, 1944.

Langer, William L., and S. E. Gleason. *The Diplomacy of Imperialism.* New York and London: Alfred A. Knopf, 1934.

———. *The Undeclared War, 1940–1941.* New York: Harper and Brothers, 1953.

Latourette, K. S. *The American Record in the Far East, 1945–1951.* New York: The Macmillan Co., 1952.

Lautensach, Hermann. *Korea: Land, Volk, Schicksal.* Stuttgart: Koehler Verlag, 1950.

Lauterbach, Richard E. *Danger from the East.* New York: Harper and Brothers, 1947.

Leckie, Robert. *Conflict: The History of the Korean War, 1950–1953.* New York: G. P. Putnam's Sons, 1962.

Leahy, William D. *I Was There.* New York: McGraw-Hill Book Co., 1950.

Lee, Chong-shik. *The Politics of Korean Nationalism.* Berkeley and Los Angeles: University of California Press, 1963.

Lee, In-sang. *La Corée et politique des puissances.* Genève: E. Droz, 1959.

Lerche, Charles O. *Foreign Policy of the American People.* New York: Prentice-Hall, 1958.

Levy, Roger. *Regards sur l'Asie.* Paris: Librairie Armand Colin, 1952.

Lewis, John P. *Reconstruction and Development in South Korea.* Washington: National Planning Association, 1955.

Lichterman, Martin. *The March to the Yalu: Case Study of Civil-Military Relations as They Affect Decision-Making.* New York: Twentieth Century Fund, 1958.

Lie, Trygve. *In the Cause of Peace.* New York: The Macmillan Co., 1955.

Lyons, Gene Martin. *Military Policy and Economic Aid: The Korean Case, 1950–1953.* Columbus: Ohio State University Press, 1961.

MacArthur, Douglas. *Reminiscences.* New York: McGraw-Hill Book Co., 1964.

McCune, George M. *Korea's Postwar Political Problems.* Secretariat Paper No. 2. New York: Institute of Pacific Relations, 1947.

McCune, George M., and Arthur L. Grey, Jr. *Korea Today,* Cambridge: Harvard University Press, 1950.

———. *The Occupation of Korea.* New York: Foreign Policy Association, 1947.

McCune, Shannon. *Korea's Heritage: A Regional and Social Geography.* Tokyo: Charles E. Tuttle Co., 1956.

———. *Korea: Land of Broken Calm.* Princeton: Van Nostrand Co., 1966.

Meade, Edward Grant. *American Military Government in Korea.* New York: King's Crown Press, 1951.

Millis, Walter. *Arms and Men: A Study in American Military History.* New York: G. P. Putnam's Sons, 1956.

Millis, Walter S. (ed.). *The Forrestal Diaries.* New York: The Viking Press, 1951.

———. (ed.). *The War Reports of General of the Army George C. Marshall, General of the Army H. H. Arnold, and Fleet Admiral Ernest J. King.* New York: J. B. Lippincott Co., 1947.

Mitchell, Clyde C. *Korea: Second Failure in Asia.* Washington: Public Affairs Institute, 1951.

Morgenthau, Hans J. *In Defense of the National Interest.* New York: Alfred A. Knopf, 1951.

———. *Politics Among Nations: The Struggle for Power and Peace.* New York: Alfred A. Knopf, 1955.

Morley, James William. *Japan and Korea: America's Allies in the Pacific.* New York: Walker and Co., 1965.

Murphy, Robert. *Diplomat Among Warriors.* New York: Doubleday and Co., 1964.

Nelson, M. Frederick. *Korea and the Old Orders in Eastern Asia.* Baton Rouge: Louisiana State University, 1946.

North, Robert C. *Moscow and Chinese Communists.* Stanford: Stanford University Press, 1953.

Oliver, Robert T. *Divided Korea.* New York: Citizens' Conference on International Economic Union, 1947.

———. *Korea: Forgotten Nation.* Washington: Public Affairs Press, 1944.

Oliver, Robert T. (ed.). *Korea's Fight for Freedom: Selected Addresses by Korean Statesmen.* 2 vols. Washington: Korean Pacific Press, 1952.

———. *The Republic of Korea Looks Ahead.* Washington: Korean Pacific Press, 1948.

———. *Syngman Rhee: The Man Behind the Myth.* New York: Dodd, Mead and Co., 1954.

———. *The Truth about Korea.* London: Putnam, 1951.

———. *Verdict in Korea.* State College, Pennsylvania: Bold Eagle Press, 1952.

———. *Why War Came in Korea.* New York: Fordham University Press, 1950.

Osgood, Cornelius. *The Koreans and Their Culture.* New York: Ronald Press Co., 1951.

Osgood, Robert E. *Ideas and Self-Interest in America's Foreign Relations: The Great Transformation of the Twentieth Century.* Chicago: University of Chicago Press, 1953.

Paige, Glenn D. *The Korean People's Democratic Republic.* Stanford: The Hoover Institution, 1966.

Pak, M. N. *Wie die amerikanische Agression in Korea vorbereitet wurde.* Berlin: Dietz Verlag, 1953.

Perkins, Dexter. *The American Approach to Foreign Policy.* Cambridge: Harvard University Press, 1952.

Poats, Rutherford M. *Decision in Korea.* New York: The McBride Co., 1954.

Portway, Donald. *Korea: Land of the Morning Calm.* London: Harrap, 1953.

Price, Harry B. *The Marshall Plan and Its Meaning.* Ithaca: Cornell University Press, 1955.

Pyun, Yong-tae. *Korea: My Country.* Washington: Korean Pacific Press, 1953.

Rees, David. *Korea, the Limited War.* New York: St. Martin's Press, 1964.

Reeve, W. D. *The Republic of Korea.* London: Oxford University Press, 1963.

Reitzel, William, *et al. United States Foreign Policy, 1945–1955.* Washington: The Brookings Institution, 1956.

Rhee, Syngman. *The Goal We Seek.* Washington: Korean Pacific Press, 1947.

———. *Korea Flaming High.* Seoul: Office of Public Information, Republic of Korea, 1953.

Ridgeway, Matthew B. *Soldier, The Memoirs of Matthew B. Ridgeway.* New York: Harper, 1956.

Riggs, Robert E. *Politics in the United Nations: A Study of United States Influence in the General Assembly.* Urbana: University of Illinois Press, 1958.

Roosevelt, Franklin D. *The Public Papers and Addresses of Franklin D. Roosevelt.* 1942 Volume. Samuel I. Rosenman (ed.). New York: Harper and Brothers, 1950.

Rosinger, Lawrence K. and Associates. *The State of Asia: A Contemporary Survey.* New York: Alfred A. Knopf, 1953.

Rovere, Richard H., and Arthur M. Schlesinger, Jr. *The General and the President.* New York: Farrar, Strauss and Young, 1951.

Royal Institute of International Affairs. *Documents on International Affairs.* London: Oxford University Press. Volumes published annually since 1933.

Rudolph, Philip. *North Korea's Political and Economic Structure.* New York: Institution of Pacific Relations, 1959.

Rubinstein, Alvin Z. *The Foreign Policy of the Soviet Union.* New York: Random House, 1960.

Sands, William F. *Undiplomatic Memories.* New York: McGraw-Hill Book Co., 1930.

Samsonov, Nikolai Ivanovich. *Economic Progress and Development of Foreign Economic Relations of North Korea.* New York: U. S. Joint Publication Research Service, 1959.

Scalapino, Robert A. (ed.). *North Korea Today*. New York: Frederick A. Praeger, Inc., 1963.

Schwarzenberger, Georg. *Power Politics: A Study of International Society*. New York: Frederick A. Praeger, Inc., 1951.

Shabshina, Fania I. *Sotsialisticheskaya Koreya* (Socialist Korea). Moscow: Eastern Literature Publishing House, 1963 (translated from Russian by U. S. Department of Defense).

Sherwood, Robert E. *Roosevelt and Hopkins: An Intimate History*. New York: Harper and Brothers, 1948.

Shoemaker, James. *Notes on Korea's Post-war Economic Position*. Secretariat Paper No. 4. New York: Institute of Pacific Relations, 1947. Mimeographed.

Snell, John L. (ed.). *The Meaning of Yalta: Big Three Diplomacy and the New Balance of Power*. Baton Rouge: Louisiana State University Press, 1956.

Snow, Edgar. *The Other Side of the River: Red China Today*. New York: Random House, 1962.

Snyder, Richard C., and Edgar S. Furniss, Jr. *American Foreign Policy: Formulation, Principles, and Programs*. New York: Rinehart, 1954.

Snyder, Richard C., and M. Burton Sapin. *The Role of the Military in American Foreign Policy*. New York: Doubleday and Co., 1954.

Spanier, John W. *The Truman-MacArthur Controversy and the Korean War*. New York: W. W. Norton Co., 1965.

Stettinius, Edward R. *Roosevelt and the Russians: The Yalta Conference*. New York: Doubleday and Co., 1949.

Stimson, Henry L., and McGeorge Bundy. *On Active Service in Peace and War*. New York: Harper and Brothers, 1948.

Stone, Isidore F. *The Hidden Story of the Korean War*. New York: Monthly Review, 1952.

Taylor, Maxwell D. *The Uncertain Trumpet*. New York: Harper, 1960.

Tewksbury, Donald G. (comp.). *Source Materials on Korean Politics and Ideology*. New York: Institute of Pacific Affairs, 1950.

Thomas, Robert C. W. *The War in Korea, 1950–1953: A Military*

Study of the War in Korea up to the Signing of the Cease-Fire in 1954. London: Aldershot Gale and Polden, Ltd., 1954.

Thompson, Kenneth W. *Political Realism and the Crisis of World Politics: An American Approach to Foreign Policy.* Princeton: Princeton University Press, 1960.

Tompkins, Pauline. *American-Russian Relations in the Far East.* New York: The Macmillan Co., 1949.

Trullinger, O. O. *Red Banners Over Asia.* Boston: The Banner Press, 1951.

Truman, Harry S. *Truman Speaks.* Three Lectures at Columbia University, April 27–29, 1959, by Truman. New York: Columbia University Press, 1960.

———. *Year of Decisions.* New York: Doubleday and Co., 1955.

———. *Years of Trial and Hope.* New York: Doubleday and Co., 1956.

Tsou, Tang. *America's Failure in China: 1941–1950.* Chicago: University of Chicago Press, 1963.

Vagts, Alfred. *Defense and Diplomacy, The Soldier and the Conduct of Foreign Relations.* New York: King's Crown Press, 1956.

Vatcher, William H. *Panmunjom; The Story of the Korean Military Armistice Negotiations.* New York: Frederick A. Praeger, Inc., 1958.

Vinacke, Harold M. *Far Eastern Politics in the Post-War Period.* New York: Appleton-Century-Crofts, 1956.

———. *The United States and the Far East: 1945–1951.* Stanford: Stanford University Press, 1952.

Wagner, Edward M. *The Korean Minority in Japan: 1904–1950.* New York: Institute of Pacific Relations, 1951.

Wedemeyer, Albert C. *Wedemeyer Reports.* New York: Henry Holt, 1958.

Weems, Benjamin. *Reform, Rebellion and the Heavenly Way.* Tucson: University of Arizona Press, 1964.

Weems, Clarence N. *Korea: Dilemma of an Underdeveloped Country.* New York: Foreign Affairs Association, 1960.

Westerfield, H. Bradford. *Foreign Policy and Party Politics: Pearl Harbor to Korea.* New Haven: Yale University Press, 1955.

Whitney, Courtney. *MacArthur: His Rendezvous with History.* New York: Alfred A. Knopf, 1956.

Whiting, Allen S. *China Crosses the Yalu: The Decision to Enter the Korean War.* New York: The Macmillan Co., 1960.

Willoughby, Charles A., and John Chamberlain. *MacArthur 1941–1951.* New York: McGraw-Hill Book Co., 1954.

Woodbridge, George. *History of the UNRRA Administration.* Vol. II. New York: Columbia University Press, 1950.

Yim, Louise. *My Forty Years Fight for Korea.* New York: A. A. Wyn, 1951.

Zaichikov, V. T. *Geography of Korea.* Translated by Albert Parry. New York: Institute of Pacific Relations, 1952. Mimeographed.

Zanzi, A. W. *Economic Reconstruction Problems in South Korea.* New York: Institute of Pacific Relations, 1954.

IV. BOOKS IN ORIENTAL LANGUAGES

Aeguk Tongji Wŏnho Hoe. *Han'guk Tongnip Undong Sa* (History of the Korean Independence Movement). Seoul: Aeguk Tongji Wŏnho Hoe, 1956.

An, Chae-hong, *Chinjŏng Minjujuŭi Ron* (Theory of True Democracy). Seoul: Ilhan Tosŏ Chusik Hoesa, 1949.

An, Ho-sang. *Ilminjuŭi Ponjil* (Essence of Monism–Ilminjuŭi). Seoul, 1950.

Chang, Ung-tae. *Chosŏn Munje ŭi Pyŏnghwajŏk Minjujui jŏk Haegyŏl ŭl wihan Ssoryŏn ŭi T'ujaeng* (Soviet's Struggle for the Peaceful Democratic Solution of Korean Problems). Pyongyang: Chosŏn Nodongtang Ch'ulp'an Sa, 1956.

Chindan Hak'hoe (ed.). *Han'guk Sa* (Korean History). 7 vols. Seoul: Ŭryu Munhwa Sa, 1959–1964.

Cho, Ki-jun. *Han'guk Kyŏngje Sa.* (Economic History of Korea). Seoul: Ilshin Sa, 1962.

Cho, Pyŏn-ok. *Minjujuŭi wa Na* (Democracy and I). Seoul: Yŏngsin Munhwa Sa, 1960.

Ch'oe, Ho-jin. *Hyŏndae Chosŏn Kyŏngje Sa Yŏn'gu* (Study of Modern Korea's Economic History). Seoul: Minjung Sŏgwan, 1947.

Ch'oe Nam-sŏn. *Taehan Tongnip Undong Sa* (History of the Korean Independence Movement). Seoul: Pangmun Ch'ulp'an Sa, 1946.

Chŏn, Yong-Sik. *Chŏnhu uri Tang Kyŏngje Kŏnsŏl ŭi Nosŏn* (Our Economic Reconstruction Policy after the War). Pyongyang: Chosŏn Nodongtang, Ch'ulp'an Sa, 1961.

Chŏng, Si-wu. *Tongnip kwa Chwa-u Hapjak* (Independence and Leftist-Rightist Collaboration). Seoul: Samŭi Sa, 1946.

Chōsen Jijō Kenkyu Kai (Society for the Study of Conditions in Korea). *Hokui 38do Sen—Kaihō Chōsen no Dōkō* (The 38th Parallel—The Conditions of Liberated Korea). Tokyo: Chōsen Jijō Kenkyu Kai, 1948.

Chōsen Minshushugi Jinmin Kyōwakoku Kagakuin, Hogaku Kenkyusho (ed.). *Chōsen ni okeru Shakaishugi no Kiso Kensetsu* (Construction of the Foundation of Socialism in Korea). Tokyo: Shin Nihon Shuppan Sha, 1962.

———. *Chōsen Minshushugi Jinmin Kyōwakoku no Kokka Shakai Taisei* (The People's Republic of Korea: State and Social System). Tokyo: Nihon Hyoron Sha, 1965.

Chōsen Rekishi Hensan Iin Kai. *Chōsen Minzoku Kaiho Tōsō Shi* (History of the Korean People's Struggle for Liberation). Translated into Japanese by Chōsen Rekishi Kenkyu Kai. Tokyo: Sanichi Shobo, 1952.

Chosŏn Rodong Tang. *Chosŏn Rodong Tang Kyuyak* (Rules and Regulations of Korean Workers Party). Tokyo: Hak-u *Sŏbang*, 1960.

———. *Chosŏn Rodongtang Yŏksa Kyojae* (Textbook for the History of the Korean Workers Party). Pyongyang: Chosŏn Rodongtang Ch'ulp'an Sa, 1964.

Chosŏn T'ongsin Sa. *Chosŏn Chung'ang Nyŏngam, 1958, 1959, 1960, 1962* (North Korean Almanac). Pyongyang: Chosŏn T'ongsin Sa.

Ham Im-hŏyk. *Kim Il-sŏng Tongji e ŭihan Chosŏn Kongsangtang Ch'anggŏn* (The Founding of the Korean Communist Party by Comrade Kim Il-sŏng). Pyongyang: Rodongtang Ch'ulp'an Sa, 1961.

Han, Tae-su. *Han'guk Chŏngtang Sa* (History of Korean Political Parties). Seoul: Sin T'aeyang Sa, 1961.

Han'guk Ŭnhaeng Chosabu. *Kyŏngje Yŏn'gam* (Annual Economic Review). Seoul: Han'guk Ŭnhaeng Chosabu, 1948– .

Han'guk Yŏn'gam P'yŏnch'anhoe (Korean Yearbook Compilation Society). *Han'guk Yŏn'gam, 1963* (Korea Yearbook, 1963). Seoul: Han'guk Yŏn'gam P'yŏnch'anhoe, 1963.

Haptong T'ongsin Sa (Haptong News Agency). *Haptong Yŏn'gam —1964* (Korea Annual—1964). Seoul: Haptong T'ongsin Sa, 1964.

Hatada, Takashi. *Chōsen Shi* (History of Korea). Tokyo: Iwanami Shoten, 1960.

Hong, Sŏng-yu. *Han'guk Kyŏngje wa Miguk Wŏnjo* (Korean Economy and U. S. Aid). Seoul: Pagyŏng Sa, 1962.

Hong, Sŭng-myŏn, *et al.* (eds.). *Haebang Isip nyŏn* (Twenty Years of Emancipation). Vol. I (Kirok P'yŏn) and Vol. II (Charyo P'yŏn). Seoul: Semun Sa, 1965.

Ikeuchi, Hiroshi. *Bunroku Keicho no Eki* (The Japanese Invasion of 1592–1596). Tokyo: Minami Manshū Tessudō Kaisha, 1914.

Im, Kwang-ch'ŏl. *Chōsen Rekishi Tokuhon* (An Introduction to Korean History). Tokyo: Hakuyosha, 1949.

Kaigai Jijō Chosashō (Foreign Affairs Research Institute). *Chōsen Yōran* (The Korean Directory). Tokyo: Musashi Shobo, 1960.

Kim, Ch'ang-sun. *Pukhan Sibo nyŏn Sa* (Fifteen Years of History in North Korea). Seoul: Chimun Kak, 1961.

Kim, Chin-hak and Ch'ŏl-yŏng Han. *Chehŏn Kukhoe Sa* (History of the Constituent Assembly). Seoul: Sinjo Ch'ulp'an Sa, 1956.

Kim, Chong-myŏng. *Chōsen Shin Minshushugi Kakumei Shi* (History of Korea's New Democratic Revolution). Tokyo: Gogatsu Shobō, 1953.

Kim, Hi-il. *Choguk ŭi P'yŏnhwajŏk T'ongil e Taehan Uri Tang ŭi Pangch'im* (The Policy of Our Party Toward the Peaceful Unification of the Fatherland). Pyongyang: Kungnip Ch'ul p'an Sa, 1962.

———. *Mije ŭi Chosŏn Ch'imyak Sa* (History of the Invasion of American Imperialism in Korea). Pyongyang: Chosŏn Rodongtang Ch'ulp'an Sa, 1962.

Kim, Koo. *Paekbŏm Ilchi* (The Autobiography of Kim Koo [Kim Ku]). Seoul: Tongmyŏng Sa, 1947.

Kim, Kwang-hyŏn. *Ch'ŏllima Chosŏn* (Flying Horse Korea). Pyongyang: Kuknip Ch'ulp'an Sa, 1961.

Kim, Sam-gyu. *Konnichi no Chōsen* (Today's Korea). Tokyo: Kawade Shobō, 1956.

———. *Chōsen no Shinjitsu* (Truth of Korea). Tokyo: Gendai Jin Sōsho, 1959.

———. *Chōsen Gendai Shi* (Modern History of Korea). Tokyo: Chikuma Shobō, 1963.

Kim, Sang-gi. *Tonghak kwa Tonghak Nan* (The East Learning School and the Tonghak Rebellion). Seoul: Taesong Ch'ulp'an Sa, 1947.

Kim Sŏk-kil. *Minju Chungnip kwa T'onghan ŭi Sin Pangan* (New Method of Democratic Neutralization and Unification). Seoul: Kukche Chŏngch'i Yŏn'guso, 1961.

Kim, Sung-sik (ed.). *Chosŏn Yŏngam—1948* (Korea Yearbook—1948). Seoul: Chosŏn T'ongsin Sa, 1947.

Kim, Tal-su. *Chōsen* (Korea). Tokyo: Iwanami Shoten, 1962.

Kim, Tu-hŏn. *Minjok Iron ŭi Chŏnmang* (Prospect of the National Ideology). Seoul: Ŭryu Munhwa Sa, 1948.

Kim, Tong-un. *Haebang Chŏnhu ŭi Chosŏn Chinsang* (The True Situation of Korea Before and After the Liberation). Seoul: Chosŏn Chunggŏn Sa, 1945.

Kiyosawa, Kiyoshi. *Gaiko Shi* (Diplomatic History). Tokyo: Tokyo Keizai Shinbun Sha, 1941.

Ko, Chih-feng. *Ch'ao-hsien Ko-ming-shih* (History of the Korean Revolution). Shanghai: Commercial Press, 1945.

Ko, Kwŏn-sam. *Chosŏn Chŏngch'i Sa* (Political History of Korea). Seoul: Ŭryu Munhwa Sa, 1948.

Ko, Sŭng-je. *Han'guk Kyŏnje Ron* (Theory of Korean Economy). Seoul: Shinmyŏn Munhwa Sa, 1958.

Kondo, Ken'ichi. *Taiheiyō Senka no Chōsen oyobi Taiwan* (Korea and Formosa Under the Pacific War). Tokyo: Chōsen Siryō Hensan Kai, 1962.

Kwahak Wŏn, Yŏksa Yŏn'gu So (North Korean Academy of Science). *Chayu wa Tongnip ŭl wihan Chosŏn Inmin ŭi Ch'ongŭi ŭi Choguk Haebang Chŏnjaeng* (The Fatherland Liberation War of the Korean People for Freedom and Independence). Pyongyang: Chosŏn Nodongtang Ch'ulp'an Sa, 1959.

———. *Chosŏn Kŭndae Hyŏngmyŏng Undong Sa* (History of Revolutionary Movement in Modern Korea). Pyongyang: Rodongtang Ch'ulp'an Sa, 1962.

———. *Chosŏn T'ongsa* (Outline History of Korea). 3 vols. Tokyo: Hak-u Sŏbang, 1959.

Kyōguchi, Motokichi. *Hideyoshi no Chōsen Keiryaku* (Hideyoshi's Korean Policy). Tokyo: Hakuyo Sha, 1939.

Kyŏngje Pŏphak Yŏn'guso. *Haebang hu Uri Nara ŭi Inmin Kyŏngje Palchŏn* (People's Economic Development After the Independence). Pyongyang: Kwahak Wŏn Ch'ulp'an Sa, 1960.

———. *P'al-iro Haebang Sibo Chunyŏn Kyŏngje Nonmunjip* (The Collected Works of the 15th Anniversary of National Independence Day). Pyongyang, Kwahakwŏn Ch'ulp'an Sa, 1960.

Lim, Kwang-ch'ŏl. *Chōsen Rekish Tokuhon* (An Introduction to Korean History). Tokyo, 1949.

Ma, Han. *Han'guk Chŏngch'i ŭi Ch'ong Pip'an* (The Whole Criticism of Korean Politics). Seoul: Han'guk Chŏngch'i Yŏn'gu Wŏn, 1959.

Maruo, Itaru, and Tsuneo Mura. *Bunretsu Kokka ni okeru Keizai Hatten no Futatsuno Ryūkei* (Two Patterns of Economic Development in the Divided Nations). Tokyo: Kokusai Mondai Kenkyū Sho, 1962.

Matsumoto, Hirokazu. *Gekidō suru Kankoku* (Korea in Turmoil). Tokyo: Iwanami Shinsho, 1963.

Minjujuŭi Minjok Chŏnsŏn. *Chosŏn Haebang Illyŏn Sa* (One Year History of Korean Liberation). Seoul, 1946.

Morita, Kazuo. *Chōsen Shūsen no Kiroku* (The Record of the End of the War in Korea). Tokyo: Gannan Tō, 1964.

Mun, Il-p'yŏng. *Hanmi osip Nyŏn Sa* (Fifty Years History of Korean American Relations). Seoul: Chogwang Sa, 1945.

Muraoka, Hirohito, *et al. Kita Chōsen no Kiroku* (Record on North Korea). Tokyo: Shin Dokusho Sha, 1960.

Nihon Kokusai Seiji Gakkai. *Nikkan Kankei no Tenkai* (Development of Japan-Korean Relations). Tokyo: Yuhi Kaku, 1963.

Okutaira, Takehiko. *Nissen Kōshō Shi* (History of Japan-Korean Relations). Tokyo: Yusan Kaku, 1942.

Onishi, Masamichi. *Minami Chōsen* (South Korea). Tokyo: Shin Dokusho Sha, 1960.

Pae, Sŏng-yong. *Chayu Chosŏn ŭi Chihyang* (The Object of a Free Korea). Seoul: Kwangmun Sa, 1948.

Pak, Chae-il. *Zainichi Chōsenjin ni kansuru Sōgo Josa-kenkyu* (Comprehensive Study on the Korean Residents in Japan). Tokyo: Shin Kigen Sha, 1957.

Pak, Ch'oi-il (ed.). *Chosŏn Minjujuŭi Inmin Kongwhaguk* (Democratic People's Republic of Korea). Pyongyang: Foreign Language Publishing House, 1958.

Pak, Chŏng-hŭi. *Kukka wa Hyŏngmyŏng kwa Na* (Korea, the Revolution and I). Seoul: Hyangmun Sa, 1963.

———. *Uri Minjŏk ŭi Nagal Kil: Sahoe Chaegŏn ŭi Inyŏm* (The Future We Ought to Have: Theory of Social Reconstruction). Seoul: Donga Ch'ulp'an Sa, 1962.

Pak, Kyŏng-sik, and Chae-ŏn Kang. *Chōsen no Rekishi* (History of Korea). Tokyo: San Ichi Shobō, 1961.

Pak, Mun-ok. *Han'guk Chŏngbu Ron* (Korean Government). Seoul: Pagyŏng Sa, 1963.

Pak, Sang-hyŏk. *Chosŏn Minjok ŭi Witaehan Yŏngdoja* (The Great Leader of the Korean Nation). Tokyo: Hyŏkshin Sa, 1964.

Pak, Tong-un. *Pukhan T'ongch'i Kigu Ron* (Theory of North Korean Government). Seoul: Korea University Press, 1964.

Pak, Un-sik. *Han'guk Tongnip Undongchi Hyŏl Sa* (The Bloody History of the Korean Independence Movement). Seoul: Seoul Shinmun Sa, 1946.

Saitō, Makoto. *America Gaikō no Ronri to Genjitsu* (Logic and Reality of American Diplomacy). Tokyo: Tokyo Daigaku Shuppan Sha, 1962.

Shin Ki-sŏk. *Tongyang Oegyo Sa* (Oriental Diplomatic History). Seoul: Tongguk Munhwa Sa, 1958.

Shinozaki, Heiji. *Zainichi Chōsenjin Undo* (Movement of Korean Ministry in Japan). Tokyo: Reibun Sha, 1956.

Tabobashi, Kiyoshi. *Kindai Nissen Kankei no Kenkyū* (Study of Modern Japanese-Korean Relations). 2 vols. Seoul: Chosen Sotoku Fu, 1940.

Tanaka, Naokichi. *Nikkan Kankei* (Japan-Korean Relations). Tokyo: Bunkyo In, 1963.

Terao, Goro. *Chōsen: Sono Kita to Minami* (Korea: Its North and South). Tokyo: Shin Nihon Shuppan Sha, 1961.

———. *Sanjuhachidosen no Kita* (North of the 38th Parallel). Tokyo: Shin Nihon Shuppan Sha, 1959.

Tōitsu Chōsen Shinbun Sha. *Tōitsu Chōsen Nenkan: 1965–1966* (One Korea Year Book: 1965–1966). Tokyo: Tōitsu Chōsen Shinbun Sha, 1966.

———. *Nansen no Kaiho Jūnen—Ri Shōman Dokusaiseiken no Jitsutai* (South Korea After Ten Years of Liberation—Facts about the Dictatorial Regime of Syngman Rhee). Tokyo: Nikkan Rōdō Tsūshinsha, 1956.

Wang, Tzu-i. *Han Kuo* (Korea). Chungking: Commercial Press, 1948.

Watanabe, Katsumi. *Chōsen Kaikoku Gaiko Shi Kenkyū* (Study on Diplomatic History for the Opening of Korea). Tokyo, 1935.

Yi, Chong-han. *Han'guk Chŏngch'i Sa* (Political History of Korea). Seoul: Pagyŏng Sa, 1963.

Yi, Dong-jun. *Hwansang kwa Hyŏnsil* (Fantasy and Fact.). Seoul: Dongbang T'ongsin Sa, 1961.

Yi, Ki-ha. *Han'guk Chŏngtang Baltal Sa* (History of the Development of Korean Political Parties). Seoul: Chŏngch'i Sa, 1961.

Yi, Kyŏng-hun, *et al. Minjok Chŏng'ŭi ŭi Hamsŏng—T'ong'il Pangan* (Indignation of Korean People—A Device of Unification). Seoul: Kukt'o T'ong'il Yŏn'guhoe, 1959.

Yi, Man-gyu. *Yŏ Un-hyŏng Sŏnsaeng T'ujaeng Sa* (The History of Yŏ Un-hyŏng's Struggle). Seoul: Minju Munhwa Sa, 1946.

Yi, Sŏn-kŭn. *Chosŏn Ch'oegŭn Chŏngch'i Sa* (Recent Political History of Korea). Seoul: Chŏng'ŭm Sa, 1950.

———. *Han'guk Tongnip Undong Sa* (History of the Korean Independence Movement). Seoul: Sangmun Wŏn, 1956.

Yi, Sŭng-man (Syngman Rhee). *Ilminjuŭi Kaesŏl* (Outline of Ilminjuŭi). Seoul: Ilmin Ch'ulp'an Sa, 1954.

Yi, Yu-gwan. *Zainichi Kankokujin no Gojūnen Shi* (Fifty Years'

History of Korean Residents in Japan). Tokyo: Shinki Bussan Co., 1960.

Yim, Ch'un-ch'u. *Hang Il Mujang T'ujaeng Shigi rŭl Hoesang Hayŏh* (In Memory of the Period of Anti-Japanese Struggle). Pyongyang: Nodongtang Ch'ulp'an Sa, 1960.

Yu, Chin-o. *Hŏnbŏp Haeŭi* (Interpretation of Constitution). Seoul: Myŏngse Tang, 1949.

———. *Minju Chŏngch'i ŭi Kil* (Way of Democratic Politics). Seoul: Iljo Kak, 1963.

Yu, Ho-il. *Gendai Chōsen no Rekishi* (History of Modern Korea). Tokyo, 1953.

Yun Ch'ŏn-ju. *Han'guk Chŏngch'i Ch'ege Sŏsŏl* (Introductory Theory of Korean Political System). Seoul: Munun Tang, 1961.

Yun, Ki-jong. *Han'guk Kongsanjuŭi Undong Pip'an* (Criticism on the Communist Movement in South Korea). With the record of the Chinpodang Incident. Seoul: T'ongil Ch'unch'u Sa, 1959.

Zhukov, E. M. (ed.). *Kyokuto Kokusai Seiji Shi: 1840–1949* (History of Far Eastern International Relations: 1840–1949). 2 vols. Tokyo: Heibon Sha, 1959.

V. PERIODICALS AND NEWSPAPERS

Asahi Shinbun. One of the most respected daily newspapers in Tokyo, Japan.

Asian Survey. Monthly, from the University of California, Berkeley.

Buhŭng Wŏlbo. Monthly bulletin, from the Ministry of Reconstruction, Seoul, Korea.

Chōsen Kenkyū. A monthly journal from Chōsen Kenkyu Sho in Tokyo, Japan.

Chōsen Shiryō. Monthly, from Chōsen Mondai Kenku Sho, Tokyo, Japan.

Chūo Kōron. A famous Japanese monthly journal in Tokyo.

Current Digest of the Soviet Press. Weekly, from the Joint Committee on Slavic Studies of the University of Washington.

Dong-A Ilbo. One of the leading daily papers in Seoul, Korea.

Far East Digest. Monthly, from the International Secretariat, Institute of Pacific Relations, New York.

The Far Eastern Quarterly. Quarterly, from the Far Eastern Association. Renamed *The Journal of Asian Studies.*

Far Eastern Survey. Fortnightly, from the American Council, Institute of Pacific Relations.

Foreign Affairs. An American Quarterly review published by the Council on Foreign Relations.

Han'guk Ŭn-haeng Chosa Wŏlbo. Monthly bulletin of the Research Department, The Bank of Korea, Seoul, Korea.

Japan Times. A daily English-language newspaper in Tokyo.

Journal of Asiatic Studies. Quarterly, from the Asiatic Research Center, Korea University, Seoul, Korea.

Korean Affairs. Quarterly, from the Council on Korean Affairs, Seoul, Korea.

Korean Information Bulletin. Monthly, from the Korean Embassy, Washington, D. C.

Korean Reviews. From the Korean American Cultural Association, Seattle, Washington. Irregular.

Korean Survey. Monthly, Korean Pacific Press, Washington, D. C.

Koreana Quarterly. Quarterly, from the International Research Center, Seoul, Korea.

Kukhoe Bo. Monthly bulletin of the National Assembly, Secretariat of the National Assembly, Republic of Korea, Seoul, Korea.

Maeil Shinbo. A daily newspaper in Seoul, Korea. On November 23, 1945, this newspaper was renamed *Seoul Shinmun.* This was one of the most important source materials for this study.

New York Times. A daily newspaper from New York.

Nodong Shinmun. An official daily newspaper of the Korean Workers Party in North Korea.

One Korea. Monthly of the Korean Unification Movement, Tokyo, Japan.

Oemu T'ongbo. Monthly Bulletin of Foreign Affairs, Bureau of International Relations, Ministry of Foreign Affairs, the Republic of Korea. Seoul, Korea.

Pacific Affairs. Quarterly, from the Institute of Pacific Relations; now from the University of British Columbia, Canada.

Sasangge (Thought World). Monthly, from Sasangge Sa, Seoul, Korea.

Sekai. A Japanese monthly journal, Tokyo, Japan.

Soviet Press Translations. Biweekly, from the University of Washington, Seattle.

The Department of State Bulletin. Weekly from U. S. Department of State, Washington, D. C.

Voice of Korea. Monthly, from the Korean Affairs Institute, Washington, D. C.

Index